My Life with Chaplin

MY LIFE
WITH CHAPLIN
AN INTIMATE MEMOIR BY LITA GREY CHAPLIN WITH MORTON COOPER

PUBLISHED BY BERNARD GEIS ASSOCIATES

Distributed by Grove Press, Inc.

SECOND PRINTING

Library of Congress Catalog Card Number: 66-13707
Manufactured in the United States of America by The Book Press Incorporated
Brattleboro, Vermont

To my sons Charles Jr. and Sydney and to my mother, for their patience, love and understanding.

"During the filming of The Gold Rush *I married for the second time. Because we have two grown sons of whom I am very fond, I will not go into any details. For two years we were married and tried to make a go of it, but it was hopeless and ended in a great deal of bitterness."*

—*Charles Chaplin*
MY AUTOBIOGRAPHY

The night outside our Pullman window was dark and the wind whistled. Lying on the bed, under the covers, I stared at the ceiling of the dimly lighted drawing room. I was keenly conscious of sounds—the sound of the train wheels beating rhythmic patterns over the track ties, the nasty sound of the wind, the sound of a laugh in the compartment next to ours, the sound of water being run in the lavatory sink less than ten feet from me.

I lay still, holding the baby inside me, when the train whistle screeched so piercingly that I sat upright in terror. A gasp of fear broke from my throat. I wished that Charlie would sense my fright and come out of the lavatory to hold me and comfort me.

He didn't. The door was still ajar, and the water kept running.

1

Soon the rhythmic sounds took over again. I lay back, not quite so frightened now, but once again as physically sick as I'd been during most of the stay in Mexico.

Everything was to have worked out so well. Once the secretive wedding and the secretive stay in Empalme were over with, the bitterness was supposed to end too. Mama had told me so: "You can't really blame him for nursing his anger, darling. No man who's forced into a marriage can be expected to leap in the air for joy. You just be patient and give him a little time. He'll come around. He'll come to see what he's known deep down all along— that he couldn't have picked a sweeter, finer girl than you if he'd waved a magic wand."

"But that's just it," I'd wept. "He didn't *pick* me! I . . . oh, Mama, I feel so—*cheap!*"

"Never let me hear you use that word again!" my mother had warned. "You come from a long and proud heritage. There's never been anyone cheap in *our* family, and there never will be. What the two of you did *was* wrong, but it was unfortunate and misguided, not cheap. But the past is past, and we won't hear any more about it, darling. You're going to make him the best wife a man ever had, and he'll wake up soon enough and be grateful."

The train's rocking motion did nothing to calm my fluttery stomach. Suddenly I was in desperate need of water. I began to raise myself heavily from the bed, feeling as though my hands and legs were chained. I couldn't make it. In a strained voice I didn't recognize, I called, "Would you bring me some water, please?"

The faucets were turned off and my husband stepped out of the lavatory, drying those expressive hands of his with a towel. I looked at the man who was then, in November, 1924, and who would remain for years to come, the most beloved and famous man in the world. He had told me, only a few months before: "I am known in parts of the world by people who have never heard of Jesus Christ." There was no doubt of that. On all continents, and in every country where a motion-picture projector and screen were available, he was known and laughed at and identified with. He was The Little Fellow, the underdog, the mute Tramp with the shabby derby, the grubby, ill-fitting shoes, the hand-me-down yet somehow elegant bamboo walking stick. He was the small man with the brush moustache and the sometimes jaunty, sometimes wistful walk. He was the symbol of the eventual victory of kindness over meanness.

Here, in this drawing room speeding toward Los Angeles, he was the immaculate, prematurely graying thirty-five-year-old master of all he surveyed, a self-educated Cockney who had built a one-man fifteen-million-dollar empire, a man of impeccable manners and love for humanity.

And he was the man who had been made to marry me, a scared sixteen-year-old girl named Lillita McMurray, because I was pregnant with his child.

"Do you really want me to get you some water?" he asked.

I nodded that I did.

"Aren't you afraid I might try to poison you?"

The nausea returned and I sank back on my pillow.

Changing to a fresh shirt, he suggested, "Why don't you get up? Put on some clothes, get out and get some fresh air. Go ahead—the observation car's just behind this one. I'll take you out to the platform."

Still uneasy, still distrusting him yet at the same time hoping his coldness would thaw, I put on a wrapper and a coat while he slipped silently into a jacket and topcoat. He opened the door for me and I preceded him, on watery legs, to the observation car.

The November night was cold, but I began to feel a bit better. With my fingers gripping the railing, watching brief patches of scenery whizzing past in the dark, feeling the wind whipping through my hair, I prayed he would be gentle. On the trip to Mexico he had avoided me. During the wedding ceremony he had been grim and had been asked to repeat "I do" because the hastily summoned judge couldn't hear him the first time. During our three long

3

days and nights there he had carefully avoided me, and only once during that period had I heard him say anything. That was when I overheard him tell one of his lieutenants, "Well, this is better than the penitentiary, I guess, but it won't last."

I had been with him so many times when he was gentle, when he was the first man in the world to say "I love you" and I was the first woman in the world to hear it. He had made me a woman, despite my years, with his love and his goodness and his care. There had been the times when the love between us was so real that we died if we were separated for longer than a day.

I was aching now for him to show some of that gentleness.

I sensed rather than saw him near me on the platform. "How are you?" he asked, not touching me.

"Not as bad as before," I said.

"But still miserable, aren't you? And you know as well as I that you're going to go on being miserable."

"No, I don't know that," I said, shaking my head, still not free enough to turn and face my husband. "Everything's going to be all right."

" 'Everything's going to be all right,' " he mocked in a soft falsetto. "If you can't cope with your misery, just mumble 'Everything's going to be all right' three times and the clouds will disappear for all us children."

Then he was standing closer to me.

"This would be a good time for you to put an end to your misery," he said. "Why don't you jump?"

Terrified, I drew back from the waist-high guard door and looked at him, standing there in the shadows. I couldn't make out the expression on his face, but I knew he wasn't joking. His quiet, matter-of-fact, almost compassionate tone scared me far more than if there had been anger in his voice. There hadn't been. He had said "Why don't you jump?" as if the suggestion were reasonable.

Chapter One

I first saw Charlie Chaplin on April 15, 1914. It was my sixth birthday, and to celebrate my mother took me to Hollywood, a short trip by trolley from our home in downtown Los Angeles. With luck, she said, we'd have a chance to see some movie stars.

He was sitting at a back table with another man when we entered the restaurant. Mama spotted him immediately and asked the owner, "Do you think it would disturb Mr. Chaplin if my daughter were introduced to him? She loves him. She sees all his pictures." She turned to me and said, "You want to tell all your friends you've met Charlie Chaplin, don't you, Lillita?"

I squirmed. Grandma had taken me to see the funny man with the big shoes and the black moustache in one picture, *Making a Living*, but he wasn't a man at all—

he was something unreal, a picture you saw cavorting along the white wall of a dark room. Yet there he was now, eating lunch, wearing a shabby suit and the black moustache and some makeup on his face. He was there, which meant he was real after all. But he wasn't like anyone I had ever seen before, and I was terrified at the thought of getting close to him.

"I'll check with him, but I'm sure it'll be all right," the owner said, showing us to a table near the front. "He's very flattered when the children want to meet him, but he's shy of grownups." He padded away and came back seconds later. "Come on, honey," he said, grinning and extending his hand to me.

I looked at Mama with an imploring "do I have to?" look. She nodded. Taking a deep breath, I got up and walked, hand in hand with the restaurant owner, to the rear table.

The man with the moustache and the makeup started to stretch out his arms and pick me up but stopped, seeming to sense that small children are scared of grown-up strangers who are too quick to make a fuss of greeting. "Well now, what would your name be, young lady?" he asked.

"Lillita McMurray."

To his friend he said, "Hasn't she lovely dark eyes and hair?" and gently pantomimed for me to sit beside him. I stood, ramrod straight. He chuckled and said, "I know a wonderful match trick. Would you like to see it?" He took some kitchen matches from his pocket and arranged them on the white tablecloth. "Now this match goes here, and—"

I heard myself cry, "I want to go back to my mother!" and I ran to her, feeling embarrassed and miserable.

Mama had seen everything, and I could tell she was displeased by the way I'd behaved. The owner followed me and shrugged. "Oh, you know how kids are. What can they say to somebody like Charlie Chaplin? How can they act? She must have been scared of his makeup—you know, all that paint on his face, the tramp clothes and all . . . Yeah, that's what it was. Mr. Chaplin makes his pictures right around the corner from here, and he comes in like that for lunch."

"Would you apologize for us, please?" Mama said evenly, frowning at me. I was distressed when I made Mama unhappy, and I made her unhappy that day because she'd been sure she and Grandpa had taught me better manners than I'd shown.

We ate without talking, and not once did I dare look in the direction of the back table. We were still eating when the man named Charlie Chaplin and his friend passed us on their way to the door. Charlie Chaplin simply walked out of the restaurant, talking to his friend. That had to mean he was mad at me.

Mama showed me some of the Hollywood sights, as she'd promised to do. But the day was already ruined.

Unlike Charlie, childhood in the slums and workhouses of England, my own in Los Angeles was relatively secure. The deprivations were emotional rather than material ones, for there was always my grandfather, William Edward Curry, to fall back on for shelter and food when my mother's marriage failed.

Until I met Charlie again—six years later and in infinitely different circumstances—Grandpa was to be the only man I saw consistently. He had been born at sea on a ship carrying the British flag. Educated at King's College in London, he came to America, became a United States citizen in 1885 and that same year married my Spanish grandmother, Louisa Seymourfina Carrillo, a member of the large and well-known Carrillo family and a descendant of Don Antonio Lugo, one of California's early Spanish land grant settlers. They settled in Los Angeles, where he and a partner opened a saloon, The Barrel House. With this and side ventures into real estate, he always provided comfortably for his family.

His and Grandma's family consisted of Lillian, my mother, and her brother Frank. Lillian resembled her British-Welsh-Irish father and Frank his Spanish mother, although both had their mother's brown hair and dark brown eyes. When Lillian was fourteen, she was sent to France to spend a year in a convent at Fontainebleau. On her return, Grandpa, who was now a diabetic, retired from business and moved them all to Hollywood, where he'd bought seven acres of land in a hilly section known as Whitley Heights. He built the first house in the entire vicinity, a Spanish-type one, and Grandma planted palm trees and other foliage around it.

Lillian, a vivacious girl with large, wonderfully expressive eyes, was eighteen when she met and fell in love with my father, Robert Earl McMurray, who was a year older (and who, incidentally, for reasons I have never learned, kept changing the spelling of his name from McMurray to MacMurray and back again). Grandpa wasn't particularly impressed by him, but after a year's courtship—spent mostly in the parlor, under Grandpa's watchful eye—they were married. A year later, in 1908, I was born.

The marriage lasted for two bickering years, and at the invitation of Grandpa, whose resentment over my mother's plight made the air stiff and testy between them, Mama took me to the Whitley Heights house to live.

Grandma, who expressed no opinion one way or the other on the subject of Mama's marriage, was a small, compact, cheerful woman who, as far as I know, rarely took a stand on anything. Grandpa, on the other hand, was a stern disciplinarian who would have been appalled to hear that he and Charlie, whom he later came to despise and once threatened to murder, were alike in a number of ways. Both were highly systematic Britishers who believed that clothes were to be brushed at specific times of the day, that a car had to be polished on a specific day of the week. Both, if it could be managed, would eat the same thing for breakfast and dinner each day. Both revered learning for its own sake. As I got older, Grandpa forced me to read his well-thumbed copies of Dickens, Thackeray, and as much of Shakespeare as I could handle. And although he wasn't religious in the formal sense, he made me read the Old and New Testaments, with the crisp explanation, "No one is completely educated until he's read the Bible."

Beyond his attention to my reading and his determination that I learn proper manners, he had little to do with me. Obviously he cared about me, because there were signs of pride from time to time—he'd taught me to read and write when I was four, and once he told Mama, "That child's smart as a whip. Picks up concepts better than a lot of adults I know"—but basically his approach to me was that of a taskmaster and teacher.

Mama, still young and pretty, would often leave me in the evenings to go out on dates. Young men would come to call for her, and her eyes would twinkle in a special, flirtatious way. She always made a point of introducing me, and the men would comment on how pretty I was, chuck me under the chin and pretend great interest. But it was clear that their interest was a fleeting thing, that they couldn't wait to get Mama out and be alone with her. In none of them did I sense the concern I so desperately needed.

One of Mama's beaus was a good-looking, good-natured man named Hal Parker. He was different from the others in that he called on Mama oftener than they did, and her eyes really lighted up when she looked at him. And he was different in that he talked to me with some sincerity in his voice.

I remember the night—just a month after I'd met and run from Charlie Chaplin—when I was wakened by loud, angry noises coming from downstairs. I left the bed Mama and I shared and crept to the top of the stairs. Mama and Grandpa were having an argument.

"You had one bad marriage—why are you in such a gawddamned hurry to rush into a second bad one?" Grandpa roared.

Mama, usually so softspoken and respectful of Grandpa, was fiery. "I won't *have* you talking about Hal that way!" she cried.

"Oh, you won't, won't you? Since when can't I size up a rotten apple? I sized up your fine Mr. McMurray far ahead of time, didn't I? And you went ahead and married him anyway. Fat lot of success you had—"

"I had Lillita, didn't I?"

"So you did, so you did," Grandpa conceded, and then, raising his voice again, said sarcastically, "That's a fine reason to hook up with another loafer—to have another child. Oh, that's a splendid reason!"

"Stop calling him a loafer! Hal loves me and wants to marry me. You don't know him. You don't know anything about him!"

"Nor do you, Lillian! You've always been too headstrong for your own good. Well, I warn you—I'm not about to stand around this time and let you reach out and beg to have your heart broken. If that young pup loafer so much as shows his face around here I'll—"

Grandpa saw me huddled at the top of the stairs and ordered me back to bed. I obeyed, shaking, and tried to bury myself beneath the covers. Was Mama going to marry that Hal Parker? Even if Grandpa didn't like it? Every child I knew and played with had a father. I wanted one, and he didn't even have to be my real one. But suppose I had one for only a little while and then he went away?

When Mama finally came into the room I pretended to be asleep. She slipped into bed and cuddled me. Soon we were curled up together in a comforting warmth.

That year Hollywood was seriously gathering steam to become the movie capital of America. A quiet and proudly dignified section of Los Angeles only a short time before, it had turned, seemingly overnight, into equal parts of gaudy carnival and lush boomtown as hundreds upon hundreds of outsiders converged to make motion pictures on a shoestring one week and sell them for awesome profits the next. The land was spacious and cheap and ideal for filming. The feeling in the fresh Southern California air was that if you had a few dollars and half a brain you could knock out a couple of quickie one-reelers and retire. It wasn't quite that simple, but in 1914 a lot of people with more nerve than artistic skill got rich in Hollywood. Customers were waiting, the price of admission in hand, to see any and all movies, and theater owners around the country were snapping up everything on celluloid they could get, whether good, or as the case more often was, bad. There were ambitious pictures such as *The Squaw Man*, made in a Vine Street barn by Samuel Goldwyn, Cecil B. De Mille, and Jesse Lasky. There were the pictures that were cranked out quickly, pictures like the Keystone Cop comedies and the cowboy and Indian chases shot anywhere and everywhere in Hollywood. Every day the trains unloaded exuberant passengers, clerks fleeing jobs behind department store counters and refugees from stranded stock companies, who had come to get on the motion picture bandwagon. If you had absolutely nothing to offer, except your presence, you could earn three dollars a day as an extra. That meant you were an actor. And that meant that nothing from that point on could stop you from becoming a star.

Almost without warning the town was besieged and occupied by deafening noise.

The feverish activity infuriated my grandfather. "What are they doing to my village?" he would roar, squinting with fury at the drastic changes in the town. The pretty name, "Hollywood," had been invented by Mrs. Daeida Hartell Wilcox, a genteel lady from the Middle West who had moved here many years earlier, intent on turning the area into what she called "a community hymn to God." For several decades she succeeded in her plan, developing her lovely paradise into a community devoted to piety and restraint. Probably it's just as well that Daeida Hartell Wilcox didn't live to see her godly heaven on earth become the stamping grounds for painted ladies who smoked on the streets and cowboy actors—or "players," as they were called—who staggered along Hollywood Boulevard at high noon, drinking in plain sight and loudly and jubilantly cursing.

My grandfather was very much alive, however, and he was perpetually incensed at what he saw. To him it was beside the point that many of the people in the movie business in 1914 were hard workers, happily married and maybe even temperate. He refused to believe that the fortunes the new citizens were earning were legitimate, and he was unmoved, even though he had a healthy respect for the virtues of money, by the fact that the new wealth was doing a lot to strengthen the economy of his beloved Los Angeles.

Nor was he dazzled by the Alice-in-Wonderland quality of sudden success. "It's hanky-panky," he growled when he heard of penniless, inexperienced girls arriving in town and, within a breathlessly short span of time, signing players' contracts guaranteeing them thousands of dollars a week.

One of the many things that irritated him about the new Hollywood was the mothers who were actually storming the studio bastions, anxious to get their children, talented or not, pretty or plain, into the movies. "If adults want to sell their souls for money that's their affair," he would grumble. "But these women who can't wait for their sweet young things to be turned into sluts—well, if I had my way they'd all be horsewhipped."

At such times Mama would smile and nod—and then would disagree when she and I were alone. "Your grandfather means well, Lillita, but he's old-fashioned. There's nothing wrong with being in the movies and being admired. You'd like to be in the movies, wouldn't you?"

"I guess so."

"Of course you would. Everyone would. And maybe some day you will be, and we'll all be so proud of you!"

Grandpa would have been outraged by such talk, but I don't think it meant any more to me than if Mama were to say, "You'd like to be a fairy princess, wouldn't you?" I had a vague awareness of the movie excitement going on near my home, but it was not a part of my young world.

Grandpa's contempt for actors had one exception— Charlie Chaplin. One evening he went to see *Mabel at the Wheel* and came home so full of praise for the comedian— "He's British, too, did you know that?"—that he became a Chaplin addict. "You mark my words, that Chaplin fellow's going to wind up famous," predicted Grandpa, who apparently hadn't learned that he was promising a great future for an already famous man. For the next few years the family never missed a Chaplin picture.

Within nine years, my grandfather would be storming across the room for his rifle, shouting, "I'm going to kill that son of a bitch for what he did to this child!"

The year I first saw Charlie Chaplin was the year Grandpa built a new apartment house, The Navarro, and moved with Grandma into one of the apartments. Mama and I moved into a smaller one in the same building, and she kept seeing Hal, over Grandpa's objections. Hal would come by for dinner, sometimes every night in the week. I liked him, and I couldn't understand why Grandpa didn't. Hal was a very tall, very handsome man who laughed a lot and never forgot to bring me a present. He paid attention to me—sometimes, it seemed, more than he paid to Mama—and he would hold me on his lap and say things like, "If your mother married me, the three of us would live together forever and ever, and you'd be my own little daughter." The idea sounded wonderful to me, and I visualized the three of us together on picnics or walking up and down the street, arm in arm, so the other kids could see I had my own daddy after all. If he moved in it would mean he'd sleep in the bed with us, but that would be all right.

But the more I questioned Mama about whether or not she was going to marry Hal Parker, the more evasive she became. I found out her decision in an abrupt way.

One night I was tucked into the bed Mama and I shared,

and I fell asleep. The next thing I knew I woke up on the living room davenport and heard voices coming from the bedroom. Mama's and a man's.

"Mama . . ." I called, afraid for some reason to get up.

"It's all right, Lillita," she called back. "Stay there and go to sleep. Everything's all right."

"Mama, who's there with you?"

Instead of Mama, Hal Parker answered. "It's me, honey. Your new daddy. Go back to sleep."

I was in Grandpa's apartment the next morning when Mama, poised and contained, told him she and Hal had been quietly married the afternoon before. I waited for Grandpa to fly into a rage. He didn't. "You've made the mistake of your life," he said, "but the damage is done. When everything collapses, just don't come crying to me."

For a time I was stunned at having been so suddenly taken from my bed and displaced. And because the wall between the living room and the bedroom was so thin, at night, when all the lights were out, I was kept rigidly awake by the squeaky sounds of bedsprings.

I soon got used to that, though, because something exciting had happened to me: I had a daddy, and a loving one. On his days off Hal would take me places—just me—and he wouldn't let Mama tell anyone I wasn't his. He had a job as assistant director to Cecil B. De Mille on Vine Street, and he took delight in bringing me to the studio and introducing me to everyone as his daughter. Once, for a lark, he even arranged for Mama and me to appear as bit players in a studio movie with Geraldine Farrar and Wallace Reid. I was delighted with the attention this brought.

Hal was a good-natured and attentive man, and it was obvious that he and Mama loved each other. But eventually he began staying home more and more, and I heard Mama picking on him for being too lazy to go to work. In time I learned, as did Mama, that he wasn't lazy but ill.

Hal was a heavy cigarette smoker in spite of the fact that he had a serious allergy to nicotine. Although one doctor after another warned him, he continued, insisting he couldn't give up cigarettes. Finally, his energy was so sapped that he couldn't get out of bed in the morning. After repeated warnings from the studio that he was missing too much work, he was fired. And Mama got a job.

Little by little her love for him diminished, but mine grew steadily stronger. One vivid recollection of him involves a silly game I played frequently. The Navarro had an automatic elevator whose sides were made of nothing but widely spaced metal slats. I would step in, push every button from the lobby to the top floor and lie on the floor of the cage with my feet between the slats, "walking" up and down. One day, though, I got one leg twisted under the other and managed to pinion them in a metal frame. The elevator kept rising; each time it passed a floor my feet would be painfully scraped. I couldn't untangle them.

I screamed in fright. I could hear both Mama and Hal calling to me, running wildly up and down the stairs because they didn't know where I was and I was too paralyzed with fear and pain to tell them.

Hal got to me first and grabbed me into his arms while Mama, just behind, was hysterical.

"There, there, baby," he said, comfortingly. "There, there . . ."

I clutched at him with every drop of strength in me and held him tight all the way to the apartment. Mama wanted me, but I refused to let go of Hal. While the doctor was being summoned I clung to Hal, even though Mama was close. And when the doctor reported that my injuries were merely bruises, I begged Hal to stay with me till I fell asleep.

I recall the incident so clearly because it made me realize not only how much my stepfather meant to me but how much I meant to him. Long after I was up and walking he was still asking whether I was completely all right and saying how relieved he was that I hadn't been hurt.

That was one of the reasons I was thrown for a loop when Mama told me—I was eight at the time—that Grandpa had been right, that her marriage to Hal Parker wasn't going to work out. "He's very sweet and I like him, darling," she acknowledged, "but the point is he just can't or won't make a living for us. I don't earn enough money at my job to take care of all of us, and Grandpa won't help. So—"

"No!" I cried. "No, no! Mama, don't leave him! Please, let's all stay together forever and ever like we said! Oh, Mama, please don't . . ."

My stepfather pleaded with her to reconsider, but Mama was a determined woman when her mind was made up. I blamed her, but I was to learn that the fault for the breakup was far from being wholly hers. Mama had striven to keep the marriage going, but Hal's unrealistic insistence that he could land a good studio job any time he chose, plus his reckless compulsion to go on smoking in spite of continual assurances that cigarettes would kill him, proved too much for her. She and I moved back in with Grandma and Grandpa.

I never saw Hal Parker again. I heard about him, though. Some years ago a circulatory disease put him in a hospital. Nearly blind, he lighted a cigarette, although he had been forbidden to. By the time a nurse got to him his mattress was in flames and he was dead. Smoking, as the doctors had predicted, killed him.

Divorced, and able to give more time to me now that Grandpa was taking care of us, Mama wasn't the same permissive mother I'd known. When I was ten she had me enrolled in school at the Blessed Sacrament—not because of any deep-rooted religious conviction, but because at the strict Catholic school my comings and goings could be more easily watched. She was going out on dates occasion- ally—she was later to marry for a third time—and where her own social life was concerned she was carefree and happy and as vivacious as ever. Where I was concerned, though, she seemed increasingly worried, and even suspicious.

Not even Grandpa was as disturbed as Mama when I came in from playing outside, and I was puzzled by her unexpected volleys of questions: "Why are you late? Who were you playing with? Didn't I tell you not to play with that Johnston boy?" The more she plied me with such questions, the more worried I was that I was doing something to displease her.

I didn't know what it might be, and I tried to find out. But all Mama would say was, "Be a good girl. Never do anything to make me ashamed of you."

"You know I'd never do that, Mama. But I'm not doing anything wrong. Why do you always ask all those funny questions?"

"Never mind. I just want you to play with nice little girls in the neighborhood," she answered, and sent me to the corner store, thus dismissing me and the subject.

Why didn't she ever answer any of *my* questions? Why did this mother I loved so dearly leave so many important questions of mine up in the air? I didn't know the word "sex," but it gradually became clear to me that Mama's concern about my playmates had something to do with it. I knew where babies came from. Mama hadn't told me; one girl my age had told me part of it, another girl a bit older had told me more and I'd filled in the rest for myself. I was afraid to go to Mama with what I knew, or thought I knew.

When I was eleven, I menstruated—something Mama had done nothing to prepare me for. I woke one morning to see blood on the bedsheet and on my nightgown. In horror I called to Mama, who looked and explained.

It made no sense. "You say this happens to all girls," I said. "Why didn't you tell me sooner?"

Mama told me she was sorry, but that there were some things some mothers are too—well—shy to talk about.

"Why?" I persisted.

"Because," sighed Mama, "there's no telling when one question won't lead to a hundred more."

I had a hundred questions. And more. I began to thrash about for someone to answer them, someone I could trust to be honest with me.

Chapter Two

By 1920, when I was twelve, Charlie Chaplin was far and away the most popular star on the screen. Audiences loved Mary Pickford and Douglas Fairbanks and William S. Hart pictures, but they adored Chaplin pictures.

And they adored Chaplin, not only in America, where movies were easily distributed, but in distant corners of the world. It was estimated that in 1920 each of his movies was seen by 300,000,000 people, including Chinese, Moslems and Hindus—at a time, remember, when the sciences of publicity and export were hardly perfected in terms of speed. Will Rogers called him "the best-known American in Zululand."

He was certainly the best-known American in America. (It was of no importance to anyone then that he was actually an English immigrant with no interest in applying for U.S. citizenship; we claimed him as our own just as, I daresay, the Orientals claimed him as their own.) The sight of him in person, crossing a street, was enough to cause traffic tie-ups. All that theater owners needed to insure standing-room-only business was to place a pasteboard cutout of him beside the ticket booth with the legend *I am here today!* The markets were profitably flooded with Chaplin statuettes and picture postcards, Chaplin dolls and toys, Chaplin shirts and hats, and dozens upon dozens of other novelties bearing the Chaplin likeness; an industrious merchandiser could grow prosperous by applying pictures of the shabby derby, brush moustache, bamboo stick and absurdly big shoes to any useless object around. We kids would hoard our pennies until Saturdays, when we would tear to the corner stores and buy Chaplin candy, Chaplin gum and Chaplin balloons. Latter-day kids have torn to the corner stores to buy Davy Crockett caps, Zorro masks, Beatle cards and Soupy Sales bow ties, I know, but these were fads that burgeoned overnight and died out almost as quickly. The Chaplin image, on the other hand, went on selling merchandise successfully year after year.

In that era before yowling autograph hunters—in 1920, despite the plethora of movie magazines, most film stars offscreen were considered mysterious and therefore untouchable—crowds gathered around him, crying, "Hyah, Charlie!" It was never "Mr. Chaplin." And although he did his best to escape from them, it wasn't because he was impatient with their too-chummy familiarity, but rather because he was genuinely dazzled by their wild affection. As he was to tell me later, "I hadn't a glimmer of how to cope with them and their feeling for me."

When Charlie was criticized during the Second World War for not entertaining our servicemen as Bob Hope and Al Jolson were, his reply was that his kind of entertainment didn't lend itself well to personal appearances. He was right, but he wasn't telling the whole of it. Actually, the apparently arrogant Charlie Chaplin was in truth an incredibly shy man who was, for all that was made public about him, not a public person at all. Having known pitifully short rations of love as a child, he was flattered by the massive love given him in 1920, but he was deeply embarrassed if any outsize attention were called to him.

In those days, Charlie was convinced he wasn't as great as the world insisted he was. He would recoil when he heard himself proclaimed a genius; the word rankled him. "I'm just a little nickel comedian trying to make people laugh. They act as if I were the King of England," he complained. Fawning irritated him, too, as on the day he was lunching in a Santa Monica restaurant with Mrs. William Vanderbilt and Sir Herbert Beerbohm Tree. Santa Monica's chief of police, no less, burst into the restaurant to put Mrs. Vanderbilt under arrest because she was committing the dastardly misdemeanor of smoking a cigarette in public. But just as he reached the table he recognized Charlie. He spent a full minute in bumbling apologies for having bothered The Little Fellow, and then tripped over himself as he backed away. Recounting the incident to me some years later, Charlie snorted, "The bloody fool. What if Mrs. Vanderbilt had been a murderess, or Typhoid Mary? The silly bastard probably would've apologized to me all the same, because she was sitting at table with me."

Still, Charlie secretly admitted elation that the affection for him and his work came from people in more than one walk of life. A few remarkable individuals, such as Bernard Shaw, Paderewski and Churchill, admired him and sought his company, but intellectuals as a class weren't to discover him for another few years. In 1920 the bulk of them dismissed him, probably because anyone that beloved by the masses was automatically suspect. However, scattered critics were beginning to see that his art could be viewed and interpreted on more than a single level. They began comparing him to Dickens, to Nijinski, to Lewis Carroll.

And the love was unalloyed by anything, even by envy. There was admiration for this Cockney who had made fifty dollars a week only a few years before and now was earning a million dollars a year, and there was sympathy—when he was the pathetic Tramp huddling in doorways against the wintry blasts, everyone's teeth chattered along with his. In fact, it was often pointed out that he had an uncanny ability to change moods and emotions with the flick of an eyelid. One awed critic called him "a chameleon in search of a color."

The admiration for him was so immense, in fact, that his marriage at twenty-nine to sixteen-year-old Mildred Harris drew gasps and condemnations only from a very small section of the public. The Little Tramp could do no wrong.

Actually, compared to the bizarre things happening in the picture industry in 1920, Charlie's marriage might have seemed perfectly normal. As Grandpa had predicted, the subject matter in pictures was getting so out of hand that censorship was right around the corner. Although my family strove to keep me from learning any of the seamy facts of Hollywood life, I knew what everybody else knew: many film players, producers, directors and others connected with motion pictures were indulging themselves, once the studio doors were closed for the day, in juicy debaucheries. The town's vast wealth and the reams of overnight success stories had brought on a general don't-give-a-damn attitude, and the scandalous tales could lead one to believe that everybody was drinking everything in sight, everybody was playing with narcotics, everybody was bedding around.

Much of the steamy gossip about the after-hours peccadilloes of film people was probably invented or at least exaggerated, but the fact remains that movies that year were intent on glamorizing sin; there was a torrent of pictures in which drugs, two-fisted drinking, casual adultery and casual divorce were made to seem fashionable as well as intriguing, and therefore to be at least tacitly condoned.

The only movies Grandpa allowed me to see were Charlie Chaplin movies. "Charlie doesn't debase life," he would say. And Grandpa was right, of course. The world picked on The Tramp, jostled him and shunted him aside, and human nastiness flared all around him. He rarely wound up saving the day from nastiness, but he invariably came out of nasty situations as sweet and dignified and optimistic as he'd been at the outset.

As far as Grandpa was concerned, Charlie Chaplin was the only justification for motion pictures. Everyone else in the industry was a rotter, a heathen, a lecher, out to corrupt decency; the movie folks, after all, were the ones who had vulgarized and changed the face and perhaps the soul of the Hollywood he loved. He was hanged if he would let me anywhere near a movie studio, in spite of Mama's—and Grandma's—gentle chidings that he was too straitlaced for his own good. He even glowered when Merna Kennedy, my best friend, came to the house to play. Merna and I had met at dancing school. She was a pretty, red-haired girl who danced well and who had had a little fling, in fact, at touring in vaudeville. This upset Grandpa, and although he was always civil with Merna, he was never really comfortable when I brought her home.

One of our neighbors, and one of Mama's friends, was Chuck Riesner, Charlie Chaplin's assistant director. One day Chuck rang our bell—Grandpa was out, fortunately—with an offer to make. "We're starting to shoot a six-reeler, and it may interest you, Lillian," he told Mama. "It's a great story—Mr. Chaplin's calling it *The Kid* for the time being—and we need some small fry for some of the sequences. If you like I can get Lillita a part. It won't pay much, and it won't take long, but it would be a nice experience for her."

Interested? Mama and I both became feverish with excitement. The following day, at Chuck's suggestion, we appeared at the Chaplin studio, having remembered to forget to say anything to Grandpa. In his office Chuck explained that California law had two rules about child players: I would have to have an adult chaperon at all times, and my schooling was not to be interrupted; the Board of Education would send a teacher to the studio every weekday for as long as I was in *The Kid*.

Before the end of the discussion it was agreed that we would be issued a contract, the terms of which were that Mama would act as chaperon in addition to her work as an extra in the picture. Chuck walked with us to the front gate, but on the way he paused at a door. "While you're here you might as well meet Mr. Chaplin, if he's not too busy," he said, and knocked.

I gaped at Mama, who seemed to be taking the earthquake in stride. I was going to come face to face with Charlie Chaplin, which for a twelve-year-old girl in 1920 was almost like coming face to face with God.

"Come in."

Motioning for us to wait, Chuck entered the room. From my side of the door, I could see Charlie Chaplin—*Charlie Chaplin!*—seated at a long desk, busily leafing through a sheaf of papers as Chuck talked to him. He wasn't wearing the tramp costume he'd worn the day I'd fled from him in the restaurant. I saw the somber-faced, mid-thirtyish Charlie Chaplin whose non-Tramp photographs were in the newspapers and magazines. I was nervous, and my knees almost buckled when Chuck beckoned us in.

However many private insecurities and self-doubts I had at twelve, I was not an ingrown kid; I had learned poise, and I was satisfied that my personality was an agreeable one—and I'd learned to enjoy meeting people. Yet when we went into that small, spare, neat office my palms were moist, and I was sure I would be tongue-tied. I felt awkward and infantile and homely. The day before I had stood, in front of our full-length mirror, melodramatically posing and admiring my developing breasts. Now, perversely, I was ashamed of them, and although I was dressed modestly enough, I wished that I were wearing a coat to hide them completely.

The great man didn't leap to his feet with courtly, expansive gestures of welcome, but he did rise and smile as the introductions were made. His eyes were violet blue, and soulful. He had small hands and feet, a disproportionately large head and a lithe body, and, I noticed, slightly protruding teeth. He was quietly refined, and he had a commanding presence.

"I'm pleased to know you," he said, nodding slightly to Mama. He was rather restrained with me as well, but he did take my hand and shake it. He saw me flinch, and evidently—and accurately—associating my flinching with the fact that my palm was disgracefully damp, his smile broadened. "You're an extremely pretty child, my dear," he said warmly, "and I'm glad Mr. Riesner found you." Before I could find my voice to thank him, he released my soggy hand and said to Chuck, as though I were no longer in the office, "She should do well with us. Those are striking eyes. She reminds me a bit of the child in the 'Age of Innocence' painting."

He appeared ready to dismiss us, and as he stepped back to his chair Chuck gave me a solemn wink. I was certainly ready to go, but that was the moment Mama decided to bubble. "Mr. Chaplin, I suppose you wouldn't remember, but—oh, quite a number of years ago—you met Lillita. It was in that restaurant right around—"

He listened politely to her pointless story. "Oh, yes, I do remember," he lied, edging closer to his chair. "Ah—now, if you will excuse me, I must get back to work."

I was furious with Mama on our way back home. I insisted that she shouldn't have brought up such a silly thing, that he was merely being polite in having us in his office for a few minutes.

"It wasn't silly at all," she said blithely. "He does remember meeting you. I could tell as soon as I reminded him."

Mama carefully signed the contracts before she told Grandpa. He hit the ceiling, as expected, and then grudgingly conceded that he could do nothing to interfere, that the damage was done, and a legal agreement was a moral obligation to be respected. After hours of calm, however, he hit the roof again. "Do you know what I'm doing here?" he demanded of no one in particular. "I'm raising a pack of streetwalkers, that's what I'm doing here!" And he pounded the table so hard that wax fruit jumped out of the glass bowl in the center.

The hustle and bustle of the Chaplin lot had me breathless. When there was actual filming, Mr. Chaplin demanded absolute silence, even though this was long before the days of talkies, when sound equipment could pick up the unwanted noise of a match struck far away—but in between takes the lot was a turmoil of activity. Electricians climbed ladders to adjust overhead lights; carpenters hammered away at sets; the wardrobe woman seemed to swarm around the extras, somehow fitting three of them simultaneously; players paced, rehearsing the action in upcoming scenes. The constant activity seemed as frantic as if Mack Sennett were directing Keystone Cop traffic.

Yet, when Mr. Chaplin arrived on the set, ready to go to work, out of this apparent chaos came splendid order. Chuck Riesner had told me that not a single detail escaped his boss's eyes during a production, that he was a supreme perfectionist. "Sometimes he blows up and laces into everyone in language you're way too young to hear," he said. "But you watch and you'll notice that the ones who let him get under their skin are the ones who haven't worked for him long. The reason the others take his lip is that they're the professionals he respects and trusts. They try to be perfectionists, too. They can't come within a country mile of him on that point—on any point, for that matter—but they try, and the boss knows it. Stick around, honey. You'll see a master at work."

I did. Charlie Chaplin had started his movie career as a hired comedian for Keystone and then Essanay, and for the most part had had little if any control over what was to go into their films. Once he became his own employer, he controlled with a vengeance. For each picture he was author, star, producer, director and chief cutter, and he had trained himself so thoroughly in every other technical and creative phase of moviemaking that he would probably, if it were humanly possible, have done everything himself.

In *The Kid,* his sixty-eighth picture, he very nearly did, or so it seemed. When I wasn't working in one of the street-urchin scenes, or at school—I thought having my very own tutor the absolute height of splendor—I would stand at the sidelines and rivet my eyes on the great man. Obviously he knew exactly what he was doing at every moment, whether it was experimenting for a precise camera angle or personally righting the seedy jacket of *The Kid,* four-year-old Jackie Coogan. I was surprised to learn that, although he had been working on the story for a full year prior to putting it into production, he had no set script yet, and in fact, only a vague idea of how the story line would develop. This flexibility seemed out of keeping in such a precise man; with so many people on his payroll, it seemed strange to me—and to Mama, who was almost continually at my side—that he was working in such an apparently loose manner.

What there was of *The Kid*'s "plot" was deceptively simple. Edna Purviance, Charlie's leading lady for a number of years past, played an unwed mother who abandons her baby. The Tramp finds the infant, takes him in and struggles to make a home for him.

That was only an idea, of course, not a plot, and any other serious filmmaker would have been asking for trouble by starting a full-scale production with such a sketchy idea. But Charlie Chaplin wasn't any other serious filmmaker, and no one on the set doubted that he would bring in anything but a gem.

During those first few days of shooting random scenes he lost his temper often, but only with grownups, never with any of us children; he was clearly fond of Jackie Coogan, for example, and his patience was limitless with the child, even when Jackie muffed one take after another. "We've plenty of time," he said, soothing the confused child. "The most difficult scenes are the simplest to do. The simplest bits of business are usually the hardest. Now let's all just relax, shall we?"

For the first couple of days he didn't seem to really notice me, even though he directed a sidewalk scene in which I appeared with some other children. Then suddenly, as if he were seeing me for the first time, he summoned one of the company's artists and said, not taking his eyes from me, "Doesn't she remind you of the girl in the 'Age of Innocence' painting?" The artist agreed, or said he did. "Paint a likeness of her, Bert, in the 'Age of Innocence' pose," Mr. Chaplin ordered. "Take your time, and make it good."

I sat for the artist for a day and a half. He didn't appear especially ecstatic over the assignment. I gathered he was indulging Mr. Chaplin, who occasionally had whims that he soon forgot completely.

Oddly, the adults were expected to call him Mr. Chaplin, but he encouraged us kids to call him Charlie. I doubt if any of us did—we were much too much in awe of him, even though he made a point during almost every workday to take a break and play with us. After a tense hour or two on the set, when he had been ranting at a technician's real or imagined inefficiency, it wasn't unusual for him to call the kids together for a game of hide-and-seek. He would play vigorously, with genuine and passionate abandon, and when he was tagged "it" his loud groan was sincere. He would run on those marvelous ballet dancer's feet of his, and he seemed to give every bit as much concentration to hide-and-seek as he did to filming his movie. We adored him because he was at once one of us and an all-knowing father.

He had no special interest in swimming himself, but there was a pool on the lot and he enjoyed watching us frolic in the water, just as he must have enjoyed fussing over us—all of us, with no favorites singled out—and saying, "Put your sweater on—take care you don't get a chill," and "Get lots of rest tonight—it's bad business not to get enough sleep." I ate it all up. I knew that his wife had had a baby that had died when it was three days old, and I'd heard someone say that one of the reasons his wife was divorcing him was that their marriage had never been the same after the baby's death, that he'd become melancholy and wouldn't talk to her. I didn't know the details. I did know that at last I had something close to a daddy.

His singling me out from the other kids, his growing interest in me, came about slowly. At first, except for the day he'd ordered the artist to paint my picture, there had been nothing to indicate that he saw me as someone separate from the pack. But then I began to catch him looking at me, as though studying me, with a rapt expression on his usually animated face. It was an expression I couldn't define, but it made me feel strange.

Occasionally he arrived late when he'd worked late the night before, and on one such morning Mama and I got to the studio before he did. When he came in he saw me alone—Mama had stepped away somewhere—and took my arm as he walked toward his dressing room.

"Come with me. I want to show you something," he said.

I went with him, puzzled and a bit nervous.

His dressing room, at the farthest end of a long row of studio offices that stretched the full length of the block between Sunset Boulevard and DeLongpre, was actually a bungalow, consisting of a plushly furnished living room with a fireplace, an alcove-like room with a three-way mirrored dressing table, a wardrobe closet and a tile bathroom. There were few physical reminders that these were his quarters—he was not a vain man—but the walls were decorated with autographed photographs of the famous. He shucked off his coat as I pretended to concentrate on the inscriptions by Galli-Curci, Winston Churchill, Enrico Caruso, George Bernard Shaw and Georges Carpentier. I was relieved when his Japanese valet materialized from somewhere and blandly, silently, began to prepare his master's costume and makeup. The room was filled with the scent of some exotic perfume.

Mr. Chaplin pointed to a chair near his dressing table and invited me to sit down. With a faint smile he produced the unframed painting the artist had done of me and asked, "Well, how do you like it?"

It was an extremely flattering likeness, but it gave my eyes a kind of wistful, reflective sadness I hadn't suspected I possessed. Blushing a little, I answered, "It's very nice, but it makes me a hundred times better looking than I am."

"Nonsense, nonsense," he said, taking the picture again and studying it absorbedly for a moment. "Whether this makes you beautiful or not doesn't concern me at all. I couldn't be more pleased by what Bert's done. I wanted him to capture that 'Age of Innocence' expression. He did, but he did even more—he caught that special elusive quality in your eyes."

"Elusive?" I repeated. I had no idea what the word meant.

Nodding, he handed the picture to Kono, the valet. "I've been peeking at you, my dear, when you haven't been looking. I've been more and more drawn to those fascinating eyes of yours. They're so very young and yet so—oh, what *is* the description? Mature, possibly. No, that isn't quite it." He smiled. "They make you seem very mysterious." He tied a large makeup cloth around his neck and turned to the mirror.

I had been told by my family and others that I had pretty eyes, but no one had ever called them, or me, mysterious. Being in the same room with this famous man scared me half to death. And being called mysterious scared me even more.

"Your name, 'Lillita' . . . you're Latin, of course." It was a statement, not a question.

"Well, sort of half," I said. "Spanish, and there's some English and Irish and Welsh thrown in." Some kids made fun of my name and called me "Spik-Mick," a nickname that angered and disgusted me.

"And only twelve years old! Amazing!" he marveled, as though no one had ever been twelve years old before. He was slapping pink greasepaint on his face as the valet moved efficiently and silently about. There was a minute of awkward quiet as Mr. Chaplin stared at his reflection in the mirror, outlined his eyes with a black pencil and mascaraed his eyelashes. Then: "My dear, have you given much thought to being a player in motion pictures? Oh, of course you have—all children have those dreams, I'm sure. But I mean, have you thought of it seriously?"

I watched him methodically put powder over the greasepaint and tint his sideburns, and I wondered if I dared confess that I didn't really care all that much about being in the movies as a career. Every other girl my age would've given anything to be a movie star like Mary Pickford—my best friend, Merna Kennedy, seldom talked about anything else—but I'd never really had any daydreams about becoming famous. I'd been thrilled when Hal Parker had arranged for Mama and me to be extras in the Geraldine Farrar and Wallace Reid picture, and I was just as thrilled now by working for Charlie Chaplin. It was fun, something exciting to do for the time being, but the thought of doing it all the time wasn't especially tantalizing. In answering him, though, I tried to soften it. "I—ah—I don't know if I'd be good enough," I said.

He laughed. " 'Good enough'?" He rubbed some spirit gum on his upper lip, pasted on the Chaplin moustache and jumped to his feet so fast that he startled me. "Perhaps I can be the better judge of that," he declared, and strode to the wall where his tramp costume was hung. The valet drew a curtain in front of him.

"There's an idea or two popping about in my head," came Mr. Chaplin's voice from behind the curtain. "I haven't figured them through, quite, but what would you think about taking a test to see whether you'd photograph well on the screen?"

He's *serious,* I thought. None of us had tested for parts as street urchins in *The Kid;* our parts were so insignificant that individual tests would have been too much trouble and taken too much time. But when you were offered a screen test, that meant you were being considered for something important. I must have been dumbfounded, because he called, "Lillita? Are you there?"

"Yes," I called back. "I'm—well, I guess I should talk with my mother . . ."

There was impatience in his tone. "She'll come into the discussion, naturally. But I'm not asking her opinion now. I'm asking *your* opinion."

"It—sounds very exciting."

There were three sharp taps at the door. As Kono opened it I turned and saw Mama, looking awfully concerned about something. Before Kono could speak she stepped in, glancing everywhere at once—at me, sitting near the dressing table, at the impassive valet, at the drawn curtain. I immediately got up, aware that Mama was upset, and just as immediately I felt guilty, although I didn't know why I should.

"Why didn't you tell me you were coming here?" Mama demanded loudly, her dark eyes now trained relentlessly on the curtain. For a second I was afraid she was going to lunge toward that curtain and pull it back.

Before I could answer, Mr. Chaplin called, "What's all that? Who's that?"

He came out, dressed in his tramp outfit except for the jacket and shoes. He regarded Mama with a slight frown, awaiting an explanation for her uninvited entrance. Now that Mr. Chaplin was in charge, Kono imperturbably slipped to a neutral corner of the bungalow.

Although she had been frowning a moment before, Mama withered under that displeased look. Her voice and her manner became timid. "Forgive me, Mr. Chaplin. I didn't mean to barge in like this . . ."

"Oh? What *did* you mean to do?"

Ruffled, she backed away slightly, closer to me. "I was

looking all over for Lillita. I was—worried . . . the studio is so big and all. Then someone said they saw her walking here with you, and I—well, I *am* her mother, after all . . ."

Now his frown was chilling. "I'm afraid I don't appreciate the form your worry takes, Mrs. McMurray. I am not in the habit of seducing twelve-year-old girls."

Apologizing, babbling an explanation about how mothers worried about their daughters, Mama only made matters worse. Mr. Chaplin nodded to the valet to fetch his shoes and jacket and then simply turned away from her, signifying that he wished the subject dropped. He had an unusual facility for making something deafening out of silence, and he demonstrated it that morning in the way he dismissed us. He made no sound or gesture—yet Mama and I were out the door without remembering how we got there.

Mr. Chaplin would never forgive me, I was sure. And I would never forgive Mama.

Chapter Three

The world didn't end. We held our breath and waited for Chuck Riesner, or *some*body, to approach us and tell us we were no longer associated with *The Kid,* but nothing of the kind happened. All morning Mr. Chaplin glanced coolly at me from time to time, but he thoroughly ignored Mama.

By afternoon his temper seemed to be under control, and he beckoned to us. He was reserved with Mama, though not stiff. "I assume that by now Lillita's told you I'm considering having a screen test done on her."

Mama agreed that I had.

He nodded. "Very well. First, I should like to explain something to you. The purposes of a test would be to determine what she looks like on screen, how she moves, to what extent her own personality comes across. I explain this to you because there can be a dozen reasons why she might fail the test, and none of the reasons need be her fault—I've seen some lovely women who've photographed poorly, and I've seen some fiery, infinitely alive women whose magnetism hasn't come through on the screen at all. Now that you know this, do you still want your daughter to have the test?"

Mama said that she did.

In the years I was to know this man there would be precious few times when he would try to soften an earlier stand he'd taken with someone he didn't wholeheartedly respect. Not that he never admitted mistakes or corrected an unwise decision, but he was one of history's most stubborn human beings by nature or background or both, and once he made a judgment of another human being, it was nearly impossible for him to backtrack from his position, even when all the facts were against him. This afternoon, though, he hadn't reached that point.

"Mrs. McMurray," he said, "I wasn't only rude this morning, I was stupid. Of course you were right in worrying about your child. Your responsibility is to her—she's got to be your first consideration. My judgment was wrong. I want to assure you that I realize that now, and that I deeply apologize."

This mixture of corn and sensitivity melted Mama. Mr. Chaplin had just recited the most moving address of the age. She indicated that her trust in him was, and forever would be, unshakable.

Whether or not he was conscious of it, he was charming Mama in order to keep her out of his way.

The following day, while my now-mesmerized mother looked on, he was all business. He took me to two of his cameramen and asked them, "How old is this girl?"

One of them guessed right: "Twelve." The other said, "Fifteen, sixteen."

Then he got intrigued with my hair. He bunched it into a mound on the top of my head, then stepped back a few inches to squint at the view as though through a frame.

He called, "Miss Prada! Miss Prada!" and the studio hair-dresser dove apprehensively toward him. "Fix this child's hair so that she'll look eighteen," he commanded.

"Eighteen, Mr. Chaplin?"

"Eighteen. Take her to Makeup and see if they can make her eighteen, too." He hurried away, back to the cameras, leaving Mama and me blinking at each other.

The test wasn't nearly so elaborately prepared as screen tests are today. I was combed, brushed, painted and dressed to look like a stranger—a grown-up stranger—and then hustled onto an unused set where the two camermen shot footage of me. I was barely able to balance on the ridiculous high heels, and I was terrified, through that hour of what seemed to be aimless filming, that everybody—meaning Mr. Chaplin—would be disappointed.

When I got to see the test I was sure that was the end.

But I was wrong. Mr. Chaplin was jubilant. "Excellent, excellent!" he exclaimed, looking around for unanimous agreement.

His chief cameraman, Rollie Totheroh, asked him, "So now that you got the test, what're you gonna do with it?"

"I'll let you know," he replied, and asked that the screen test be delivered to his home.

That was on a Friday, and he was missing from the lot the following Monday. We soon discovered why: he had spent the weekend and Monday rethinking the latter portion of *The Kid*. And his plan centered around me.

The plan staggered me. Edna Purviance would remain the leading lady in the picture and be billed as such, but her original role would be shifted and trimmed in order that a new second half could be fashioned. The new version contained the famous Dream Sequence, wherein The Tramp, exhausted from the countless scrapes and frustrations he goes through to care for Jackie Coogan in his dingy garret, falls asleep on his doorstep and dreams he is in heaven, where the streets are paved with gold, where everything is free and everyone is kind. I was cast as the Flirting Angel who sweetly teases the shy Tramp.

Mr. Chaplin was obviously delighted by the way his brainstorm was fitting so smoothly into his overall concept of *The Kid*. And he was delighted—as he repeatedly told me and everyone within hearing distance, including Mama —that his long-forming hunch about me was paying off. For a thoroughly inexperienced girl, he said, I was exquisitely natural.

Perhaps it seemed so to him; actually, I was terrified from first to last.

He grew so enthusiastic about my work, in fact, that he did something no other leading lady I've since come upon would tolerate: he had Edna Purviance removed from her ultra-comfortable dressing room and had me installed in it!

Miss Purviance was a fetching blonde with classically beautiful shoulders and neck and alabaster skin, an extremely capable comedienne with a singularly placid nature. As I was later to find out, she had been Charlie's mistress before his marriage to Mildred Harris, had stayed as a semi-mistress during his two stormy years of marriage, and at the time of *The Kid,* was winding up her long affair with him, although she didn't quite know it yet. She was an extraordinarily patient woman, chiefly because he invariably returned to her after straying, and she remained pleasant and understanding even when he yelled at her on the set.

But she was far from serene when I was given her dressing room and, for a time, a taste of the star treatment. She clearly was hurt, and indeed stopped being civil to me; when our paths crossed anywhere on the lot, she would stride regally past, her nose in the air. Yet, peculiarly, she continued—in public, at least—to be unfailingly pleasant with Mr. Chaplin.

My original contract was torn up, and I was signed to a new one-year contract with the Chaplin studio. That meant I was now officially a member of what was un-officially called the Charlie Chaplin Stock Company. Mr. Chaplin disliked the term, saying, "It sounds like a closed corporation, an inflexible family affair that no outsiders can penetrate." He did prefer a steady company of players, nonetheless, and for a perfectly sound reason. He knew the virtues and limitations of people like Edna Purviance, Mack Swain, Henry Bergman, Albert Austin and his own half-brother Sydney, and he rarely had the inclination or the time to squander on trying out new players for parts that no doubt could be handled just as adequately by his own company. I was one exception, and Georgia Hale and Virginia Cherill and Paulette Goddard were to be others, but for the most part he was disinclined to view himself as a discoverer of untested talent.

Mama reveled in my new status, and she walked on clouds for days after I finished my stint in *The Kid*. Mr. Chaplin informed her that he predicted a glorious future for me in films. Grandpa, who refused to go near the studio, grunted. And as for me, I was getting to like the idea of being part of the Chaplin team.

During the screen test, and all through the Flirting Angel scenes, I still hadn't come to terms with the fact that I was actually in the movies. What I was doing was a dream, a romp, a nice game that would soon come to an end. When it finally hit me that the new contract meant I was wanted for more pictures, though, all the reservations I'd felt were dissolved and I began to take my status seriously.

One practical advantage of belonging to the company was that I could brag about my "career" to the jealous Merna Kennedy. Another advantage was that I received my seventy-five-dollar salary every week, whether I worked or not. It wasn't a terribly impressive salary—no one on the Chaplin payroll, for that matter, received a terribly impressive salary—but it did help to increase my allow-ance.

One distinct disadvantage was that, for a period of time

after *The Kid* was completed, I saw Mr. Chaplin either rarely or not at all. He had a reputation for hibernating after a picture, to think out the one to follow. I discovered myself missing him, missing the fuss he made over me. We hadn't exchanged more than a dozen words other than as boss and player once the Dream Sequence had got under way, but I had developed a twelve-year-old's crush on him and I could hardly wait to see him again.

Charlie Chaplin did go into hibernation right after *The Kid*, but not to concentrate on his next movie, *The Idle Class*. Mildred Harris sued him for divorce.

I understood only a little of the newspaper accounts of his troubles at the time; the rest was explained later. Mildred was charging him with mental cruelty, and her attorneys were not only demanding temporary alimony for her and trying to prevent him from disposing of his assets, but they were seeking an order as well for a division of community property. He had fled to Utah in the dead of night with the negative of *The Kid* under his arm, aware if the picture were to remain in California, half of the profits from its eventual distribution would legally be his wife's, under the community property law. By fleeing, he could escape his own state's power to attach his assets— and the most significant asset at the time was the negative of *The Kid*.

But even Mr. Chaplin realized that he couldn't stay away from California forever. He went to Europe and then came back to find himself in the middle of a long-distance tug-of-war between his lawyer, Nathan Burkan, in New York and Mildred Harris' attorneys on the Coast, and a daily lurid running account of the Chaplin-Harris marital battle in the papers. The fight went on for weeks, in court and in headlines, before both sides agreed to negotiate. Mildred never did receive a penny from the receipts of *The Kid* as such, but she did get a more than handsome settlement—$100,000 in cash and some of the community property—which depressed those of us from the studio who were in wholehearted sympathy with his plight. I, for one, was positive that the so-called cruelty was entirely on Mildred Harris' part. How dare a gold digger like that make so much trouble—any trouble—for the kindest, gentlest, finest man who'd ever lived?

Then Mama and I got word to report to the studio. We returned, along with the rest of the company, prepared to see a dejected, melancholy Mr. Chaplin. Instead we saw a lively, deeply tanned, relaxed boss, looking years younger and eager to get back to work. *The Kid* had just opened in New York, to unanimous critical raves and to stupendous business.

We were all happy for him. I was overjoyed that he was back where he belonged and looking so fit, so unbruised.

I was troubled, too, that very first day back, when he managed to dispose of Mama for a minute and beckoned to me. His smile wrapped itself around me.

"Have you heard of Mae Collins?" he asked.

I nodded. "Oh, yes." Everyone knew the popular actress.

"She's a close friend of mine, and I'm giving a birthday party in her honor this Friday evening at my home," he confided. "Would you like to come? There won't be any other children there, but you're getting to look eighteen more and more every day, even without the Flirting Angel makeup. You won't feel out of place, I assure you."

"I'd love to come," I said, and began to talk about asking my mother's permission.

His eyes narrowed. "Let's—ah—not discuss this birthday party with your mother, shall we? This is to be a no-mothers-allowed party. It will be all perfectly proper, of course, but it will be so much more fun if you're not chaperoned."

"Well . . ."

"Could you steal out on Friday evening, early, and not be missed?"

"I—gee, I don't think so."

I saw Mama, directly behind Mr. Chaplin. He half turned and saw her, too. She must have gotten the drift of the conversation, because her eyes were blazing.

"My daughter has homework to do this Friday evening, Mr. Chaplin," she snapped. "As a matter of fact, she'll be having homework to do every evening for quite a number of years to come."

Mama steered me home.

Once again we waited to be fired. And weren't. We went on working for the Charles Chaplin Film Corporation, although Mr. Chaplin himself gave both of us the cold shoulder. We were cast as maids in *The Idle Class*, and that was it. At the end of the year the option to my contract wasn't picked up.

Grandpa sighed with relief because the foolish fling was over and done with. Mama was sorry, she said, because she believed she was to blame for what had happened; maybe she'd found fault too fast, without having waited to examine all the details. I was disconsolate because I was positive I would never see Mr. Chaplin again.

Chapter Four

Teachers frequently sent notes to Mama complaining that I had a good mind and an uncommonly good capacity to learn, but that I was an indifferent student. They were right. Reading fascinated me, and I had a mammoth curiosity about many things. But I was my own kind of student; I stubbornly insisted on learning at my own pace and on my own terms.

This bothered Grandpa, who had always stressed the virtues of formal education. I tried to please him. Transferred from Blessed Sacrament to U. S. Grant Grammar School, I buckled down to study and I did graduate from the eighth grade at U. S. Grant, though hardly with distinction. Then I took a course at the Hollywood Secretarial School, but I set no worlds afire there, either. Compromising, though with reservations, Grandpa enrolled me at

Cummnock's School of Dramatics, an accredited school that carried a full scholastic program and that, in addition, featured extracurricular courses in dramatic training.

I did better at Cummnock's, though my daydreaming mind was still wandering down the roads of fantasy.

I was fourteen now and living with Mama in a house she'd taken over in Hollywood during one of her periodic attempts to be financially independent of Grandpa. She turned it into a rooming house, and though she had only a meager business sense, there were signs for a while that she just might make a success of it.

For a while she certainly made a success with one of her roomers. He was a rangy, handsome engineer with an iron-thick Alabama drawl. He had barely moved in, it seemed, before he swept Mama off her feet and became her third husband.

In several ways Bob Spicer was practically indistinguishable from Mama's other husbands: he was robust, good-looking, initially attentive and not overly ambitious. He had a wealthy father in Birmingham, but Bob's independent streak made him want to be on his own, and so, after college, he'd drifted to California and taken a job as a surveyor.

It wasn't long before serious quarrels began to spring up between him and Mama. "You're an engineer, and here you are frittering your talent away with that surveying outfit," she would say sharply. "When are you going to wake up and really try to make a career for yourself?"

"There aren't that many solid openings for engineers around right now, honey," he would reply. "Everybody in Los Angeles County is a graduate engineer."

"That's no excuse, Bob. You just don't apply yourself enough."

Then one day Bob burst into the house with the excited news that he'd been offered a chance to go into the movies: "I'm not too hard on the eyes, if I do say so myself. Maybe I'll become a big star and we can all retire young. Hey, you want my autograph?"

Mama blew up. The surveying job was bad enough, but to turn actor! "That's the most brainless, irresponsible thing I've ever heard!" she shouted.

Nevertheless, Bob put all his enthusiastic eggs into the movie basket. For months he waited for the nibble to become a real bite. But nothing happened.

Mama's fear that anyone or anything could put improper thoughts in her daughter's head overnight was well-meaning but plainly naive. I was already filled with them.

Not that they were anything more than thoughts. I wasn't allowed to have dates, even chaperoned dates, but if I had had them, and if a boy had touched me with even a hint of suggestiveness, I'm sure I would have darted for safety. Sex, nonetheless, was uppermost in my mind a great portion of the time as I approached my fifteenth birthday.

Without knowing it, Mama had set the stage for such preoccupation early in my life—with those tantalizing moans I listened to while she and Hal Parker were in bed, with her shocked reaction when I asked her where I'd come from and her nervous, jumbled answer, with her continual insistence that I stay away from boys, with all her groundless suspicions. Her motives in protecting me were sincerely intended—but they were clumsy. So much so, in fact, that I was guiltily intrigued by every conceivably lewd aspect of what went on between a woman and a man.

Of my few good friends, Merna Kennedy was the only one to whom I dared talk about the subject that made me so giddy. To my relief I discovered that she was totally absorbed in it too.

Except for having been on the outer edges of show business—she and her brother Merle had toured the Pantages Theatre Circuit with a dance act and I had worked for Charlie Chaplin—we were about as unalike as any two girls could be. Merna had brick-red hair, fair skin and blue eyes; I had the dark hair, dark skin, dark eyes and high cheekbones of my Spanish grandmother.

Her figure was lithe and as graceful as a dancer's; I was tall and big-boned. She was inclined to be aggressive; I was more reserved. Yet we were genuinely close—and our mutual fascination with boys brought us even closer, as though we were the only two girls our age who felt that way.

While Merna envied me for having been in movies, I envied her for being allowed to move about pretty much on her own without being constantly under the watchful, suspicious scrutiny of her family. On one of our walks I admitted my envy and sighed that my mother was trying to keep me a baby forever.

"Well, why don't you cut loose some day?" she drawled. "Have yourself some fun with a fella. Your mother can't keep on the lookout for you every second."

"Fun? You mean—uh—*fun?*"

Merna grinned wickedly. We were nearly the same age, but she had been everywhere on the theatrical circuit, and her sophisticated manner made me feel like a bumpkin. "Sure, we're talking about the same thing. But you make fun sound like pimples or something. Now don't hand me that wide-eyed look. You've been in the haystack once or twice, haven't you?"

"The what?"

"Oh, don't play it so sappy!" she said. "You've been jazzed. I can tell."

I'd never heard that word before, but I understood immediately what it meant. And I was shocked. Was Merna trying to kid around with show-off gutter talk like that, or was she being serious?

"That's all you know," I said soberly, looking straight ahead. "I haven't even been kissed by a boy."

"You're kidding!" Merna yelled, as though I'd confessed I'd never taken a bath.

"No I'm not."

"*Wow . . .*" she breathed, and shook her head slowly. "You better not let news like that get around or you'll really be up the creek. I'm a good friend, though, Lillita.

You can trust me. If anybody asks me about you, I won't let on."

I laughed sheepishly. "You act like I ought to be ashamed that I'm a virgin. Gee, I'm hardly even fifteen!"

"If you're big enough you're old enough," she said airily. "Hell's bells, what're you waiting for, you dope, Christmas or something? Getting jazzed is the best thing can ever happen. And don't give me the excuse that your mother's on your trail all the time."

I didn't want Merna to disapprove of me, but at the same time I didn't want her to get a completely wrong picture of me. I said, "There are *some* things a girl doesn't rush into. Like handing out—uh—favors too freely." It sounded horribly stuffy.

We were at the corner leading to my house, and I let my steps flag as Merna stopped dead in her tracks. "You know something, stick-in-the-mud?" she declared in a tone of affectionate impatience. "You and me'd better have a down-to-earth talk. With those notions you're gonna end up in the loony bin!"

We went to the second floor of Mama's rooming house, down the hall, and into the little cell of a room to which I'd been assigned when Mama married Bob Spicer. We closed the door, sat down, and Merna Kennedy, just turned a worldly fifteen, began to lecture me. And, in the process, to educate me.

What I wouldn't get through my thick head, she complained, was that some girls were grown up at twenty-one, some at fourteen and fifteen, and some would never grow up. She honestly considered herself an adult, with enough sense to go after and enjoy an adult's fun, and she quietly, sternly let me have it for thinking it was so darned honorable to be a pill. She had not only done her share of necking and petting, she confided, but she had waved a relieved good-by to her virginity a year before, and she was jazzing all over the place, and what her folks and teachers and neighbors didn't know about her wouldn't hurt them. In the past year she had gone all the way with five boys and one man, and the oftener she did it, she said, the more she liked it. Sure, there was the possibility that you could get a baby from doing it, she conceded, but she had learned to make sure ahead of time that her date had a condom. If he didn't, she always carried a supply with her.

A condom?

Merna explained it.

And she explained lots more. Didn't I understand, for Pete's sake, that there was nothing wrong with jazzing with a good-looking boy so long as you knew how to cover up your tracks so your folks wouldn't jump on your neck? Where was the harm in fooling around and getting the boys to like you? And liking them, and liking what they were able to do to you and for you?

Sitting across from me like a depraved urchin, Merna detailed the peak experience in her sexual adventures. They sounded marvelous. And they sounded like adventures I could never, in a million years, bring myself to participate in with abandon even remotely as great as hers. I was intrigued, certainly, I agreed, but not won over. Fun or no fun, electricity or no electricity, popularity or no popularity, I wasn't about to try it.

Merna snorted.

In less than two years Merna was to visit me again— not the me who was gawky Lillita McMurray but the me who was Lita Grey Chaplin, wife of the greatest creative artist of our time—and snicker, "Everything I told you in your mother's rooming house that day was a blowhard lie. I was as untouched then as the day I was born!"

At the time of our close friendship, though, the more Merna baited me with detailed erotic descriptions of her heavenly boudoir romps the more scared—and the more intrigued—I became. We spent weeks together on this giggling tack as I asked her a thousand breathless questions and got a thousand big-shot answers, not suspecting for a moment that my leg was being pulled.

Then one day I came home from school to find Mama,

alone, sitting in the rocking chair in her bedroom, her hands folded lifelessly in her lap, her face drawn. Across the bureau mirror Bob had written, in giant lipstick letters, I CAN'T TAKE IT ANY MORE ! ! ! !

He never came back, or telephoned, or sent a letter.

And we moved back to my grandparents' home.

In the two years between the time I was dropped by the studio and the time I next saw Charlie Chaplin, his fame had reached a zenith that not even his front-page divorce from Mildred Harris could disturb. *The Kid* was a smashing success, and it was followed by *The Idle Class* and *Pay Day,* two two-reelers, and a longer one called *The Pilgrim.* Those serious critics who had originally either ignored him or sloughed him off as being just what he'd called himself—"a little nickel comedian"—had long since hopped on the bandwagon to extol him as the sole presiding genius in motion pictures.

Newspaper interviews—which he still granted frequently—indicated that he would never again refer to himself as a little nickel comedian. Although he was still utterly free of arrogance or self-inflation as far as the press was concerned, the signs were becoming unmistakable that he was taking the critics' serious views of him seriously. An imperceptible trace of pomposity was creeping gradually into his observations about his work.

He surprised everyone after *The Pilgrim* by making *A Woman of Paris,* a drama he wrote and directed but did not appear in, except in the bit part of a train porter. The picture made a star of Adolphe Menjou—who some years later, incidentally, was to loudly and publicly denounce Charlie's politics. *A Woman of Paris* was fairly well received, in spite of dire predictions that by shelving his forte, comedy, he was courting box-office disaster.

The movie also served as Edna Purviance's involuntary swan song as an actress. During the making of *The Kid* she had begun to drink—not heavily, but enough to displease Charlie, who viewed drinking during working hours as unprofessional and therefore intolerable. More and more often she would approach the camera with her face just a bit pinker, her walk just a bit unsteadier, and Charlie, who never missed a trick, would quietly chide, "Watch yourself. It all comes out on film. You can hide these things from the camera for only so long."

He was right, for by 1923 Edna had undergone a sadly evident change. Her face was still attractive, but now it was bloated. She had developed a rather ungainly, toes-turned-outward walk that was almost Chaplinesque. She had put on so much weight that Wardrobe had to corset her severely to make her believable as Menjou's delectable mistress. Her affair with Charlie was long a thing of the past.

Another boss might have simply arranged for her to sit out her contract and then sent her out to pasture. But Charlie, who could be and often was ruthless in his dealings with those closest to him, also had a deep sentimental strain, which he demonstrated in Edna's case. He felt he owed her a debt of gratitude for their nearly eight basically good years together, so he built *A Woman of Paris* around her, giving her responsible dramatic scenes that salved her tipsy ego and treating her with utmost kindness. The reviews praised him and Menjou and the overall production, but for the most part they dismissed Edna as merely adequate. (This short shrift incensed Charlie, who was fond of Edna and who had been eager for her to leave pictures in a blaze of critical glory. She appeared in one more film, a non-Chaplin French picture titled *Woman of the Sea,* and then drifted, for all practical purposes, out of sight. Charlie kept her on the payroll, however, with a monthly $350 check until her death in 1956.)

With *A Woman of Paris* completed, an announcement was made in the newspapers that Charlie Chaplin was preparing his most ambitious work to date, a full-length picture to be called *The Gold Rush.* It also said that he was casting about in search of a young actress to play his leading lady.

The newspaper announcement didn't imply that Charlie's search was in the nature of a dedicated talent hunt, but it did mark a departure—at that point in his career —from his only nominal interest in discovering new talent and developing it to hopeful heights.

I wanted the part. And I decided to take the first major independent step of my life. I would go after it.

My decision to try for the part was hardened by Merna's prediction that I wouldn't have the nerve. Mostly, though, I was just cocky and filled with enough intermittent self-assurance at fifteen to believe there was nothing I couldn't achieve if I put my mind to it. If I didn't get the part, I thought philosophically, who was to arrest me for trying?

On the Saturday morning when I set out for the studio of the Charles Chaplin Film Corporation, though, I was only a shadow of my former cocky self. I went largely because Merna's dare wouldn't let me backtrack. But I made her go with me, to bolster my faltering courage.

In the studio reception room I gave my name to the busy lady at the desk and bravely asked if Chuck Riesner were in. It had been a long while since I'd seen Chuck, and I had no right to expect him to roll out a red carpet, or even bother to come out to say hello. Besides, I might not be welcome on a Chaplin lot. The receptionist told us to wait and went to look for him.

Merna and I waited half an hour. Merna was fidgeting and I was just about ready to give up and run when Chuck Riesner flung open the reception room door and greeted me. He was genial, though not so spontaneously warm as he'd been in the past. He sat between Merna and me on the beige office sofa and asked, "Well, what can I do for you, Lillita?"

Okay, you big brave bluffer, I told myself. You've come this far on gall. Now how do you put what you want into words?

Somehow I got it out without sounding too childish. "I read that Mr. Chaplin's looking for a girl to play in *The Gold Rush*," I said with astonishing smoothness. "I've had a lot of dramatic training since I—ah—was here last, and I thought . . ."

Merna, so bold and confident outside, sat straight, not moving. I was entirely on my own.

Chuck regarded me and nibbled at his upper lip. Then, gently, he said, "You don't know much about the picture business, do you, honey? Nobody, not even an established professional, comes to a studio out of the blue to ask for a test. It's done through agents, and sometimes it's done through pull—a lot more pull than I have around here, by the way, for a feature part like this one—but it's never done this way."

"I'm . . . sorry." I was ashamed of myself, ashamed that I'd shown myself to be so stupid and ashamed that he had the impression I'd come here to ask him to pull strings for me. His impression wasn't wrong, of course, but trying to take advantage of knowing him hadn't seemed this baldly aggressive to me earlier.

But Chuck wasn't sore. Rising, he smiled and said, "Look, I've got to hustle on back, but you young ladies are welcome to come along and watch us all go crazy in there if you like. What do you say?"

Of course we said yes. Chuck let us through the arcade onto the lot that was so familiar to me. Except for more flowers than usual, and some new greenery around the pool, and a new office that had been added, the studio looked no different than it had the last time I'd seen it. The hustle and bustle were the same: the handpicked noisy crew not only knew their business, they knew how to get it done in minimum time and with maximum efficiency. Crossing the large, elevated shooting stage, we came upon the busy set, which consisted of the ramshackle cabin that was to be *The Gold Rush*'s most important interior; it was tipped at a slant, suspended by pulleys.

Chuck moved us along through a maze of props, boxes, tangles of ropes and wires, cameras, chairs and bags of fake snow, and past a wind machine the electricians were testing. I saw Mr. Chaplin in the distance, taking charge of everything and everyone, alternately shouting oaths and compliments. I thought he looked a little grayer, a little older—and, if possible, even more magnetic. He didn't see Merna or me.

Chuck summoned camp chairs for us, placed them near a wall where we wouldn't be in anyone's way and excused himself. He hurried away. Everyone at the Chaplin studio hurried.

Merna was impressed, not only by the big-league activity but by the fact that so many of the studio company recognized me at different points during the afternoon and stopped by for half a minute to say hello. I was impressed, too, and very flattered—but I wasn't about to confess that to Merna; maybe she knew what men were like in bed, but who knew her at any movie studio, let alone the Chaplin studio? I was recognized first that day by one of the prop boys, who must have told another prop boy, who spread the word that the Flirting Angel was on the lot. Mack Swain, the big funny walrus who played the bullies in some of the Chaplin pictures and whom Charlie sincerely admired, came by. So did the cameramen, Rollie Totheroh and Jack Wilson, who said they couldn't get over how I'd grown and how pretty I was.

And so did Henry Bergman, who greeted me with enthusiastic warmth. Henry was Charlie's studio sidekick, an upbeat, perennially jolly man who ran errands, worked in bit parts, sat in on the few story conferences held and served in general as a kind of court jester.

"Hey, does Charlie know you're here, beautiful?" he asked. I said that I doubted it. "Well, stick around," he suggested. "Charlie'll catch up with you. He's up to his neck today, but he doesn't miss a pretty face."

Henry was right. Minutes later I noticed him holding Mr. Chaplin's arm—Henry Bergman was one of the very few Chaplin employees who could get away with being this chummy with the boss—saying something I couldn't hear and pointing in my direction.

Mr. Chaplin looked our way and frowned. I went stiff;

52

that frown could only mean that he recognized me immediately, remembered the embarrassment of the Mae Collins party years before and was going to have me summarily banished.

Instead, though still frowning, he waved. He turned his back to confer with a carpenter, but half a minute later he glanced at me again—this time, I sensed, in an effort to place me. Over the next hour he glanced at me again and again. Then I saw him in conversation with Chuck Riesner, and saw him looking at me for a moment longer than before. There seemed to be little question that Chuck was telling him why I'd come.

I tingled with embarrassment.

In a short while he came toward us. Merna froze. I was afraid I would be sick.

He took my hand, and his smile was affable. "Yes, yes, indeed," he said. "My 'Age of Innocence' girl! My word, what a young lady you've become . . . here, stand up, let me have a look at you." I stood, my hands still in his. "Oh, splendid, splendid! Where've you been keeping yourself?"

"I've been going to school," I answered hesitantly, and then remembered to introduce Merna, who was in a state of shock.

Ignoring her, giving rapt attention to me, he was doing more than going through the motions of being polite to a visitor. He was clearly glad to see me, and as he turned me around again, cheerfully repeating how grown up I'd become, I could almost hear wheels clicking in his head.

It was near the end of the work day and most of the company was getting ready to leave for home, but Mr. Chaplin insisted on showing me the cabin set he and the crew had been struggling with. Merna tagged along. He ushered us "inside" the three-walled cabin and pointed through one of the windows to a complex series of pulleys. "We have some interesting technical problems here, and I think we're just on the verge of solving them," he said. He explained that in the picture, laid in Alaska, the cabin would look as if it were teetering precariously over the edge of a precipice, and he would attempt to squeeze every last ounce of suspense out of making the audience think the cabin, with him in it, would topple into the abyss. He took his time in explaining the technical problems, and it was obvious that he was thrilled to be so near mastering them.

It was obvious, too, that he was studying me as he talked and answered my questions. Walking us to the lot arcade, he said, "Chuck Riesner informs me you'd like to test for the part of the dance hall girl in the picture."

I blushed. "Well, it—uh—did seem like a good idea at the time," I acknowledged with a total absence of confidence. "I've had some dramatic training, and I thought —uh—but it was awful for me to come barging in and— ah—"

"Oh, come now, I'm delighted you did. Tomorrow morning—no, tomorrow's Sunday—on Monday morning, call here and ask for Mr. Reeves. He'll work out the details and set up the test. We've tested a dozen others for the part, and we may have to test a dozen more. Who knows? Perhaps you'll be the right one for it." Patting my arm, he said briskly, "I must go now. You can find your way out, can't you?"

Not waiting for an answer, and still ignoring Merna, he strode back to the lot.

There was a reverent silence for a moment, like one that follows an awesome storm. "I'll die," gasped the sophisticated Merna. "I'll just die . . ."

I did a bit of dying myself as I tried to decide how to break the news to Mama. I'd gone to the studio without telling her. If the day had been uneventful I wouldn't have told her where Merna and I had been. But now she would have to know that I'd seen Charlie Chaplin. Screen test or not, I was afraid she would be livid.

She was, though not for long. If the offer was a genuine

one—and she definitely would be on hand to find out!— then the opportunity was, to be realistic, too good to pass up. In addition, although she couldn't wholly forgive him for having invited me to a party in such a secretive fashion, she had been sure for some time that the great Mr. Chaplin would never be so unbalanced as to seduce a young girl. "I know about that Mildred Harris being so young," she affirmed, "but everyone knows what a fallen woman she was, even at that age." Moreover, Mama had been reading about Mr. Chaplin's current lady friends, Claire Windsor and Clare Sheridan and the like. And many seemingly well-founded rumors were making the rounds that he was going to marry the famous actress Pola Negri. Mama seemed to be satisfied that Mr. Chaplin was too busy with his active love life to give a roving eye to anyone new.

So I made the test.

I was told that Mr. Chaplin had it run over and over again in the studio projection room and that he grew more hopeful each time he saw it. I was also told that Rollie Totheroh wasn't particularly pleased with how I came across on the screen, and that the company's publicity man, Jim Tully, strongly disapproved of how I looked and moved on film and tried to dampen the boss's growing enthusiasm.

Mr. Chaplin listened to the criticisms—and then called his manager, Alf Reeves, to draw up a contract at once.

Mama and I were summoned to the studio, and Mr. Chaplin, beaming, met us with the contract in his hand. He was civil if not overly cordial with Mama, but every time he turned to look at me it was unmistakably evident that he didn't regret his decision. Jim Tully, the brick-haired ex-hobo who had written a book about his wanderings, *Beggars of Life,* suggested that some stills be shot of us signing the contract. Mr. Chaplin, who regarded publicity as he regarded stage mothers—as necessary evils— agreed. He had invented a new name for me. I was now, he advised us, to be known as Lita Grey.

The formalities done, he rubbed his hands and exclaimed, "Well, now we can all roll up our sleeves!" He informed us that not a minute was to be wasted from here on out. In the week needed to finish constructing the interior sets we would travel to Truckee, California, for location shots; Truckee was ideal, he'd learned, because you could count on plenty of snow even at the beginning of summer, and snow was to be an intrinsic part of *The Gold Rush.*

Although there seemed to be no immediate reason why I should be part of that long trek in which only exterior locations were to be shot, it was expected that I go along with other members of the company, who probably wouldn't be called on to work, either. Charlie Chaplin was a totally unorthodox moviemaker. Once he had the fundamental idea of how a picture was to progress, he extemporized a great deal, having learned from experience that spontaneous thoughts for a scene can sometimes be the best ones. He had no way of knowing in advance whether it might occur to him in Truckee to do some closeups—in which case I most certainly would be needed.

About fifteen of us were to make the journey. Preparing for it, the busiest people were those in Wardrobe, for they not only had to find or make costumes to be taken to location, but they also had to scurry about in search of winter coats, boots and hats—items not easily obtained in Southern California—for us to wear during our stay in the frigid climate.

The morning finally came for us all to meet at the train station. Mama made it perfectly clear to me that she intended to watch me like a hawk—a warning I didn't appreciate, because I was fifteen now, not an infant. Besides, she was acting as if she didn't trust Mr. Chaplin after all.

"Oh, I trust him, all right," Mama said. "About as much as I trust any man—even a gentleman."

"What does that mean?"

"Never mind. Come on or we'll be late."

"Mama, why don't you *ever* answer a question?"

She blinked her large, dark eyes. "Why, what a thing to

say!" she declared. "When haven't I answered your questions? Now come on, I said, or we'll miss the train."

Boarding the train, I made my hundredth vain attempt to sort out my flood of feelings. I had pretty well come to accept the fact that I was no longer Lillita McMurray but Lita Grey now, and that I was going to play an important role in a major motion picture that would be seen by millions of people. I was exhilarated by the fact and petrified by the responsibility.

But what worried me far more was my feelings about the man I dared call—when no one was listening—Charlie. I was old enough to know there was a difference between having a crush on a man and being in love with him, but I wasn't old enough, or bright enough, to know what the feelings I had for him added up to. The wishful daydream of his making love to me—the one thing Mama was determined to guard zealously against—had been an almost continuous one for weeks, although the fantasy wasn't nearly so much erotic as it was romantic. I kept reminding myself that it made no sense at all, that dreaming of being alone with him for even five minutes was a foolish dream because it could never possibly come true, that I would die if it did come true. I was scared of my shadow, scared of most men, scared even to be near most boys—yet I was consumed by the fantasy of being held and kissed and protected by Charlie.

That morning I didn't know that I wouldn't have long to wait.

Chapter Five

The trip to Truckee was long, but far from dull; the private cars occupied by *The Gold Rush* company were bursting with excitement. Mama and I were hardly settled in our drawing room when Jim Tully knocked at the door, came in with pencil and pad and recommended we get right down to the business of publicity. "We can't start too soon getting the public to know you," he said. "The newspapers and magazines will want to run stuff on you, and of course we'll want to give them every bit of cooperation we can." He crossed his legs and yawned, as if to convey to us that he was here merely to earn a living, that he was full of disdain over this chore that had befallen him.

Despite the unfriendly atmosphere we worked to come up with what he kept referring to as "hot copy." I admitted that there was nothing particularly "hot"—a word that didn't sit at all well with Mama—to report, but could he do anything with the fact that an ancestor, José Anton Navarro, had given the city of Los Angeles its name in 1781, and that another ancestor, Henry T. Gage, had once been a governor of California and ambassador to Portugal? Tully nodded and took notes. Mama added that we also were descended from such colonial families as the Picos, Rimpaus, Alvarados and Sepulvedas, all of whose names, for what it was worth, now adorned Southern California boulevards. I considered this musty history, and additional information about my hobbies, aspirations, pet peeves, favorite foods and the like seemed to be pretty insipid material, but I must have been wrong. After that superficial interview and scores of other interviews and photographing sessions in the weeks that followed, someone named Lita Grey came across in the magazines and newspapers as a lively and even colorful girl.

At what point did it become incontestably clear that the feeling Charlie harbored for me was more than a professional one? I can track it to a specific place and time—at lunch in the dining car on the way to Truckee.

Charlie was lunching with two studio workers at his table, and Mama and I were lunching at the table directly across the narrow aisle. He glanced up and saw me, and from the way he looked at me I suddenly got the feeling that he was seeing me for the first time—and that he very much approved of what he saw. All his guardedness, all his reserve was stripped away, and his distinctly intimate gaze sent such erotic waves across the aisle that a shiver tore through me.

I couldn't avert my own gaze, even though I understood the significance of his look and was scared. It was a voluptuous moment, and one that I was the first to break by pretending to return my attention to my salad, not so much because I was afraid that Mama would realize what was happening as because I hadn't a notion of how to respond to his insistent stare an instant longer.

The remainder of the train trip was exquisite torture

for me, and my fantasies ran riot. Merna Kennedy had bragged that she knew all there was to know about men, but her boasts were restricted to cheap thrills. Although I'd never been alone with a man—or even a boy—for experimental purposes, I was sure I knew reams more about what went on between a man and woman than Merna ever would. The way you got worked up, she'd claimed, was to have a fellow kiss you with his tongue and feel your private places with his hand. Merna had never talked about exchanging glances, and that meant she was ignorant. And I'd been ignorant, too, for having been taken in by her fake revelations. I knew more than she did because she hadn't been looked at by Charlie—my Charlie—and I had.

We were met at the train station by a fleet of horse-driven carriage sleighs and taken to Truckee's single decent hotel, a rundown inn complete with wood-whittling natives in red hunting caps sitting around a potbelly stove in the lobby. Mama and I were shown to our quarters, a tiny room that contained a lumpy brassbound bed with a chamber pot beneath it, a thready carpet that had been scrubbed so often you couldn't guess what its original color had been, a small maple bureau, a few low three-legged stools instead of chairs, three (!) cuspidors, and on one of the mottled walls, a print of a kitten wrestling with a ball of yarn.

"Well, this isn't exactly the Ritz," said Mama, beginning to unpack.

I didn't care. I stood at the window, fascinated by something I'd never seen before except in pictures—snow.

My fascination was short-lived. The weather was so bitterly cold that spring of 1924 that before the first two days there were over I'd had my fill. I wanted only to stay indoors as much as possible. The hotel was inadequately heated—for this Southern Californian, at any rate—but it was better than the unbelievable cold outside.

Over those first few days I saw relatively little of Charlie

—I was still referring to him, aloud, as Mr. Chaplin—but he'd meant it when he'd said a minute wasn't to be wasted. He personally scouted every inch of the area for suitable backgrounds, and he had the cameramen shoot thousands upon thousands of feet of film, aware that he might wind up using little or even none of it, yet eager to get the feel of vast expanses of snow.

There was little doubt that Charlie was anxious that *The Gold Rush* be more than just a good movie. Although he still had no solid story line worked out, as was his custom, he had given fastidious care to the preparation of the film. He'd read everything available on the search for gold in Alaska in 1898, a search so frantic that the hunger for gold had turned human beings into cannibals. (The scene in which Mack Swain as the food-starved prospector has the hallucination that Charlie is a chicken and tries to eat him was the result of Charlie's research into the cannibalism of those desperate days.) He was determined to capture the authentic quality of 1898 Alaska.

He was so determined that he wore the entire crew, and himself, to a near frazzle. He spent a disproportionate amount of time directing a long line of people—most of them natives he'd hired as extras—to trudge, like an army of ants, up the side of a big, rugged mountain. This long-shot scene, depicting a gang of prospectors on their hopeful way to riches, was to become the first scene in the picture, and one of the most memorable. I, as well as everyone else around who wasn't in the crew, was conscripted into the prospecting party.

This diligence of Charlie's was fine, except that before the week was out the Truckee natives—and I, for some reason—were the only people who hadn't come down with bad colds. Day after day we trudged the hilly slopes of that mountain, only to stagger back to the hotel at night, weary and chilblained. Even Mama, who hadn't been exposed to the unceasing cold as much as the rest of us, took to our bed with a fever of a hundred and two.

The plan had been for all of us to stay in Truckee for

no longer than a week. Then Charlie caught the flu and was ordered to bed, and the production was halted for four days.

No one was pleased by this respite, least of all Charlie, who viewed bed rest at such a crucial time as idiotic. Spirits in general were low, especially among those of the company who were well enough to move about and who wanted some fun during the standstill. There was nowhere to find it; Truckee was a pretty desolate and depressing town, and it simply provided no outlets for anyone who wanted to let off steam.

Charlie knew this. He knew, too, that low morale in a picture company can become contagious and can damage the end product. So, though it wasn't his style to be overly chummy with workers during a production, he sent word that he wanted to have the company visit him from time to time—not to talk shop but just to socialize. Knowing him as I was soon to know him, I'm sure that Charlie flinched inwardly when he made this offer, for he wasn't a man to engage in chitchat. But the invitation did have a wonderful effect on the cast and crew. Each of them made a short, individual pilgrimage to his room and came out with spirits buoyed.

The afternoon came when Henry Bergman walked over to me in the lobby and said, "Charlie wonders why you haven't dropped by to say hello."

"Maybe I will," I said, glad that we were in the lobby and Mama was upstairs—and immediately nervous about actually, at long last, being alone with Charlie. In fantasy I'd been audaciously bold and grown up. But that was fantasy.

I took a pot of tea to Mama, who sneezed, thanked me and complained that she just couldn't seem to rouse any energy, that all she wanted to do was doze. I sat with her while she sipped half a cup of tea, and I tiptoed out the minute I was sure she was asleep.

Heart thumping, I guiltily made my way down the

dimly lighted corridor to Room One at the end of the hall. I told myself I was being melodramatic, that he wished merely to see me and chat with me, not rip my clothes off. He *had* given me that unmistakable look, of course; but he was Charlie Chaplin, with a million things crowding his active brain, not some one-track-minded simpleton. He had Pola Negri, a mature woman of the world, for a fiancée, didn't he? What could a passably pretty kid of fifteen, who made fifteen-year-old conversation, possibly have that would interest him?

I hesitated at the door. Then, closing my eyes, I knocked. "Come in."

He was sitting up in bed, two large pillows behind him, reading a book. A broad smile broke over his face and he lowered the book to greet me. "Well, finally!" he said jokingly. "I was beginning to feel that being a leading lady had gone to your head and I wasn't important enough for you to waste your time on."

Moving with careful steps into the large, comparatively luxurious room—it had chairs instead of stools—I said, "That shows how much you know, Mr. Chaplin. I was scared to death to come till now. I was sure you'd think I was an awful upstart."

"You're joking! What a preposterous thing to think!" he objected. Then, patting the edge of his bed, he said, "Come sit down by me, Lillita—no, forgive me, it's Lita now, isn't it?"

I sat where he directed, stiffly and impersonally so I wouldn't give the impression that I considered the visit even remotely improper. I tried to make my smile impersonal, too, the smile of an utterly naive and unconcerned teen-ager. It was a pose, of course, and an outrageously dishonest one at that. I *was* there to impress him, to make him approve of me. I *was* intrigued by what would happen if he touched me—the romantically receptive young woman, not the dumb, dopey kid. Tension was mounting inside me. I wanted to be his little girl—and yet I wanted him to put his tongue in my mouth. I knew I was playing with fire by not getting up and sitting safely in one of the chairs, but I wasn't honest enough to admit just how little fire I was prepared to play with.

"Are you feeling any better?" I asked. "You don't look sick at all." His eyes were rimmed with red and his nose was pink and a little puffy, but otherwise he looked marvelously alive. I'd never been so struck till now by the beauty of his eyes, by how long his lashes were. By no stretch of the imagination could he be called handsome in the Fairbanks-Valentino-John Gilbert sense, but it was no accident that so many discerning women found him desirable; the magnetism of the man was immediate and overwhelming.

He gave me that shy, bucktoothed grin. "I'm not the match for wintry blasts I expected I would be, but I'm much better, much better—for an antique."

I frowned. "Why do you talk like that? 'Fossil,' 'antique.' Do you really think you're old?"

"No. Truthfully, I like to believe I'm not even approaching the prime of life yet. But I'm thirty-five, and most people your age see thirty-five as far over the hill."

"Well, I'm not most people my age," I said. "I think— well, I think of you as just about the youngest man in the world."

That reached him, for the grin widened and he took one of my hands from my lap and pressed it. "You're very kind, Lita. Turnabout is fair play. I think of you as just about the most adult young lady in the world."

If I was going to escape the time was now. I could have done it with a show of casualness, too, for his hand wasn't pressing mine with any force. I could easily have slipped away and drifted to a chair without appearing to be ill at ease.

I stayed.

"You're hard for me to understand," I said. "How do you mean, I'm adult? We haven't talked together very much before today, and when we have I've always sounded like a nitwit. I mean, I get embarrassed when you ask me something or want me to talk. I—well, I always feel like I'm anything but adult . . ."

Slowly, he leaned a bit closer toward me. "Are you embarrassed now?"

I nodded and withdrew my hand from his, but I continued to sit where I was. I was both glad and distressed that I'd closed the door when I'd come in. And both thrilled and frightened by those eyes that had now left mine to scan the contours of my body.

It was his turn to speak, but he was silent, leaving me more rattled than ever. Desperate to see this meeting through, yet just as desperate to change the fearsome mood, I indicated the book he'd put aside and asked, "What's that book about?" as if it were urgent that I know.

Apparently sensing my discomfort, he leaned back again and picked it up. "This is a biography of Napoleon and Josephine—an excellent one, by the way. You know who Napoleon was, don't you? Of course you do. Do you know who Josephine was?"

"She was his wife, wasn't she?"

"Not exactly. Not in the beginning. She was his mistress."

He pronounced the word with relish and looked at me once more as he said it. It was now obvious that he was embarking on a serious game of cat and mouse, to judge how far he might go.

Not blinking at the word, I asked, "Was she beautiful?"

"Only the most beautiful woman in all France," he said. "She wasn't French, you know. She was Creole, a mixture of two pure Latin strains. She looked like you, Lita."

"Is there—ah, could I see a picture of her?" I asked, fixing my eyes on the book, trying to make the question sound light, knowing that the thing I was ardently hoping for and ardently dreading was about to happen.

His hand circled my wrist, his face suddenly dark and

intense. I began to babble senseless words about anything and everything I could think of, and I kept on as he pulled me to him. Then I stopped abruptly, for there was no breath left in me.

For an instant I felt he would be gentle. If he'd only go slowly, if he'd only be nice, I thought, then somehow all my panic would magically evaporate and I could accept anything.

But instead he pushed me back roughly on the bed. He kissed my mouth and neck and his fingers darted over my alarmed body. I found my voice and implored in a ragged whisper, "Please . . . stop . . ." but he rolled on top of me and covered my mouth with a deep-drawn kiss.

One of his hands snaked under me; his other hand squeezed my breast with almost brutal force. His body writhed furiously against mine, and suddenly some of my fright gave way to revulsion. His animal movements might have made some semblance of sense if we were naked, but we weren't; he was wearing red silk pajamas and I was wearing a blouse and skirt. He was heavy on me, and the thing he was doing was hateful because it had no tenderness, no recognition of me as a person.

His mouth drew away and once more I pleaded with him to stop. I pushed him and started to roll toward safety, but he caught me and pulled me back.

Then, abruptly, he sat up, looked at the door and whispered, "What's that?"

I leaped to my feet and hurried as far from him and the bed as I could get. I heard something, too, the sounds of muffled voices and the shuffling of feet on the other side of the door. Upset and obviously angry, he rose and moved conspiratorially over to the door, where he stood and listened. He peered at me and put his finger against his lips.

I stood at the window, terribly shaken, terribly disappointed, terribly confused. If this was what sex was all about, I wanted none of it—ever. It was vile and it was savage, and the fact that it was made so by this man I adored—or thought I did—revolted me all the more. The world saw him as a man of taste and sensitivity and compassion, which struck me now as bitterly laughable. Did he do these grotesque, dismally unromantic things with sophisticated women like Claire Windsor and Pola Negri? No, probably not. Only with a ninny like me, who had almost no conception of what being a woman was.

I tried to smooth my wrinkled skirt, and then I began to comb my hair. The sounds of feet and voices moved on down the hall, and he came back, muttering, "Bloody bastards." I was afraid he was going to come near me again, but he didn't; he sat in a chair, crossed his legs and watched me comb my hair.

"You look unhappy, Lita."

I nodded.

"I'm going to make love to you," he said, as casually as if he had said, "I'm going to tie my shoelaces." Then he said, "When the time and the place are right, we're going to make love."

I found the courage to say, quietly but resolutely, "No. We're not."

He was calmly curious. "Why? Because of middle-class scruples, or because I didn't touch you sweetly?"

"Both, I guess. Please. I don't want to talk about it."

"But we must," he said, still without a hint of urgency. "I'm not a caveman, Lita, even if I behaved like one for a minute. I'm really quite human, and you're very beautiful. But you don't know what it is to be a woman yet. You want to grow up, don't you, and live life to its fullest? I'll be your teacher, Lita."

I was no longer scared or revolted, just drained. "I'm going to my room," I said, walking past him, not looking at him.

He didn't get up, but his soft voice held me. "I assume you won't mention a word of this visit to your mother." It was not a question.

"Of course not."

He nodded. "That's very wise. If you must go now, will you kiss me good-by? My flu has just about flown. You needn't worry about catching it."

I walked to the door. "Good-by," I said and left, too troubled to say or hear another word.

Mama was still asleep when I returned to our room. I stared at the waist-high snow drifts through the window, sure that the bath I was going to take would never cleanse me.

Charlie was up and ready to resume work the next morning. We stayed in Truckee for four more busy days, to everyone's loud dissatisfaction. Charlie didn't speak to me for the rest of our stay there, but every time he caught my eye, whether we were near one another or separated by yards, his probingly intimate look seemed to tell me he would have his way, that it was indeed merely a matter of the right time and place.

I became silent and withdrawn, so much so that Mama kept feeling my forehead, convinced that I was coming down with a cold after all. If I was outwardly listless, though, I was a maze of anguished emotions inside. I was still disappointed and hurt that he had tried to use me instead of making love. But, no matter how ugly his gross approach had been, it was impossible to deny that giant waves of weakness coursed through me when I thought of his body pressing against mine.

On the train back to Los Angeles, Mama and I were summoned to his compartment. Henry Bergman let us in, but Charlie got up and greeted us cordially, acting so elaborately friendly with Mama, inquiring about her health after her flu attack and personally escorting her to the best chair in the room, that I was amazed she didn't get suspicious.

"This is as good a time as any, I think, to discuss your characterization in the picture, Lita," he said, sitting across from me like a thoroughly relaxed man. "Any objections?"

"Of course not."

"Good, good." He began to talk, repeating, perhaps for his own sake as well as for mine, bits of details I already knew: "The little fellow"—that was the way he always referred to the role he played—"has a deeply respectful attitude toward all females, good or bad. He can recognize guile and selfishness and evil in men, but it would never occur to him that a girl could be anything but grand and worthy of being placed on a pedestal. The moment he sees you in the dance hall he falls in love with you. He doesn't dream that you've 'been around,' as the saying goes—everyone else in the picture and in the audience knows, but not the little fellow. On the other hand he's not an idiot, so what you must do as the dance hall girl is to be blithely tolerant of him at first—you can't imagine yourself getting serious about this overgrown child. It is a tricky problem: you must convey the impression that you're far from straitlaced, but there must be no hardness in you."

Although the plot of *The Gold Rush* was still incomplete in his mind, he obviously had done a lot of thinking about the dance hall girl. We spent an hour in his compartment talking about her, he describing her in exacting detail, I breaking in occasionally to ask him to explain this or amplify that. He seemed pleased that I was getting a clearer picture of the role.

We got so absorbed that I forgot for solid patches of time that this masterly man was the same one who had ground himself against me in the hotel bed. But every so often during the hour we spent together that very private look of his reminded me. In a way, this was one of his most brilliant acting performances. He was all business, but even while he was deftly discussing characterization and even though Mama and Henry Bergman were sitting and listening and watching, his insolent eyes were telling me of his careful plan to take me to bed.

I could, of course, read his meaning, and his colossal nerve, with my mother so close, made me more than uncomfortable. I did nothing with my own eyes to encourage him in the slightest. I do know, though, that that hour under his erotic scrutiny strengthened my decision. If we were alone again, I would be ready for him. Eagerly ready.

We returned to Los Angeles on a Saturday and were told to be at the studio on Monday morning. Sunday was an endlessly restless day for me. My flipflops were agonizing— one minute I was certain I couldn't possibly go through with it, the next I was wondering if I could survive until I saw him again.

When Mama and I got there Monday, we found all the sets completely built and everything in prime order. But at the lunch break my heart sank. I saw Charlie scurrying to a young woman who had just arrived and embracing her with cheerful affection. She wasn't Pola Negri, his supposed fiancée, whom I would have recognized. She was dark and exotic looking, with long, faultlessly lacquered red fingernails and a willowy figure, and she embraced him in return. They went off together, arm in arm, to the commissary.

Pretending I didn't much care, I asked Mack Swain if he knew who she was. "That's Thelma Morgan Converse," he said. "Gloria Vanderbilt's twin sister."

Impressed by the reflected glory of the Vanderbilt name, Mama asked if they were having a romance.

Big Mack shrugged his beefy shoulders. "Well, that's the rumor, but who knows? The story's going around now that Charlie and Negri have cooled off and he's all warmed up about this Converse dish. Somebody was telling me that they were writing love letters back and forth every day while we were in Truckee. But like I say, who knows? Charlie's the most close-mouthed cuss there is when it comes to his love life."

The news devastated me. After that time with me in the Truckee hotel room, had he sat down and written a love letter to somebody else? If he had any feeling for me, how could he have any for anyone else?

After lunch they came back to the cabin set together,

and Charlie had a chair brought for her so she could watch in comfort. We were shooting the scene in which he and Mack Swain wake up in the morning, neither aware that during the night the cabin has been blown to the brink of a cliff and is dangerously near toppling over. Charlie walks to the side of the shack where Mack is still lying in bed—the side that is leaning over the precipice. Both men realize something is wrong, but because the windowpanes are frosted, they are not quite sure what. Bewildered, they agree that they feel as if the floor is tipping. They jump up and down, testing it, and then follow with a dozen brilliant sight gags, each more excruciatingly suspenseful and hilarious than the one before, until the door flies open and Charlie goes sliding out, saving himself from falling into the abyss only by grabbing the doorsill in the nick of time.

It was a stubbornly hard scene requiring exquisite precision, and it seemed that Charlie would have every step reshot again and again forever.

I watched Thelma Converse, hating her for being so interested and for being so beautiful—and hating myself for having believed he cared for me. He wanted to use my body—I was convinced it was as simple as that. All right, why shouldn't he? I had a good body, and he was a man, and as Merna had said and as Mama had implied, most men want sex for its own sake. So why had I fluttered in awe that he wanted to make love to me? It could just as easily have been the chambermaid.

My mind was changed again, and this time I was certain I would stick by my decision. I was fifteen, but I wasn't brainless. Why should he get what he wanted and then simply forget me? It wasn't a fair exchange, and I wasn't going to let it happen. I wasn't going to become another conquest.

Late that afternoon, after Thelma Converse had left and while Mama was talking with someone, Charlie beckoned me to a corner and said, smiling, "You're making it very difficult for me to concentrate on my work."

Haughtily I said, "Don't you mean Thelma Morgan Converse?"

That amused him. "Good God, is that jealousy I hear? Thelma's a friend of mine."

"I'll bet. Do you give her the kind of looks you give me?"

I was being awfully pompous, childishly pompous and sassy, and I didn't like the fact that I sounded clearly concerned. But my concern appeared to amuse him all the more. "That's for you to guess at if you like. What I won't make you guess at is the fact that you've become an obsession with me. It's absolutely vital that we be alone soon."

I faced him. "I've got to make something clear. Nothing is going to happen between us. If that means I won't be in the picture, well, then it's not really too late to get someone else. But nothing is going to happen."

Unfazed, he said, "Lita, you're managing to make me seem to be the worst sort of lecher—and a petty one, at that. I do want you, but I assure you I'm neither a lecher nor petty. I'm a planful man. And Thelma Converse happens to be part of my plan."

"I don't understand."

"You will, gradually. You will."

Satisfied that he had successfully filmed the most complicated of the teetering cabin scenes, Charlie began on the dance hall sequences, which meant that he would now be focusing much of his professional attention on me. Before going to Truckee, and since our return, he and Wardrobe had taken great pains to select the right basic costume for me to wear as the breezy dance hall girl in the Alaska saloon. At one point nothing would do but that I wear something satirically brief and baubled to highlight my legs and thighs and bosom—"Let's make the outfit so ridiculously oversexed that it's comical," he said. At another point he junked that idea and ordered a completely different costume. "Put her in something that really covers her, that displays only the vaguest outlines of curves. The result will be much more effective if we have to surmise, if we can get her eyes and her mouth and her hands to convey appeal."

He and Wardrobe finally agreed on a costume somewhere between those two extremes, a gown that was tight enough to show that I had curves but modest enough to cover thighs and bosom. Mama was happy.

By the time the dance hall sequences were under way, my name and picture were popping up more and more in the newspapers and the movie magazines. Jim Tully was seeing to that; although he was a sour man who made no secret of disliking me—and, for that matter, of disliking nearly everyone in the *Gold Rush* company—he was doing a professional job as publicist for the Charles Chaplin Film Corporation.

About this time, having paid extravagantly polite court to Mama, Charlie went to her with a proposition: for the sake of the picture, he felt it was necessary for him to be seen with me in public. "The more she's seen and the more she's identified, the better it will be not only for the film but for her own career beyond the film," he said. "I'm not suggesting for a moment that Lita and I go to premieres and dinner parties alone. My fiancée, Thelma Morgan Converse—Thelma *Vanderbilt*—will always be with us. I'm anxious to introduce Lita as my protégée. I'm sure it can do nothing but good."

Mama asked many questions. And conferred with Grandpa. Finally, she told Charlie it would be all right, on condition that we always be accompanied by another adult and that I be delivered home at a reasonable hour.

I could have told Mama she was making a big mistake. But I didn't.

Chapter Six

It began.

It began with an invitation to the premiere of a Douglas Fairbanks movie, to be attended in evening clothes. The day before the premiere, a full-length gown was sent to the house for the occasion—not by Charlie, whose name on the card might have caused suspicion in the family, but by the Charles Chaplin Film Corporation, thus making it a perfectly impersonalized gift. Mama and Grandma were thrilled. Grandpa walked around the gown a few times, ordered the low-cut bodice to be remedied, and then gave his reluctant approval.

Charlie's Locomobile pulled up in front of the house and the chauffeur came to the door. Charlie didn't get out, but he made sure that he and Thelma Converse could be seen from our front window. Seeing Thelma satisfied

Grandpa. I was kissed and sent on my very first important evening out. I felt quite grown up.

Charlie greeted me, moving so I could sit between him and his date, and introduced her. She was smiling, though a little stiffly. I admitted to stomach butterflies, which made him laugh. "Get rid of them," he declared. "I'm accompanying two stunning belles of the ball tonight."

The activity outside the theater was glittering and glamorous. Movie stars were everywhere, and many of them greeted Charlie. Some of them—Lionel Barrymore, Mary Miles Minter, Jean Hersholt and Mae Murray—indicated that they didn't need to be told my name, that they knew me already from the newspaper publicity, and they were kind with their compliments. Mary Pickford was nowhere to be seen, but Douglas Fairbanks, who reminded me of a handsome, carefree trapeze artist, embarrassed Charlie by giving him a crushing bearhug in the crowded lobby. Charlie introduced me to Tom Mix, who reeked of whiskey and who looked quite out of place in elaborate white cowboy garb. Charlie was pleasant enough with Mix, whom he called "my cross-the-street neighbor," but when the actor left and we were shown to our seats, he muttered, "I can't stand that fellow. There's enough showing off in acting—why carry it over away from the studio? And what part of the West is he from, anyway? West Hollywood?"

I remember nothing of the Fairbanks movie except that I was in nervous seventh heaven. We filed out when the lights went up, and the chauffeur drove us to a small, out-of-the-way restaurant, a quiet and inexpensive one most motion picture people didn't frequent. Charlie ordered steaks for the three of us, not asking us how we preferred them prepared but instructing the waiter to make sure they were "intensely" well done. Only then did he begin to comment on the movie. "A trifle, of course, and a highly forgettable one," he said. "But it's a mistake to take Doug Fairbanks lightly. He can't act worth pins, but he has a powerful personality that the most tiresome, tawdry film can't squash. I think it's nonsense for critics to waste their time and everyone else's roasting the Fairbanks and the Valentinos—and all right, even the Tom Mixes—for being such inadequate actors. If you can project yourself on the screen in scenes with other performers and make the audience see only you, that's art enough right there. And Fairbanks dominates absolutely everything."

They took me home and the chauffeur saw me to the door. Inside, the family was waiting up to hear about the evening. Grandpa retired to bed within five minutes, but I found out that in the morning he asked Grandma for all the details.

A week later I went with Charlie and Thelma to a small dinner party given by Mr. and Mrs. Sam Goldwyn. I was a little uneasy in the company of Goldwyn's wife, Frances, and of the other guests, a woman attorney and her husband, but I liked Mr. Goldwyn almost at once. Charlie was extremely fond of him, and always roared when recalling some of Sam's soon-to-be-famous convolutions of the English language. As he told Thelma and me on the way to the dinner, "If Sam made those mistakes of his on purpose, the humor would be lost and some of his charm along with it. It's his unaffected naivete that makes him so endearing." Then he remembered his favorite Goldwynism: "One time Sam asked a young actor where he came from, and the boy said, 'Idaho, sir.' Sam looked at him and said, 'That's fine, young man, but out here we pronounce it "Ohio." ' " Laughing, Charlie added, "But don't let his shaky English fool you. Sam Goldwyn has impeccable taste."

I was to attend half a dozen dinner parties at the Goldwyn home over the following year, and I was to get to know him well, but his simplicity and comfortable warmth impressed me keenly that very first evening. I was only dimly aware then of his reputation for integrity both as a producer and a human being, but I was to hear much about it in later years. And when Charlie was being plagued by patriotic groups and woman troubles in the 1950's, though many people of influence in Hollywood privately mourned his problems, Sam Goldwyn was one of the very few who stood up publicly in Charlie's defense.

Pictures were barely discussed during dinner, which was unusual, for in 1924 as today pictures and the picture business were almost the sole topic of conversation in Hollywood. After dessert we were shown a screening of Josef Von Sternberg's *The Salvation Hunters,* which marked the debut of a young actress named Georgia Hale. I thought it a plodding, overly arty film in which the camera spent great amounts of time viewing garbage cans in shadowy alleys. More than once I saw Mr. Goldwyn stifling a yawn.

Charlie, who had little tolerance for artless artiness, had many good things to say about it, though. "This Von Sternberg chap pathetically misses the boat," he said over coffee, "but you have to give him a lot of credit. He obviously takes the camera seriously. He sees what too few directors around have the wit or the energy to see—that the opportunities to use the motion picture camera creatively are practically limitless. Lubitsch is another one of those few. He can do more to show the grace and humor of sex in a non-lustful way than any director I've heard of."

I was afraid to open my mouth, but everyone else joined in—including Thelma Converse, who made me mad because she was so pretty and could talk so well. She listened to Charlie condemn most of the movies being made in Europe as well as in Hollywood for their slavish mediocrity and unwillingness to take artistic chances, and then she quietly set about putting holes in his charges by listing people and pictures she thought were worthy of respect, and explaining why she thought so. Charlie patiently heard her out.

Feeling smaller every minute, I wondered for the thousandth time what he could see in me when stunning, bright, intelligent women like Thelma Converse were available to him. And I wondered why, now, even as he nodded at her speech, he was giving me that special look again.

The dinner party and the unresolved discussion ended early, as most week-night evenings did when there was picture work to be done the next day. The butler was ready to help me on with my jacket, but Charlie, seeing Thelma talking with the Goldwyns, took it from him and did the job himself. Softly he said to me, "You're interfering with my work. I can't concentrate for thinking about you. It's going to happen for us, Lita. It's got to, and soon."

At the door, Mr. Goldwyn took my hand between both of his and beamed. "You're working for the master when you're working for Charlie Chaplin. What he doesn't know about the picture business the rest of us would be lucky to forget. And I think *he's* lucky, too. You are a delightful girl, Lena."

"*Lita!*" Charlie shouted, and laughed so hard he missed his step and fell across a chair.

Charlie drove himself hard, and he sneered at pseudo-artists who claimed they couldn't work unless they were inspired by the Muse. But he was smart enough to realize that it was fruitless for him to push for creativity on days when he felt himself completely empty. On those days he would phone the studio with one command: "Send everyone home. I don't feel funny today."

On these days, and on weekends, he often relaxed by going to the Santa Monica Swimming Club. And occasionally he took Thelma and me with him, although it was becoming evident that coolly self-sufficient Thelma Morgan Converse sensed that Charlie was using her as a blind. She never confronted me with this awareness, but although she kept seeing him, even with me tagging along, she was gradually becoming less and less communicative.

The swimming club was my idea of the ultimate in sophistication. Lush and lively, it swarmed with film stars happily cavorting in the comfortable knowledge that they symbolized the closest thing to royalty in twentieth-century America. Here was John Gilbert, friendly and outgoing, soon to be taken seriously as an actor with the release of *The Big Parade*. Here was Gloria Swanson, radiant yet vaguely haughty, a star who appeared just a trifle too aware of being one. Here was Greta Garbo, slightly aloof yet far more sociable than she was in time to become (a year or so later, on the several occasions I was to meet her at San Simeon, William Randolph Hearst's estate, it was increasingly evident that her aloofness was gradually overshadowing the rest of her). Here was Clara Bow, the vivacious cutup not much older than I, a bona fide celebrity now but with a long way to go before being dubbed The It Girl, gingerly flirting, boisterously enjoying her popularity.

And always there was Charlie, mercurial in his moods, now convivial and now withdrawn, yet usually the center of attraction. He had, when he chose, a rare knack for being in the middle of everything one moment and then suddenly disappearing the next. A couple of times he arranged for me to disappear with him, and we strolled the unpopulated areas around the club while he talked out tricky scenes he was trying to master for *The Gold Rush*. We both knew I served as nothing more than a sounding board, but he assured me that this was a skill in itself and that he felt good when I was with him.

We inevitably ended up sitting together on a lonely stretch of beach. Sometimes Charlie would talk ceaselessly, and at other times not a word passed between us. I was becoming acutely aware, though, that whatever there was between us was growing steadily. Consequently, when he told me to precede him to our stretch of beach one day at dusk, I understood perfectly that everything up till now had been a mere preliminary.

I knew, somehow, that the threatened, promised time had come, and I went there without a qualm.

I stood at the water's edge, watching the ocean waves running with swift little feet up onto the sand. He came directly behind me, spanning my waist with his arms, and said, "It's lovely at this time of day, isn't it?" He kissed my shoulder. "You're lovely at any time of every day."

I didn't move. Fear was more manageable here and now than it had been in Truckee, not because I knew him better now—I really didn't—but because his whole approach was so radically different from his terrifying lunge in the hotel. He was softer; even before he touched me I sensed I wouldn't have to struggle, that he would be tender, that he would be sensitive and kind. He was pressing lightly against me and I felt his excitement, but I didn't flinch or go to pieces at the knowledge of what was to come.

"Do you like this?"

"Yes," I breathed. "Like" was scarcely the right word to describe my sensation as he began to move slowly, rhythmically against me. I was frightened, I was in awe, I was breathless; "like" was much too pallid, but I dared not tell him.

"Has this ever happened to you before?"

"Once . . . with you."

"Yes, with me," he whispered. "I'm so grateful there's never been a man before me, Lita. I'm going to bring you awake. There will be none of that juvenile wrestling we had the first time we were together." His laced fingers slid upward from my waist to the round curves of my breasts. "You must not be frightened any more. You must trust me. I would never hurt you. You must know that. You must always know that."

As his lips brushed my ear and neck, his fingers lowered the bathing suit straps from my shoulders and over my arms and he cupped my tingling breasts in his palms. A gasp broke from my throat, for the first time my knees weakened and I came close to losing balance. Then, smoothly, he turned me around to him, and I saw him gazing at my breasts with a lover's pure, uncritical delight.

We sank together to the sand. I silently appreciated his kissing my lips before he kissed my breasts, if only because it told me that now he was with *me,* the whole of me, not merely a body. Perversely, my physical desire for him sprang from the fact that he had started off kissing me chastely, almost reverently, rather than with openmouthed fervor. I was embarrassed by my nakedness and the thunder of my heart, yet I threw my arms aggressively around him and hugged him, bringing him closer.

After another and then another straining embrace, he freed himself. With deft, still unhurried movements he peeled the bathing suit off me and sat back on his knees to look at me nude. Instinctively I began to cover with my hands the parts of me that no man had seen till this moment, but looking at him again, I saw the absence of lewdness in his eyes, and abruptly there was no shame. My hands fell to my sides.

Lying prone, I reveled in the admiration of his gaze, in the nearly inaudible words he was muttering to himself . . . "Beautiful, incredibly beautiful . . ." and I loved this man who had released me from all my shame and doubt. It was a miraculous time of day, shadowy, yet light enough for us to look at each other unashamed. He stayed where he was, viewing me as though he were studying a painting. Waiting for him to touch me once more, I was conscious of a fresh surge of giddiness. To ease it, I kept my eyes on the knuckles of his hands, which, in their stillness, might have been carved from brown wood. Their quietness betrayed no need to probe, no urgency to prove their strength, no desire to possess what they did not have.

"You *are* Josephine, aren't you?" he said. "Virgin and

vixen, innocent and knowing." He got to his feet and began to remove his striped bathing suit. "Will it shock you to see me, young Josephine?"

I shook my head.

"Will it thrill you?" he asked, now standing proudly naked. I nodded, not meaning it but nodding because he clearly wanted me to be roused by the sight of him. My curiosity was intense, of course, but even more intense was my hunger to hold him, this man who loved me, this man I worshipped.

Then he was kneeling over me, and I was astonished that I seemed to feel no fear. Would it happen easily, or would this loving act be broken by something other than love? One of the girls at school—not Merna—had warned me that the first time it happens there is blood and pain. I didn't know anything—except that there couldn't be pain associated with someone as perfect as Charlie.

He lowered himself against me, and I gasped at the sudden knowledge of what lovemaking was all about. Merna had told me this, surely, but I had been so captivated by the thought of sex—not as an invasion of my body, but as someone who would hold and love me—that I didn't realize what they had told me until this minute. And I was gripped by fear.

"Born . . . we're both being born . . ." he mumbled, moving with small, steady increases of force. I clutched at his back. I knew he didn't want to hurt me, but now he *was* hurting me, and terror swarmed through me. It wasn't too late yet. I couldn't go through with it. I couldn't have him tear me open and plunge into me. I needed to be a child again. I couldn't have this. This was for animals. This was for grown-up people.

"No," I whimpered, shaking my head wildly, taking my arms from around him, trying to close my legs. "Oh, I can't, I can't!"

I felt his crushing weight lifted from me. Maybe he would swear at me, maybe even hit me, but I didn't care. I turned on my side away from him and wished the tears would unlock and pour out. There was guilt, and there was stinging shame, and I wanted to die.

"There, there, there," he whispered, holding me so sweetly and understandingly that the tears did erupt. He cradled me and kissed my eyes and soothed me: "It's all right, Lita. Truly it is. There won't be any more now. There, there, there . . ."

Eventually, with his support, I was able to gather myself together, but I was embarrassed that I needed him to help me to my feet, even to help me back into my bathing suit. "I tried to tell you," I said bitterly.

"Tell me what?"

"That I'm not only a virgin, but a scared and ignorant one."

He laughed easily, without reproach. We started to walk back. "You sound apologetic," he said, holding my arm gently.

I nodded. "Sort of. I wanted to make you happy. All I did was to act like a stupid virgin."

"Stop using that word to mean something horrid," he said. "Do you think for an instant I would have been this irresistibly drawn to you if you were some sailor's sweetheart? There are many things attractive about you, Lita, but the most appealing is your virginal innocence. And long after you're no longer a virgin you'll retain that innocence. That's what separates you from the carloads of girls around here."

The more ashamed I was of my almost total ignorance about the act of lovemaking, and the more I wanted to avoid confessing it, the more I seemed to have the compulsion now to speak. "Do you really want to laugh? Can I tell you how really dumb I was? You can believe this or not, but till you got going back there I honestly didn't know how deep you were supposed to put your"—I gulped —"thing." It was a dreary kid's word, I knew, but the kinds of names Merna gave it were disgusting, and I was afraid the word "penis" would sound too textbookish.

He was good-humoredly amused, not by my confession

but by the word. "Breaking the hymen does hurt a bit," he conceded, "but it's hardly excruciating. No female, to my knowledge, has ever died from the pain. If we'd kept on, the deed would likely've been done by now and all the discomfort forgotten. Past that initial discomfort, Lita, there's nothing but pleasure."

"Why—didn't you keep on, then?"

"Because you were so fearful."

"But you say that first part is over fast," I pursued. Why was I doing another turnabout? Why was I blaming him now for not doing what I had begged him not to do?

Patiently he explained, "For the simplest of reasons. I am not a violent man. I am a passionate man, I admit, and sometimes I get so carried away that I'm mortified by my conduct. But I don't want merely to use you, Lita, and then have us go our merry way. If it were only a matter of quick sex, I have enough opportunities in this shallow town . . . That kind of thing is for pigs, though. It's infinitely more rewarding to develop the sort of relationship you and I are going to have. And we shall have one—a most memorable and beautiful one."

We returned to the club, which I dreaded doing. I was sure everyone would read our secret immediately, but if we'd been seriously missed, no one greeted us with a smirk. Thelma didn't appear overly happy to see us together, but as far as I know she didn't say anything about it to Charlie.

On the set we successfully gave the impression that we were strictly business, two people related only through making a movie. When Charlie was directing me he seemed to make a point of treating me impersonally, of placing me here or suggesting a bit of action there in much the same way he dealt with players like Mack Swain or Tom Murray, the two grizzled prospectors—in firm, professional, no-fooling-around fashion. His private glances at me were no less meaningful than before, but he took more care now to keep people from getting the idea that he saw me as anything other than the picture's leading lady. The less friendly attention he gave me on the set, the warmer he was with Mama. Their chats were brief, but he was obviously out to charm her into regarding him as thoroughly trustworthy as far as her daughter was concerned. And by the way she talked about him to me on our trips home from the studio, he had been eminently successful; he had manipulated her so subtly and so cleverly that she was persuaded he was as safe for me to be around as a maiden aunt.

The newspapers helped, too. Once or twice a week, the trio of Charlie Chaplin, Thelma Morgan Converse and Lita Grey was photographed attending a film premiere, a concert, a restaurant—the master, his fiancée and his protégée. The pictures always caught us smiling, and the captions always alluded to the two women in Charlie's life, one the girl friend and the other simply the girl. Even Grandpa, who had taken a dim view of my having gone into *The Gold Rush* in the first place—"She needs a normal adolescence, not this wasteful type of cotton candy life"—had to come around to admitting that I did look nice in the photographs, and that he was glad I was keeping my wits about me and not putting on airs.

The only one besides Charlie and me who recognized the sham for what it was was Thelma. During dinner one evening at Musso Frank's Restaurant, she watched and listened to his flattering attentions to me for a while, then pushed her plate forward and her chair back. "I've been in the way long enough," she snapped, shot up and marched out of the restaurant. Charlie went after her, but was back within seconds.

"Poor Thelma, I think she's peeved," he remarked in classic understatement.

"I wish you'd go after her and bring her back."

"Do you want her back?"

"Well—not really," I confessed. "But she looked awfully angry. I'd hate to be the cause of trouble."

His grin was devilish. "Would you?" he said, baiting me.

"I mean, she's important to you, isn't she?"

He nodded. "You're right, Lita, Thelma *has* been important—to us. If she doesn't answer my telephone calls past tonight, and I have a sneaking hunch she might not—that was fire in her eye—we may have a bit of a problem about being seen together in public. I'm sure the newspapers with their filthy minds would stop the presses if they suspected for a minute that I love you. Or anyone your age."

"Did I hear you right?" I asked. "Did you say you love me?"

"Great Christ, you know I do!"

There was more food on the table. We barely touched it. The Locomobile was waiting when we came out of the restaurant. While the doorman opened the rear door, Charlie paused a moment to tell Frank something I couldn't hear. Then he joined me, and once the door was closed and the car was moving, he leaned forward and turned a crank that drew a black divider curtain across, shielding us from Frank's view.

"Frank knows where you live, and we'll take you home," he said. "But it's still early, and it's a delightful evening. We'll take the long way."

I had been in this big car before, but I had never known it could be curtained off.

"You think of everything," I said.

"Absolutely everything." He grinned and leaned back.

I thought I knew Hollywood well, but not more than a minute passed before we were cruising on roads so unlighted and unmarked that we might have been far in the country. Vaguely I suspected what was coming: when he thought the time was right, Charlie would reach out for me in this broad, cushiony rear seat. I had met Frank and was not particularly worried about his judgments of me, if he had any; he was ageless, faceless and human only to the degree that he could drive a car and had the back of a neck.

There was a light in the rear seat, but Charlie didn't

switch it on. Instead he busied himself in closing the curtains over his window and then leaning over to close the ones over mine. We were in almost pitch blackness.

"How do you like all the comforts of home?" he asked. He began to fondle my hair.

I couldn't tell him I felt as if I were riding in a hearse. "I like being with you," I said.

This time, when he kissed me, I responded instantly and fully. Fear of him and anguish over what he wanted us to do together were still riding hard within me, but I knew now that I loved and needed him. And he had said he loved me . . . I not only let him kiss me, I clung to him, and my lips formed a small oval.

His soft hand dug into the bodice of my dress until it was snared inside my brassiere. I moaned weakly and held him all the tighter. "How can we get this blasted harness free?" he asked in a queerly croaking voice.

"It's sort of complicated. Everything's sort of all fastened together."

He made a harsh noise of frustration. His other hand darted under my skirt and danced all the way up my thigh until it found the material of my underpants. "What about this? Is this part of the ensemble?"

The pants could be pulled off, but I was apprehensive again. In Truckee Charlie had been a panting animal. At the swimming club in Santa Monica he had been calmly masterful. Now he was somewhere between the two—not wild yet not calm, either—and I was worried. "I'm yours—you know that," I said. "But please don't do anything here. This is such a—bleak place. Please . . . not here."

Wordlessly he found his way to the top of the elastic-banded underpants, and wordlessly he yanked them down; I murmured for him to stop, though without much force, for he was kissing me again. Then he was struggling with his own clothing and pulling me over on top of him. I heard his labored breathing, and I was distantly conscious of the insanity of his trying again—not on a Truckee bed or a Santa Monica beach but in the unlighted back seat of an automobile with a driver not four feet away from us. . . .

Again I cried out in pain, and again he stopped. He brought me back to the seat, caressed me with more kisses. "I understand, darling . . . no more, no more for now," he whispered.

Slowly his breathing quieted. He drew the black curtain aside and mumbled something to the chauffeur. "Home you go, Lita dear," he said, cradling me once again. "Don't shiver so. There are only good things ahead."

I slept badly and ate almost not at all. Mama was worried, but I blamed my nervousness on the pressures of the movie, and she soon accepted the explanation.

To some extent I was telling the truth. I did everything I was told to do as the dance hall girl, and Charlie complimented me on the set. Even Rollie Totheroh took the time to assure me, "You're treating the camera just fine, kid. It's catching all your animation, all the bubbles." But I didn't feel animated or bubbly. I felt clumsy and inadequate in this crowd of professionals, bumbler without a notion of how to act naturally before a camera. Dozens of times I wanted out, and I didn't dare say so; I was afraid that if Charlie suspected my misgivings, he would start to have second thoughts about my capabilities as an actress—personal closeness or not.

What oppressed me more on the set, though, were Charlie's eyes, ceaselessly pursuing me, continually reminding me—as if I needed reminding—of what was yet unfinished. Then, three interminable days after our dark ride in his town car, he got me alone for a moment and said, "I can't bear any more of this punishment, Lita. Tomorrow at noon I'm going to get a blistering headache and dismiss everyone for the day. You and I will go to my house. Can you arrange for your mother to be off on other business?"

Boldly I said, "I'll think of something," but my mouth was dry.

When the headache was announced the following noon, I found getting rid of Mama no problem. I simply told her I wanted to see a movie matinee with a girl friend, and that was that. She had some shopping to do anyway, she said.

The plans to meet Charlie at a certain corner at a certain hour were elaborately timed to perfection. I saw the Locomobile approach and slow down, and I hopped in. "We should make a spy picture together," Charlie said, grinning, as the chauffeur whooshed us away. I grinned back feebly, still not able to look directly at him.

The trip to his estate in Beverly Hills was long and oddly quiet; now, when I wanted and needed him to be near, he sat unaccountably silent at the far end of the seat, his eyes fixed on the divider curtain straight ahead. I certainly wouldn't have appreciated banter, but his solemnity hurt. It was as though we were on our way to a joint dental appointment, not a lovers' tryst. Part of me wanted to hurtle into his arms and beg him to hold me, but that surely would have startled him. Charlie feasted on genuine bursts of emotion, but as I guessed now and was later to learn for sure, he would go into a momentary state of shock if those bursts were directed squarely at him without his having intentionally prompted them.

It was a relief when the big car neared the imposing Cove Way mansion. The Georgian house sat on a plateau overlooking Beverly Hills, all her adjacent hamlets, and the Pacific Ocean coastline. The steep driveway made a perfect circle at the summit of the plateau, around a park-like area lush with rose bushes.

The car came to a full stop in front of the porch. A young Japanese in white coat and black trousers bounded down the steps and opened the car door, bowing while Charlie emerged, and helped me out. We were still silent as the Japanese followed us up the front steps and the car whisked away.

Kono, the secretary who was seldom far from Charlie, admitted us with that semi-smirky grin of his, the grin that suggested he knew precisely why I had been brought here. He took my wrap, handed Charlie some mail and asked, "You'll ring when you're ready for tea?"

"Yes, yes," Charlie said, impatient for him to go away, and as Kono vanished, began to sort the mail.

As I waited, I looked around curiously. My initial impression was that the house was a hodgepodge of English, French and American contemporary, wedded oddly to Chinese and Japanese decor. The overall aura was Oriental, from the profusion of jade to the faces of the servants. The room we were standing in was like a theater. To our right was an organ console, and to our left, on the first landing of the stairs leading to the upper story, was the window of a projection booth. At the far end of the room was a picture screen that came down from the ceiling. It was a huge room; the ceiling, two stories high, was beamed with great rafters of solid oak, and the massive furniture was upholstered in heavy burnt-orange velour. Leading away from us, and right down the center of the house, was a hallway carpeted in black-and-white checks.

Turning finally to look at me, Charlie was amused by the expression of enchantment on my face. "Come along, Lita, I'll show you around," he said, taking my arm. We started down the checkerboard hall and entered the living room. Scattered throughout this vast, proudly masculine room were what seemed to be scores and scores of pieces of jade, most of them nude figurines. Charlie picked one up lovingly and showed it to me. "This cherub is my favorite," he declared, and I was a bit embarrassed at his preference for the one without the fig leaf. He walked to an array of figurines of fish, Oriental gods and miniature edifices, but he carried the nude cherub with him. "I'm partial to cherubs," he explained. "They have both knowledge and love, and they're without wickedness or guile." Smiling, he added, "I think of you as a cherub, Lita."

My feeble grin returned, but I could think of no answer.

Above the bookshelves hung a pair of etchings depicting London in a fog, the trunks and limbs of the trees bare and melancholy. I felt his presence near me, studying the etchings. His face was sad, reflective. For the first time the surprising thought struck me that maybe this famous, beloved man had been as lonely and inwardly homeless as I.

He led me to the walnut-paneled dining room. The furnishings matched the walls. The heavy carved table could seat eight, but the chairs were so huge that only six were able to fit comfortably around the table. The master chair had an exceptionally high back, and with its ornate carving and its thick orange velvet armrests, it was distinctly a throne. Charlie guided me to the smaller chair opposite, pulled it back and commanded, "Sit, my queen." I sat and saw him smile approvingly at me. "Perfect, perfect, absolutely perfect!" he exclaimed. "You're a perfect Josephine—regal, yet relaxed. Empresses are the epitome of relaxation."

"You're not talking about me," I argued. "I'm about as relaxed as—"

"Don't argue," he said, smiling again. "If I say you're Josephine, then you're Josephine." He crossed the dining room to some heavy velvet draperies whose valances almost touched the ceiling, pulled a silk cord and exposed an enormous window. "Come here," he commanded, and I did.

The view was extraordinary. Before me was a broad expanse of well-cared-for, terraced lawn, with thick shrubbery on either side. "Wait till you see this view from upstairs!" he said enthusiastically. "From here you can't even see the swimming pool. It's below the lowest terrace. But from upstairs the panorama is breathtaking!"

The drapes closed as fast and as easily as they had opened, and he took my arm to show me through the other rooms on the ground floor. Next to the dining room was a bright, cheerful breakfast room with wrought iron furniture and a kitchen at least twice the size of the bedroom I shared with Mama. I was shown the powder room, the sunporch, the projection room. My host led me into the garden, where we saw the tennis courts and the pool, and we walked down narrow paths under vine-covered arbors. And he kept talking and talking and talking, just the way a boy my age might talk if he had just come into possession of such magnificent splendor, as if he wasn't entirely sure he deserved all these material rewards of his fame. It was still another facet of him I had never seen before.

Climbing to the second floor with him, I was impressed as well by his nervousness, again like a teen-age boy's, which seemed to increase with each step. He kept repeating how wonderful the view would be from the upstairs windows, as though trying to fool me into believing we were headed there for no other reason. I was touched by his nervousness, and indeed, it made me feel less nervous myself.

The bedroom was done in the same expensive taste as the rooms on the first floor, except for the carpeting; it was flowered and ordinary and cheap-looking, and it did nothing to grace a room that otherwise was luxurious and airy. "This carpet doesn't go with my Chinese bedroom suite," he said defensively at once, although I'd made no reference to it. "I like it, though." Then, with that startling inconsistency of his, he added, "You know, it only cost three dollars a yard!"

The room had two exposures. We went to the windows on the west. Near one of them, on top of a decidedly masculine bureau, stood a bottle of cologne marked *Guerlain's Mitsuk*o. "Is that what I smell all the time?" I asked. "In your dressing room at the studio, in your car, on your clothes, on—you?"

"You like it, eh?"

"Oh, yes! I've never smelled that scent anywhere else but on you."

I hadn't meant it to sound that way, and I began to explain what I did mean. Charlie laughed, picked up the bottle and lifted the stopper. "Here," he said, and rubbed some of the exotic-smelling cologne on my arm. "It is quite a remarkable odor, isn't it?"

"Mmm," I nodded, smelling my arm. "I guess it'll always remind me of everything about you." That came out sounding too loaded, too. But as long as I could keep looking through the window and not at him, I supposed I could get away with such talk for at least a while.

Not touching me, although he was close, he stood silently for a minute. Then he said, "Let's go over to the east side of the house. On the way I'll show you my pride and joy."

I followed him through a narrow passageway and a glass-paneled door to the bathroom, all white tile and white marble. At first it appeared to be merely a bathroom —an opulent one, to be sure, but just a bathroom. But then he pointed to an anteroom containing a built-in slab of marble and said, "My private steam room."

I was awed. "Steam room? I've heard of actresses taking champagne baths, but your own steam room! My grandfather takes steam baths sometimes down at the—" I stopped, realizing I was babbling idiotically.

"Here's the place to relax, Empress Josephine," he said softly. "And the operation is so simple, even a cherub can do it." He directed me to some handles on one wall. "Turn the handle marked 'steam.' Step in. That's all there is to it. Ah—of course, you leave your bathrobe on the hook. As I'm certain your—ah—grandfather has told you."

Instead of pressing the subject further, he said abruptly, "Come." He guided me to another room, the guest room. This room was unlike the others in the house in that it was essentially feminine. Graceful taffeta curtains were hung at the windows, and the dominating colors were pastel pink and blue. The furniture was delicate, and in an ivory color. A vanity table displayed an ample supply of women's toiletries, and a ladies' terrycloth robe lay over the pink satin-covered bed.

Jarred by the display, but pretending to ignore it, I moved over to the window. I could see beyond the estate, a sweeping view of the whole eastern end of Beverly Hills; nearby were the undulating, perpendicular, purple hills of Hollywood, and in the distance a snowcapped mountain silhouetted itself against a cloudless blue sky. But all the while I was keenly conscious of the purpose of the room, and what he was leading up to.

He took the letters Kono had given him out of his jacket pocket. "I've got to glance over these for a bit," he said. "While you're waiting, why don't you try that steam bath? There's everything you'll need, and there are plenty of towels in the linen closet here."

"If you say so."

"Oh, you'll love it! When I've had a hard day at the studio, a few minutes of steam and I come out ready to fight wildcats! You—ah—make yourself at home. You won't be disturbed." And he trotted out.

Having a glimmer now of how his mind functioned, I was reasonably sure I wouldn't be disturbed—by servants, at least. If he hadn't done it already, he was doubtless on his way now to warn them. I marveled at how much I'd changed since Truckee. Preparing to knock on his door there, I'd felt I was about to enter the lion's mouth, but my fear had been tempered by the childish certainty that nothing could harm me. Here, in this Beverly Hills mansion, scarcely a month later, I was brazenly, almost matter-of-factly, ready to give this man anything he wanted, without qualm or reservation.

Avoiding both of the mirrors in the guest room, I undressed quickly, put on the terrycloth robe and stepped into the bathroom. For a moment I wondered if I would be frightened by inhaling steam. I turned the handle Charlie had shown me, and immediately a hissing sound began. I took off the robe, hung it on a hook, stepped over the tiled threshold into the small room, and waited. Nothing seemed to be happening, and then all at once steam was chugging at me from everywhere, clouding the walls and the air. My eyes began to smart and I hesitated at taking a deep breath, but soon the warmth was soft and soothing.

The foglike mist billowed, grew thicker and thicker, finally filled every inch of the room. I couldn't see anything. The steam, gently caressing me, was making me drowsy, and I lay down on the marble slab and closed my eyes. Every picture and movie I'd ever seen of queens and princesses bathing in royal tubs, with slave girls drying them and anointing their bodies with perfumed oils, danced in front of me. I draped my arm over my forehead and crossed my ankles, wondering what was to happen next.

What happened next was Charlie, lying beside me and teasing my neck with swift, darting kisses. "It's easier this way," he said huskily. "We can't see each other."

On the beach and in his car he had been determinedly in charge, yet rather gentle. Now, though, he was suddenly the man from Truckee again, roughly using me rather than loving me. But it no longer mattered. I hugged him frantically. Then there was a sharp, piercing pain inside me and I cried out, but I did not release my grip. The pain blinded me far more than the encircling steam, but I writhed wildly, as though in ecstasy, to let him know I belonged to him—and then I received all of him.

For minutes after he left I lay still on the slab. The steam had started to recede. Cool drops of water fell from the ceiling, and the moisture on the walls was trickling down in rivulets to an indented nickel drain in the floor. Finally I was able to raise myself. I stood weakly, aghast at all the blood. I was dazed. And I was still in pain.

I was supposed to be a woman now. I was fifteen, but I felt younger than fifteen. It was crazy, of course, to think I would have a baby. Charlie had told me not to worry.

Chapter Seven

One fear stood out above all others: that all he'd wanted was a conquest, that now, with the mission accomplished, he would find some way to put me out of his life.

I was sure I couldn't survive that.

As I showered, I kept repeating, with a mixture of wonder, shame and unsteady relief, *You're not a virgin any more.* Except for the lessening throbs of pain, my body felt no different, and I supposed I looked the same as I'd looked an hour before. I *was* different, though. Mama had made it plain that decent girls were virgins, that girls who gave in to men before marriage were sluts. Was I a slut? I felt strange, but not cheap. I loved this man, this father turned lover, and I had given myself to him because I loved him. Sluts gave themselves for other reasons, didn't they?

Wrapped in a Turkish towel and carrying the robe over my arm, I went back to the guest room, trying not to cringe. Charlie was there, in a bathrobe, and he saved my life by greeting me with a smile that radiated warmth. The pink satin coverlet had been folded back from the top of the bed, and my clothes, even my underclothes, lay neatly arranged across the foot.

He crooked a finger under my chin and said softly, "You're divine."

"I love you," I whispered solemnly.

"I want you to," he said, and unwrapped the towel from around me to pat me dry. "Isn't it strange? There's been such a wealth of poetry—beautiful, soaring poetry—written over the ages to describe love, and yet none of it can match the perfect simplicity of those words 'I love you.'" He paused, looked at me soberly and said, "I love you. I love you, Lita dearest, I love you."

I was so deeply moved that I began to cry—no longer in fear or regret or confusion, but in quiet joy, for this was the most blissful moment of my life.

The narrow bed reached up to welcome us. I joined Charlie willingly, unafraid now because I had never been safer. This time he was gentler, and this time I tried as hard as I could to be less stiff, to make him think my body was relaxed. I sought his lips and kissed them, repeating "I love you" as the kiss softened. Sunlight flooded the room, but there was no shame in seeing him or being seen. I still hurt when he entered, though not nearly so agonizingly as before. I clutched at him, feeling the rigid insistence of him and waiting—hoping—to share a particle of his pleasure. When it happened for him I was remotely disappointed that it—whatever "it" was—wasn't happening for me, too, but I was disappointed for only a moment. He collapsed, panting, in my arms, and I was filled with an overwhelming sense of reward for having pleased him so. I needed nothing else.

As we dressed, I asked, "Was I any good?" It was a dumb question, and it embarrassed me—Pola Negri and his other sophisticated women wouldn't have asked such a silly question, I knew—but I couldn't stop myself.

Charlie laughed. "No," he said.

I looked at him sharply.

"Why should you be, yet? No art can be learned at once. And lovemaking is a sublime art that needs practice if it's to be true and significant. But I suspect you're going to be an excellent student, Lita."

"You shouldn't put it that way," I said, vaguely offended. "I want to be more than—well, just a student. You make it sound like I'm learning to play the piano or something."

He laughed again. "Don't talk back to the teacher, young lady. Hurry along now, don't dawdle. We'll have some nice sandwiches and tea downstairs and then scoot you home safe and sound to Mother."

At the bedroom door he kissed me once more and said, "I'm really quite mad about you."

After that day we were alone at every possible opportunity—sometimes for as long as an hour or two, sometimes only for snatches of minutes. When time was short we were barely able to keep our hands off each other. I was nowhere near experiencing the torrential passion he assured me I would soon know, but I was thrilled when Charlie gazed at me with such frank approval after each act of love. Who was a slut? Certainly not this adoring girl who belonged, body and soul, to Charlie.

Working out elaborate schemes to escape Mama's watchful eye became a game between Charlie and me, and we grew adept at it. The more we were together, especially after he had spent himself, the less guilt I felt. There was no question that sex was the bond in our relationship, but gradually it became equally clear that we were more than merely two sex organs. We were comfortable together. Charlie, who wasn't ordinarily a compulsive talker, enjoyed talking out scene ideas, studio problems and random thoughts with me, and I reveled in listening to him, even when I didn't understand him. I was never under any illusion that I could satisfy him on any intellectual level, and I would say so with regret.

"You help me just by being around, Lita," he said once. "I feel peaceful with you. I don't have to be The Little Tramp or the big executive. I can be myself. I don't have to be frightened of you."

"Frightened? Does anyone frighten you?" I asked, incredulous.

A little too lightly, he said, "Of course. Almost everyone frightens me. Always has."

It was a queer statement for this supremely confident man to make. I asked him what he meant, but he brushed the question aside.

For a few weeks after my first visit to his house, Charlie got a mischievous kick out of devising the ruses that would put Mama off our trail, and at the same time figuring out excuses to allow him and me to spend an hour or so less on the set on days when absolute concentration wasn't necessary. Then one day we were in the garden outside his house—he'd suddenly been hit with an awful headache, he'd told the company manager, and I was supposed to be off at the public library—and he turned to me in a brief fit of anger.

"Damn it," he complained, "I'm getting tired of this back-alley sneaking about, dreaming up these stupid methods for chasing people out of our hair so we can be alone. It's a tawdry business. What are we doing that's so wrong that we have to lie about our every move?"

I reminded him.

"Just a moment, Miss Guilt-ridden," Charlie said. "Aren't you overlooking something? The last two times we've been alone we could've gone to bed. We didn't. Nor do we have to today. Just what the hell is it we're doing that's so ghastly?"

My eyebrows shot up. He was right. Without sending up red flares we had stopped—at least temporarily—tearing at one another the instant we were by ourselves. We had begun using being alone to walk and talk and be together simply because it was good and natural to be together. We had kissed, to be sure, and we were intensely aware of the feel of our bodies touching. But without our fully recognizing it, sex was no longer the single force that brought and kept us together.

I nodded. "You're right."

"Naturally I'm right! I love you, damn it! I love being with you. I hate deception. Your mother looks sturdy enough. Would she really wither or shoot me dead if she were told how innocent our friendship is?"

"Innocent?" I teased.

Charlie looked at me, then nodded. "No, I guess not," he conceded, still serious. "But it's a blasted irritating thing, though. I want to tell your mother and the whole world that I'm not an evil, lecherous man, that being with you keeps me young, keeps me happy and stimulated, gives me the strength to live and work in this dirty cesspool of a world. Oh, Lita, why can't life be sweet and simple, just sometimes?"

There were days when I wasn't needed on the set, but Charlie wanted me there anyway. In the old stock company tradition, he wanted all his players and crew continually near at hand, whether they were to work on a particular day or not; he never could be sure that he might not be hit by a sudden inspiration for a different scene, so everyone had to be available. I was glad merely to stand around, not only to be close to this man who was my whole life, but to watch a giant at work. With the fewest words and movements, Charlie could get more out of a cast and crew than any director I've ever watched. When he knew exactly what he wanted, he could convey it simply and clearly. When he wasn't completely certain what he wanted, he could convey the general idea so effectively that people strove all the harder to satisfy him, and did.

He was always tense while directing, and he seemed

always on the verge of a temper tantrum, but he never lost his temper to the degree that work was held up for any appreciable length of time. Inefficiency irked him, and he had no patience with incompetence, but then incompetent people didn't stay with a picture of his for long; they were soon fired—never by him, incidentally, for he couldn't bring himself to fire the most hopeless dolt personally—but by Alf Reeves or Chuck Riesner or some other lieutenant.

He was often almost indulgently patient with players and technicians when a point wasn't getting across with crystal clarity and he believed the fault to be his. Unlike many directors who storm at others because they themselves aren't articulate, Charlie would take great pains to explain himself. Now and then he could be sarcastic and even insulting, but when the going got rough he invariably made it clear to people who made mistakes that he was a mortal with faults of his own. "Don't misunderstand me," he would say. "If you've got questions fire away. Now's the time to ask them." I heard members of the company grumble to each other about Chaplin the man; they criticized him for working them harder and longer than they deemed necessary, and they criticized him, a multimillionaire, for paying what they called coolie wages. But they never criticized Chaplin the artist. In his work he could do no wrong.

In that ecstatic summer of 1924 I knew better than anyone that he could do no wrong. I was so bursting with love that I could barely hold myself back from running up and down the world to share the news of my incredible fortune with everybody. I caught myself several times on the verge of blurting out to Merna that Charlie loved me. Once I came perilously close to telling Mama, of all people, just to see whether she would understand that what was happening between him and me was beautiful, good, glorious, everything real love should be.

As time went on Charlie found the furtiveness of our

meetings less and less appealing, and he threatened to tell Mama we were seeing each other. "I'll spill none of the important beans, naturally," he said, "but your mother seems to be a reasonable woman. Maybe you give her less credit than she deserves. I'll simply say that I like your company and I want to be with you, which is the truth."

I begged him not to go to her. I warned him that I gave her exactly the credit she deserved, that one hint from him about us and Mama would see that we'd never be together again.

He gave in, though not without an argument. I was as frustrated by the secret nature of our meetings as he, because I could not make myself believe anything we had done was truly wrong. I was well aware that the love Charlie felt was for a young girl, not a woman, but there was purity in this love; the age difference made it unusual, to be sure, but it was about as ugly and perverse as a sunrise. (In the 1950's, some newspapermen compared Errol Flynn and Beverly Aadland with Charlie and me, an understandable though wildly inaccurate comparison. Flynn was a self-proclaimed hedonist who, for all his public defense of the free life, was essentially a deeply troubled moralist, as he proved—to me, at least—in the noisy and often constant way in which he called attention to his affair with a girl less than half his age; he fairly smacked his lips when he alluded to their sexual athletics. Despite his young blonde lady friend's hysterically dramatic assertions that their love affair had "depth" and "tempestuous thunder cracking all the time," Flynn was content just to have the folks know that he was bedding down with a young girl.)

It's hardly a secret that Charlie had a penchant for young girls. He approached them as projects, and indeed, cared for some of them. He liked to cultivate them, to gain their trust, to be their first—never their second or third lover, and to create them as scrupulously as he created a motion picture. To me he admitted his preference for the company of inexperienced girls over experienced women. "It's so damned difficult to explain this to even sensitive people, so I've stopped trying. They have a fixed conviction that if Mr. November sets his eye on Miss May, there's only one reason. As far as an artist is concerned, that's rubbish. The most beautiful form of human life is the very young girl just starting to bloom. Some Mr. Novembers can be disgusting when they're with some Miss Mays—no doubt of it. I see them all about, old grandfathers peering through rheumy eyes, eager to corrupt innocence. I'm not like that—God, I *know* I'm not. I want to build you, not destroy you. You know that, don't you, Lita?"

Not waiting for me to answer—I gave him my answer every time we met, for walks, for bed, for brief kisses—he talked of Mildred Harris. "Mildred was a pretty thing —not breathtaking and not overly bright, but she had a way about her that made me think I could do something for her, educate her, wake her up to all the wonders of the universe. I tried, and she seemed willing to let me help to develop her." He sighed. "It didn't work. I was very fond of her, and we got married, and for a while I kept hoping she wouldn't let go of her youth—the spirit of youth, the spirit of being gay and forever incorruptible— but she lost it. In the long run she turned out to be as selfish and cynical as a brawling fishwife."

Charlie began to "create" me. Though he was never comfortable with the press—chiefly, I think, because he sensed the press was never comfortable with him; reporters and photographers couldn't understand why he wouldn't clown and put on funny hats—he granted frequent interviews, during each of which he never failed to mention me and praise my looks and acting. His praise, in fact, was so extravagant that inevitably someone would ask if there was a romance going on between him and Lita Grey. At first the question annoyed him, but it became such a natural part of each interview that he learned how to handle it with consummate skill. His interest in Miss Grey, he announced, was an artist's interest in another artist and in her potential.

I was thrilled, but worried. "Why did you build me up like that, calling me an 'artist' and everything? What's going to happen when the picture opens and everybody finds out I'm not as great as you said?"

"Just a moment," he cautioned. "The word 'great' was not uttered. 'Someday great,' perhaps. 'Great,' not. I'm not a Hollywood flack, Lita. I've got Tully to feed the Through the Looking Glass pap to the public. May the Lord strike me dead if I'm ever caught saying Hollywood words like 'stupendous' and 'colossal' to describe anything so unstupendous and uncolossal as an actor. I told the press the truth. I said your potentialities are great. And I believe it, if you work hard, and above all, if you stay young."

"You mean stay fifteen years old forever?"

"No, damn it, I don't mean that at all! You didn't understand what I was telling you about Mildred. Of course people get older. The only thing sad about getting older is that some people, the ones we most want to hold in time, mislay and then lose for good the marvelous spirit of being young. That needn't happen. When it does it's because the lovely glow of all that's sweet in youth has been allowed to die out. I want you to stay young, Lita. I want you to be young and curious and excited by life when you're a hundred years old. I want you never to be bitter, or bored."

Charlie brought me books to read, sometimes with pages paper-clipped to direct me to passages he considered particularly valuable. None of them concerned show business. Most of them were introductions to various arts and sciences, from ballet to anthropology and one of them—a book by H. G. Wells, dealing with the future—he paper-clipped copiously. I did my best to plough through each and every one of them, although I seldom succeeded, in spite of encouragement from Mama, who had been let in on his Educate Lita plan and who was all in favor of it.

"You should keep reading, dear," Mama maintained. "If Mr. Chaplin believes you have the capacity to take in these subjects, and if he goes to the trouble to give you these books, then you owe it to him—and yourself—to stretch your mind as far as it can possibly go."

It went next to nowhere, mainly because this fifteen-year-old nongenius found the bulk of the books rough going. One of them I worked at studiously, though, and that was the Napoleon biography Charlie had had in Truckee. For a long while, he told me, he'd been playing with the idea of making a serious movie about Napoleon, with himself in the central role." There've been a few films about Bonaparte, but none have even scratched the surface of this complex man," he said. "I may make it my next picture, once *The Gold Rush* is out of the way. And who do you think would be perfect as Josephine?"

I suppose I should have been exhilarated, but I wasn't. Charlie had absolute faith in me as an actress, but I didn't. In spite of his faith, and the apparent confidence of the people on the lot that I was doing a good job, I was convinced I merited neither faith nor confidence. True, I was getting into the part of the dance hall girl who befriends the tramp, and I had lost many of my initial fears that I would make a fool of myself; but if I was good there were two reasons: the part wasn't the most demanding in movie history, and I had a flawless director shepherding me every step of the way. As Josephine, though, I was positive I would fall smack on my face. And my ambition to be an actress, much less a star, had never been that consuming.

Charlie paid no attention to the doubts I voiced. "Your modesty is refreshing, but you'd do best to calm it a bit," he said. "How does it look for me to go to the public and praise you to the skies, and there you sit without a jot of confidence?" In one of his bursts of enthusiasm he confided his plan for his next picture project to Mama. Mama supplied the exuberance I lacked.

In bed with Charlie I wasn't quite so unsure of myself.

I was still having nothing close to an orgasm, but he was teaching me—and I rather thought I was teaching myself as well—how to give him the maximum of pleasure. I even began to be relieved when each act was finished and I hadn't reached a climax, for I told myself, in my gross ignorance, that you won't have a baby if you don't have an orgasm.

Once, only once, had we discussed the danger of my becoming pregnant. Charlie had assured me I was perfectly safe, and that had been that; out of trust in him, out of my own ignorance, I hadn't pursued the subject. Merna had told me about the rubber thing called a condom, and though I never saw him with one, I assumed that when he guaranteed my safety he meant I was always protected. Soon I stopped worrying about the possibility of an accident, if only because it made no sense that the famous, unmarried Charlie Chaplin would risk fathering a baby.

Although we were careful to cover our tracks, in time Mama began to sense that something out of the ordinary was going on. One day she asked me, point-blank, "Are you by any chance getting a crush on Mr. Chaplin?"

Understatement of the age though this was, I was nonetheless jolted. "That's a silly thing to say," I declared. "I like him, sure, but then so does everyone else. And anyway, he's more than twice as old as I am."

"That's very true—he is," Mama said. "He's also very attractive. I've been noticing—well, I don't know what I've been noticing. I can't put my finger on it, but there's something a little peculiar when you two look at each other. I'm not sure, but it doesn't seem like the kind of look that's right between a child and a man old enough to be her father."

"Oh, Mama, what sort of a terrible mind do you have?" I cried. "If you can't trust a man like Charlie, can't you at least trust your own daughter?" I was pleased and horrified at how convincing I sounded.

"Well, it's 'Charlie' now, isn't it?"

"Yes, it's 'Charlie'—when he's not listening!" I improvised desperately. "Really, you're just terrible! You shouldn't talk about anything like that."

Her voice lowered in the kind of calm that always scared me. "I'll thank you to keep a civil tongue, Lillita. I'm still your mother, and I'm determined that you're going to stay decent. I have nothing against Mr. Chaplin, but he *is* divorced, and he *does* have a reputation as a ladies' man."

"That has nothing to do with—"

"You be still and listen to me. I may not be the most intelligent woman, but I do know a great deal about men."

"Oh, are you going to start that lecture again?"

She slapped my wrist—not hard, but hard enough to let me know she meant business. "Stop that snippy backtalk. Yes, I'm going to start that lecture again. Whether it's for better or worse, you're a pretty and—well, attractive—child. *Child,* I said—at fifteen you're still a child without a mind of your own. You matured too early physically, but that doesn't make you grown up, and neither does the fact that you're in the movies. Now, I'm not so old-fashioned that I don't realize a girl your age can have certain emotions about which the less said the better. But I *am* old-fashioned enough to know that if you ever let a man get free with you before you're married you'll regret it for the rest of your days. Are you *lis*tening to me, Lillita?"

Nodding, I stared at the ceiling, pretending to be suffering through an unendurable sermon. Mama kept it up, no longer referring to Charlie but cataloguing the horrible things that can happen to a decent girl's self-respect if she stops being decent. I was behaving like a brat, partly because I'd heard the lecture so many times before and partly to mask my guilt, because much of what Mama was saying contained enough obvious truth to make me uncomfortable.

The next free moment I had with Charlie, I told him of the encounter. "Don't fall apart—I'll come up with something," he said. And he did, the same day.

He would give a swimming-buffet dinner party at his house and invite about ten carefully chosen guests, none of them from the swimming club crowd. Mama would be the honored guest. I would be the innocent, wide-eyed visitor. Seeing us together in a relaxed setting, surrounded by people not connected with the studio, would dispel her suspicions about us. All I'd have to remember was to pretend I'd never been to the estate before. He would instruct the servants to show no sign of recognition when they saw me.

Pleased by the fact that Charlie invited her to the party personally, Mama said she'd be delighted to come. But she almost didn't make it, because a day before the party she suddenly doubled up in pain and had to be helped to bed. I flew to phone the doctor next door, who was luckily in and who agreed to come right over. When I returned to Mama, the color was back in her cheeks, but she clutched her stomach and complained of stabbing cramps.

The doctor arrived, poked about, said he could fairly safely rule out appendicitis and after examining her for another five minutes or so, said, "You're in good condition, Mrs. Spicer. You gave yourself a bellyache, that's all. Come to my office tomorrow if you like and we'll run some tests, but I'm sure it's nothing to be alarmed about."

The pain seemed to vanish as quickly as it had started, and soon Mama got up and walked around as if nothing had happened. I was about to shrug it off when she startled me by admitting, a bit too offhandedly, that this hadn't been the first time she'd had a seizure like this.

"Why didn't you tell me?" I asked, horrified. "Haven't you seen a doctor?"

"No, and I don't intend to," she said. "I hate to fuss with doctors. I'll be all right."

Although she appeared fit the next morning, I was all

for calling Charlie's house to say we wouldn't be there, but Mama wouldn't hear of it. She was fine, she insisted.

When we arrived at four o'clock on that sunny but cool Saturday afternoon, we found Charlie, in excellent spirits, in his bathing suit. We'd brought our own swim suits at his recommendation, and he suggested now that we change and take a dip before the weather got too brisk. Mama declined, saying she didn't feel much like swimming after all, but I was eager to try the pool.

Most of the guests had already come, and they were chatting comfortably about the unusual midsummer weather. I knew Alf Reeves, who had brought his wife, Amy. We were introduced to Dr. Cecil Reynolds, a very tall skeleton of a man, and his wife, Nora. The other guests looked like substantial citizens; they were people in various professions, all of them polite and rather sedately reserved. Roughly half of them were in bathing suits, but Charlie appeared to be the only one who had actually been in the water.

As I swam—alone—I saw him and Mama sitting in deck chairs, deep in what looked like sober conversation. I was terribly curious, of course, and at the first opportunity I asked Mama what they'd been talking about.

"You, mostly," she answered, pleased. "Mr. Chaplin is all excited about your work in the picture. He says you take direction well and you have a beautifully unspoiled way about you. He was raving about how refined you are, what good manners you have." She smiled. "He's a real flatterer. He said I could take most of the credit for what a nice girl you are. And he called me Lillian."

"There, you see? Does he sound like a vulture?"

"I never called him anything like that and you know it!" she said with a sniff. "I'm—well, I'm sure he's a real gentleman."

We all stayed near the pool till the sun went down, and then Charlie took Mama and me on a proud though lightning tour through most of the estate. Mama was enthralled. As for me, for someone who knew the house pretty well from stem to stern, I gave a superb performance —my "oohs" and "ahhs" sounded as genuine as Mama's. And none of the servants let on they knew me.

The buffet dinner was leisurely and almost, if not entirely, opulent; I was captivated by the sight of caviar and guinea hen being served on paper plates and imported wine being poured into paper cups. Charlie was both frustrated and tolerantly amused by a discussion he was trying to have with Dr. Reynolds; he was asking questions about medicine, but the doctor was interested only in discussing movies. At one point Charlie turned to Mama, who was on his left, and said, grinning, "What am I going to do, Lillian? This skinny horror happens to be one of the most deservedly noted brain surgeons of our time, and I'm honored that he's here. I have a thousand things I want to ask him, and he won't give me the chance. Do you know why? Because this great man wants to chuck the important work he's doing and become a *player* in motion pictures! Can you imagine?" Charlie made "player" sound like "panhandler."

Dr. Reynolds, his prominent Adam's apple bobbing, protested. "When did I say I want to chuck what I'm doing? All I've ever said is that I'd like to tackle acting for a while. Don't make me sound like a maniac, you maniac. You have no peer in the movies, Charlie, but your sophistication leaves a lot to be desired. Surgery stops being fascinating as a topic for conversation after the first ten minutes. The world of entertainment never stops being fascinating. I simply won't have my brain picked by a low Cockney like you."

Obviously relishing the game, Charlie countered, "All right then, I won't have my brain picked by a ha'penny brain doctor like you. Consider the matter closed. I have better things to do with my time than frittering it on underweight quacks." He turned again to Mama. "What can we do with this overpriced pill pusher, Lillian?" he

110

asked in mock severity. "I didn't invite him, you know—his lovely wife, yes, but not him. He crashed the party."

Mama was so flabbergasted by the attention paid her that she could make only tiny "oh dear" sounds.

The evening went smoothly until the first few guests began to leave. Then, suddenly, Mama fell ill again, this time so violently that Charlie had to help one of the servants and me steer her upstairs to the first available bed—which was in the feminized guest room I had seen so often. We set her down, and after watching her grasp her stomach and listening, helplessly, to her moans, Charlie snapped to the servant, "Find Dr. Reynolds. Get him up here at once."

"I'm all right . . ." Mama gasped, but she was surely not all right; her face was ashen and she writhed in an agony that paralyzed me with fright.

Dr. Reynolds stalked into the room and cleared us out into the hall, closing the door after us.

"We're lucky he was here," Charlie said to me.

I went to pieces. He put a comforting arm around me and stayed with me in the hallway for perhaps twenty minutes, until Dr. Reynolds emerged.

"I've given her a sedative," the doctor said. "She oughtn't to be moved, Charlie. She ought to sleep here tonight."

"Of course!" Charlie agreed. "What is it? Can I get anything for her?"

"No, she'll be all right. The sedative should take effect immediately, and she'll sleep through till morning." He shook his head. "She's quite a stubborn woman. She tells me she's had a few other attacks like this one, but she won't see a doctor. She's afraid of what a doctor might tell her. It's absolutely senseless."

"Please," I said. "What's the matter with my mother?"

"There's no sure way of judging without an X ray," he answered. "It could be an ulcer, it could be her appendix, it could be—this is my hunch—some disorder in the fallopian tubes. In any event, it would be idiocy not to have

111

a complete checkup." He began to scribble something on his prescription pad. "Here's the name of an internist I can recommend highly." He tore the top sheet off the pad and handed it to me. "Getting your mother there might involve a lot of work on your part, young lady. But I strongly advise that you waste no time."

In a scared whisper, I asked, "Can she die?"

A kindly smile spread over his normally expressionless face. "Not for a great many years." I said I wanted to go into the room to be with her, but he shook his head. "I'd rather you didn't. Give the sedative a chance to go to work. She should have as few disturbances as possible. The best thing you can do is take care of yourself. You've had a scare and you look it. Relax. Your mother will be perfectly fine tonight."

The three of us went back downstairs, where the remaining guests were solicitous about Mama. Dr. Reynolds assured them that everything was under control and then signaled to his wife that it was time to leave. I thanked him for what he'd done, and so did Charlie. A quarter of an hour later the last of the guests had said good night and gone, leaving Charlie and me alone in the mammoth sitting room.

He brought me a glass with a dark liquid in it and said, "This is brandy. Drink it. It'll settle your nerves."

I sipped it and coughed. I sipped it again, and coughed again, but soon I stopped coughing; the brandy tasted dreadful, but after a moment it felt warm and wonderful in my stomach. Charlie had poured a drink for himself, but he only held it and sniffed it occasionally. Unlike lots of people in the picture industry, Charlie had no interest in alcohol. At dinners and parties he would always accept a drink, though more out of courtesy than thirst, and he would nurse it. He would rarely have a second. At the dinners and parties he gave in his house, liquor was always available to his guests but little drinking was done, chiefly because people who got drunk irritated and bored him.

Only once did I ever see him very drunk.

"How is it?" he asked.

"Full of fire."

He chuckled. "A few drops can't hurt you. You'll be able to sleep well."

"I think I'm a little scared," I said slowly. "I believe Dr. Reynolds—that my mother will be all right tonight—but I'm still a little scared."

"Of course. That's because you're a compassionate, sensitive person. But fretting is going to help neither you nor your mother. You should do what Dr. Reynolds advised—take care of yourself. Worrying about your mother will only make the night endless for you."

"What am I supposed to do? Ignore her?"

"No. Just be practical. There's nothing you can do for her tonight. But there's something you can do for yourself—and for me."

I looked at him.

And he was looking at me, meaningfully. "It's the first night we've ever had together. Make use of it."

The suggestion upset me. "How could you even think of such a thing at a time like this?" I said angrily.

His manner became even more low-keyed, and I wished he weren't so close. "Are you going to disappoint me, Lita? Are you going to go in for black magic?"

"What do you mean?"

"I mean that obviously your joining me in my room will have no bearing one way or another on your mother's recovery. Superstition may tell you that if you join me your mother will die, and if you don't join me she'll spring back to health immediately. But that's pretty childish, isn't it?"

I kept shaking my head. And drank more of the brandy. And melted enough in the next few minutes to agree that he was right, as usual.

We parted in the second-floor corridor, and I entered the guest room quietly. From the light of the table lamp I could see that Mama, lying on her back, was quite asleep, moving slightly now and then but definitely asleep. She was well covered, and I was grateful that her face had

113

color again. I leaned down to kiss her cheek. She didn't stir.

I sat in the chair beside the bed, watching her and listening to her breathing, which was regular and deep. I wondered what kind of heartless animal I was—my mother was ill, maybe very ill, and I could barely wait to get into bed with Charlie. But I had talked myself into agreeing that he indeed was right, that I could do nothing for her by staying here. After another couple of hesitant minutes I got up and tiptoed across the soft carpeting toward the bathroom, not taking my eyes from Mama. I went into the bathroom, closed the door soundlessly behind me, and rapped ever so softly at the connecting door to Charlie's room. He whispered, "Come in."

A small light was on and he was in bed, lying naked atop the blankets, his arms extended. I began to unbutton my blouse as I went to him, amazed that my body was so stoked with passion even though he hadn't touched me, amazed that I could undress myself so boldly in front of him. Until now I had waited for him to peel my clothes off; until now I had been passive, or what I supposed a girl should be if she was to be called feminine. Now, though, I was acting exactly the way I was sure sluts acted. In taking off my blouse without the preliminaries of seduction I was announcing that I was *eager* for sex. Surely decent girls *never* behaved like this. Now, standing at the side of the bed, I freed the single button at my skirt waist. The skirt fell to the carpet and I stepped out of the ring it made around my feet.

"You step away from a skirt like an empress, Josephine," he said softly.

My instinct was to warn him to make no sound, but I realized he was talking normally and that even if Mama were awake she couldn't hear anything. Not amused, not proud of myself, I answered, "I don't feel like an empress. I feel—hot." The vulgar description just popped out of me. I was at a loss to understand the sensual abandon I felt, it didn't occur to me that the brandy might have had something to do with it. Feeling irresponsible, yet swelling with explicit urges, I pulled the panties down over my hips. Without a word, I conveyed the idea to Charlie that the fearfully timid Lita had been replaced—hopefully forever—by an unapologetic wildcat.

He sat up, his eyes grave. I was just about to step out of my shoes when he muttered, "No, wait. Keep them on." He pulled me down on top of him, encircled me with his arms and gripped me with fantastic strength. I kissed him with my tongue, teasing lightly at first and then driving deeper and deeper, with heightening intensity, into his mouth. His fingers found the clasp of my bra, released it, and thrust it away.

He pushed me off and maneuvered his torso toward my mouth, urging me to do the thing I had refused to do so many times before. Less inhibited now than ever, I was on the verge of doing what he wanted, but at the last moment I turned my head away and refused again. Charlie tried once more, again without success, and then invaded me quickly and unceremoniously.

For me, the rapturous joy of making love with Charlie lay in those serene moments afterward when we huddled together, still deliciously sweaty, embracing each other protectively against the world. This night, though, scant minutes had elapsed before he was aroused again, and we were locked together once more.

When we were still again I asked, "Do all men do it like this, one right after the other?"

He laughed. "No, if you must know. Most men need a rest between—ah—bouts. I don't. I'm either lucky or divinely blessed. I'm a stallion, Lita, and you'd better resign yourself to it."

Later on I was to learn that this was no idle boast. There were nights, after our marriage, when Charlie was good for as many as six "bouts," as he called them, in succession, with scarcely five minutes' rest in between. But tonight was to be merely a preliminary.

Continuing the banter, he teased me: "Considering

that I get no real cooperation from you, you pretty bitch, I think I'm the Eighth Wonder of the World, at least."

"Cooperate? Who says I don't cooperate?"

In a suddenly serious tone, he said, "You've got to learn something, Lita. Nothing is wrong if two people love each other. Love is not only sharing but giving. What I want you to do isn't all that monstrous. But I'm not a fiend, an ogre. Maybe I'd better just bide my time till you love me."

"I *do* love you."

A pause. "Then why this ridiculous holding back?"

"Because—because the thought of it makes me—makes me gag. I love you, and I'll always love you. But I can't do that."

He cuddled me. "Very well, then. Not now, not yet. You'll change your mind in time, though. You'll come to see that love has no fences around it."

"Yes, I'll try," I murmured. I reached over and kissed his beautiful lips, marveling at the fact that this man I adored, who had not yet propelled me to the promised clouds, was able, by his presence and even by the thought of him, to send me into a feverish frenzy of desire.

In the room's purring softness, in each other's arms, we talked. About nothing and about everything.

And heard the doorknob squeak in turning.

The door opened and Mama tottered weakly into the room and saw us there, without our clothes on.

Chapter Eight

As we sat there, frozen, she stood in the doorway, staring at us with a glazed, unseeing look on her face, and then staggered back and closed the door, leaving us alone.

I scrambled to my feet and dressed hurriedly. Charlie reached for his robe, but, oddly, seemed only mildly upset. "In a way, it's good she saw us," he said. I was sure he had to be raving mad to talk like that, but I didn't answer him. All that mattered now was that I go to my mother. I would say nothing because there was nothing that could be said, but I had to see her and have her see me.

Mama was in bed, her hands lifeless, her full eyes trained on the ceiling. Her cheeks were moist with tears, but she would not look at me. I wept, and I kissed her cheeks desperately, in urgent need not so much to be forgiven as to let her know I was aware of the pain I'd caused her. Still not looking at me, she finally said, in a fuzzy voice befogged by dope, "I dreamed that . . . it didn't happen . . . I dreamed . . ."

She turned to me, but her eyes were still far away. "I woke up. I went to the bathroom. I heard you and him, I thought I heard you, I was there and dreaming and I heard you. So sleepy . . . I want to leave here . . . so sleepy . . ."

Charlie knocked and marched into the room, ignoring me in order to give all his attention to Mama. He sat on the edge of the bed and took her hand. "Lillian, listen to me. This wasn't the way it appeared. I love your daughter, do you hear me, Lillian? I love her, and she loves me, and I'm going to marry her."

Mama blinked. I was thunderstruck.

"Are you listening to me, Lillian?" he said intensely. "I've been planning to make Lita my wife for months now. I adore her. There aren't five minutes that pass that I don't think of her. I'm not a bad man, Lillian. I'm going to do the right thing. We'll make the arrangements, and when the picture's finished we'll have the biggest wedding the world has ever seen."

He was talking fast but with emphasis, knowing her sedated brain couldn't take everything in, yet intent on making her understand that everything was all right. Mama began to talk, but her words and thoughts rambled. Suddenly she was asleep again.

I studied his face as he rose, trying to determine whether he'd said what he had merely to appease Mama for the time being or because he really meant that he wanted to marry me. His expression was still grave, but he looked like a man greatly relieved. "I've wanted to do this for so long," he said softly. "I do want us to marry. Why did I wait so long to say it?" He came to me, and at last he smiled. "You'll be my wife, won't you?"

Everything was happening much too fast, and I told him I couldn't talk about it yet. Then, with unusual insensitivity, he said, "Now that that's settled, come back with me to my room. We'll celebrate our decision."

"No," I breathed. "Please go. Please let me stay with my mother."

Charlie shrugged, then left. I felt too cheap, too dirty, to get into bed beside Mama, so I sat in the chair near the window, folding my legs under me, and watched her. Nothing would ever be the same again, I mourned. Mama wouldn't cast me out, wouldn't stop being my mother, but we were set apart now, all the same. I had begun to love Charlie and to make love with him for a number of reasons, simple and complex ones, but I had never thought of marrying him—not seriously. I didn't want to marry him. I didn't want to marry anybody. I wanted to be a fifteen-year-old girl. Perhaps I wanted to be a virgin again. But everything would be different now.

I wept for Mama. And petrified by the thought of Grandpa finding out about Charlie and me, I wept for myself, for my maze of confusion, for the loss of my childhood.

When I woke up in the morning, the bed was empty and Mama was nowhere to be seen. I'd fallen asleep in the chair, and someone had covered my legs with a blanket.

Mama, fully dressed and looking well, entered the room and walked to the bureau mirror to comb her hair, which obviously had already been combed. She was remote but not hostile. She had just telephoned Grandma, she said, to say we'd decided to sleep here overnight, that everything was all right and that we would be home soon. I expected her to start right in on the night before, but she didn't. Her composure worried me.

Kono met us at the foot of the stairs and said, "Mr. Chaplin rarely takes his Sunday breakfast till late in the morning, but I can see that you're served now, if you like." Mama answered that we wished to leave and asked if he could call a taxi for us. "That won't be necessary," he said. "I'll have Frank drive you."

The faceless chauffeur took us home in the Locomobile. Most of the ride was silent and strained. Finally, unable to hold my anxiety in any longer, I urged, "You won't tell Grandpa what happened, will you?"

"I don't know yet what I'm going to do about anything. I do know that sometime today you and I are going to spend of lot of time together, talking."

Grandpa was waiting for us in front of the house, and motioning for Frank to stay at the wheel, he opened the car door for us himself. "This is a dandy time for you two to be straggling home," he said gruffly, but I could tell he wasn't angry. Fortunately he and Grandma had turned in early, so there had been no chance for them to worry about our safety; fortunately, too, they hadn't missed us this morning till Mama had phoned.

Grandma poured coffee and asked for all the glamorous details about the Chaplin party. Grandpa, who never admitted interest in such goings-on, managed to stay within earshot even while pretending no curiosity. I must say that Mama gave an absorbing, succinct account of the afternoon and evening without alluding even fleetingly to me or to her illness. At any rate, my grandparents seemed to be satisfied that nothing was amiss.

Around noon, Mama and I took a long walk. And we talked. She spoke unemotionally, which made it seem at first that she was indifferent to what had taken place. But I knew she was upset, and hurt, and confused. Her first question was, "How long has it been going on?"

I had lied long enough. I answered her truthfully. I began at the beginning and told her everything, from the time in Truckee to the time last night. I defended Charlie, insisting that I had been the one who'd chased after him. Mama listened, her eyes now showing revulsion, now looking sad. But she appeared calm—ominously calm.

"I thought about calling the police," she said, "about having him arrested."

"Mama!"

"And I decided against it—not to save your lordly Mr. Chaplin, but to save you the ugliness of being drawn into a courtroom. Then I thought about telling Grandpa, and I decided against that, too, because Grandpa would take a gun and shoot him, and that would involve a courtroom, too." She paused. "Lillita, it's too late now, obviously, for me to give you any more—well, you call them lectures, don't you? I'm going to insist on one thing, though. You'll finish the picture, mainly because I can't imagine how we could explain to people—your grandfather, especially— why you suddenly stopped being in the movie. But from now until your work in the movie is done, you and this man are not to have a single word with each other, much less spend a minute together, except where the picture is concerned. You're to give me your word about this. If you don't, if you disobey me, I can assure you that you, and he, will regret it."

"He said he wants to marry me," I reminded her weakly.

Mama looked at me and frowned. "Is that really what you want, Lillita—to be married at fifteen, and to a man his age? What would you get out of it? The physical part of it wears off awfully fast—believe me, I know. Money and comforts? Yes, they would be nice, but look at what you'd be giving up to get them. Your youth, Lillita. You'd never get the chance to grow into womanhood normally, to find yourself. You'd be the tiny shadow of a man who lives only for himself, who'd stay with you for a time and then, the second another girl came by, who'd—"

I insisted she was all wrong, but something inside me knew she wasn't.

In the afternoon, the telephone rang. Mama answered and motioned me out of the room. She told Grandma that the call had been from a friend, but she told me privately that the call had been from Charlie. "The gall of the man is almost completely unbelievable. He phoned to ask how I'm faring after my attack last night, but he acted as if that's all that happened at his house."

"But he did call," I said timidly. "That means he's thoughtful. Why else would he call except that he was worried about you?"

"To judge how worried he should be about himself. Well, I told him. I told him everything I told you—that he's forbidden to have anything to do with you except *Gold Rush* work. I told him that if he wished to take you off the picture I'd agree to letting him cancel the contract, but under no circumstances was he ever to see you again."

Mortified, I asked, "What did he say?"

"Oh, he acted terribly hurt that I was taking such a position when he'd assured me about his so-called love for you, and on and on and on. But he ended up saying that if that's the way I wanted it, that's the way it would be. Incidentally, you might be interested to know that he didn't refer to marriage even once."

I ran upstairs and slammed the door, unendurably humiliated. How could she have been so heartless, so horrible? I lay on the bed in misery. Strangely there were perverse instants of relief that it was finally over at last— I'd never truly reconciled myself to what we did in bed— but they were only instants; we loved each other, and I could never face him again.

On the lot the next morning Alf Reeves announced that the whole company was dismissed till the following morning. Charlie had called in and said that it was one of his Don't Feel Funny days. I was dying to go to the Beverly Hills house, but I didn't dare to leave Mama's sight.

That same day she confessed that she'd phoned the internist Dr. Reynolds had recommended and asked for an appointment. She wasn't feeling in tiptop shape, she said, even though there'd been no more attacks since Saturday night. She'd just decided that probably she'd been wrong —that if there was anything wrong with her it would be foolhardy not to see a doctor. This uncharacteristic concern for her own health automatically dissolved my anger toward her and made me apprehensive.

I was concerned, but the moment I was sure it was safe

I went to the telephone and called Charlie's house. Kono answered. I identified myself and asked to speak with Mr. Chaplin. In a minute I heard Charlie's voice, guarded, a bit remote.

"Where are you calling from?"

"My home," I said. "It's all right. I'm alone. I . . . do you hate me?"

"Of course not, you simpleton." He laughed, sounding magically more familiar now that he gathered I hadn't been forced to make the call. "You can believe this or not, but just this moment I was standing here, thinking about you, wishing you'd ring me up. I think your mother's being terribly unfair—she said some disgraceful things to me that I wouldn't take from anyone else—but I'm an incurable optimist, dear. She'll come around some day. She'll see that we've done nothing to be ashamed of. Ah—will she be away long? Could you get out and come here?"

"Oh, gosh, no, I wouldn't dare, not with the way she's been carrying on. And anyway, aren't you a little scared? That she'd do something bad to you if we see each other again, I mean?"

"Now you know that's just a pack of maternal noises," he said lightly. "She's not likely to report me to anyone, and the three of us know it perfectly well. I don't like not seeing you, but I'm willing to go along with her annoying little hysterics for a while. She'll be over them soon. In the meantime, I do wish you could come here. I'm feeling very lonesome and very naughty."

"I'll bet you could have any one of a hundred girls there in two minutes."

"A hundred? No, a thousand. But I want to be naughty with you, not with them."

We didn't talk long, but long enough for each of us to convince the other that our feelings were as strong as ever, maybe stronger. I replaced the receiver, frustrated that we weren't together but grateful that he still cared for me.

On the set, Mama and Charlie were formal but polite. Then, early one evening after leaving the studio, Mama kept her appointment with the internist and took me along. I said nothing to her, but I was getting mildly interested in seeing a doctor myself. I was a number of days late in getting my period this month. I wasn't worried about being pregnant, certainly. My periods were erratic more often than not. What bothered me was that for the past few days, instead of my usual premenstrual aches, I had been having moments of weakness and dizziness, plus a general physical feeling of uneasiness.

As I waited alone in the outer office while Mama was being examined, I was suddenly engulfed by a wave of nausea. It was frightening, but the moment it passed I attributed it to concern over Mama's health.

The reports came in. Dr. Finney hastened to assure Mama that she had nothing serious. He did see what he called a baby tumor in one fallopian tube, however, and he urged her, to be on the safe side, to check into a hospital and have it removed. "It's the kind of thing you might be able to live with for the rest of your life without being troubled by it ever again, except for those pain attacks. On the other hand, why fool around? Get it over with, and you'll be out of the hospital in less than a week."

"I'll get back to you, Doctor. Thank you."

I knew what that meant, because I knew how scared she was of doctors and hospitals. I begged her to take Dr. Finney's recommendation seriously. She promised she would. Then she made me promise, on my solemn word, that I wouldn't breathe a word of any of this to Grandma or Grandpa. "They're worry warts," she reminded me. "Doctors always make things more frightening than they are. We'd just worry your grandparents into a fast grave."

From nowhere it suddenly occurred to me that night that maybe Dr. Finney hadn't made Mama's diagnosis sound as frightening as it really was. Maybe the news was worse than he'd let her know. Maybe he'd sensed that she couldn't have taken bad news point-blank and had colored it for her, but maybe it was really important for her to have an early operation.

The next morning I called his office and asked to see him. His nurse gave me an appointment, two days later, at half-past four.

On the morning of the appointment I awakened in the grip of a severe siege of nausea. Fleeing to the bathroom, I began to vomit helplessly. I leaned over the toilet bowl, retching seemingly without end, glad that the family was already downstairs. Finally done, I sank to my knees on the cold floor, feeling shaky and still violently ill, marveling at how fast the pinwheels were spinning around and around in my head.

I'd read somewhere about morning sickness, about its being one way your body has of telling you you're going to have a baby.

A *baby?* No!

I'd eaten something last night, that was all. I couldn't remember what, but I'd eaten something bad and now I was throwing it up. I couldn't be pregnant. If you didn't have an orgasm, how could you be pregnant? True, I hadn't had my period yet. But then I was usually late, or early. Charlie had been calm, had told me not to worry.

No! O God in Heaven, no!

I got up, went to the bathroom window and took at least a dozen deep breaths. They helped. I flushed the toilet, grabbed a washcloth, ran it under the cold water tap and retraced my steps to the hall to clean up any traces. I went back to the bedroom, purposely walking straight, purposely breathing deeply, and began to dress to go to the studio. I didn't want to pray, because I was ashamed. But I prayed.

The shakiness receded. I descended the stairs to the kitchen with a surely overdone display of poise. The family was at breakfast. Grandma was the first to see me and the first to say that I was pale. Then Mama and Grandpa looked up, and both agreeing I was pale, demanded to know why.

"I'm all right," I said haughtily, and sat at the table.

Mama felt my forehead, then said it was damp and that she was sure I was coming down with a cold. Grandpa grunted that I should stay home and get busy with mustard plasters. He knew, as I'd heard him say countless times before, that the only way to lick a cold was with mustard plasters. I kept insisting I was all right.

And in fact, I was. By noon on the set I had nearly completely forgotten how sick and fearful I'd been in the bathroom. We'd shot the scene in the dance hall in which Charlie, smitten with me, sees me smile and wave and assumes I'm smiling and waving at him. Shyly he waves back. I approach him—and then walk past him, for I've really been smiling at a man behind him. Charlie had us do it twice, announced he liked it, and then had us do it twice more, just to be sure. He was happy, in good form that day, and he made no pretense of it. "Some days, everything goes beautifully on a set, without rhyme or reason. This is one of them," he confided to those nearest him, making certain that Mama was one of them.

At three-thirty I asked Chuck Riesner to ask Mr. Chaplin, quietly, if I could be excused for the day. Fifteen minutes later Chuck caught my eye and nodded. I went to my dressing room, got out of my makeup and costume, changed to street clothes and left the lot by a side door. Mama wouldn't like not being able to keep tabs on me, but at least she would know that Charlie and I weren't together.

Dr. Finney welcomed me into his office, and I got straight to the point about Mama. "Does she have cancer, or is there any possibility of it in your mind?" I asked. "Deep down, she's not very sturdy. Have you been holding anything back?"

Lacing his fingers across his chest, Dr. Finney smiled a contagious smile. "The answer is No, definitely No. Purely and simply, No. Is there anything else I can tell you?"

He didn't see me squeeze the arms of the chair. "May

I ask you something, and will you tell me without telling my mother?"

"I'll try."

"Will you tell me if I'm pregnant?"

Dr. Finney asked me questions. Charlie's name was never mentioned. I was tested and told to phone the next afternoon.

I did, and got the results. I was carrying a child. There was no doubt about it.

Chapter Nine

First there was numbness. Then there was panic.

I called Charlie's house. Kono said the master had left the city for the weekend and couldn't be reached, but that he might telephone. Did I wish to leave a message? Could I be called anywhere? "No," I said.

I hung up and sat in the booth for a very long time. It seemed preposterous that the only person I felt I could talk to was Merna Kennedy, and I certainly wasn't going to go to her. Dr. Finney had been solicitous, had invited me to come to see him, but I couldn't do that—not yet. I left the booth and walked in a half daze, unbearably alone. There was a church up ahead. I hurried to it— but stopped at the door, too ashamed to enter.

Mama would have to know, of course, yet the prospect of telling her was chilling. In bed with her that night,

I tossed as she slept, wondering how long I could keep the news from her. If only I could have reached Charlie—he would have known what to do.

In the morning I did exactly the thing I had spent most of the night promising myself I wouldn't do. I told her.

She immediately covered her mouth with her hand, as though to keep from crying out. She made me tell her again, and then she wept so hard and so uncontrollably that I was afraid Grandma would hear and come running in. When I tried to comfort her she slapped me across the face. And then she took me in her arms and cradled me.

When she was able to compose herself, Mama phoned Dr. Finney. Then she phoned the house in Beverly Hills, even though I told her that Kono had said Charlie was out of town. Kono repeated the information that Mr. Chaplin wasn't due back till late Sunday night.

At the studio on Monday morning, she found Charlie and insisted on seeing him at once, in private.

He frowned. "Can't it wait? We've lots to do."

"It can't wait."

He looked at her, then at me, then back at her again. Then he nodded and preceded her to his office. He glanced over his shoulder once, seeming surprised that I wasn't coming along. She'd ordered me to stay where I was.

They were together for perhaps a quarter of an hour, and then he came storming out in a red fury. "Close down the set! Send everyone home! No work today!" he bellowed at Alf Reeves, stomping about like an insane man. Every eyebrow lifted. The company knew he had a temper, but bellowing had never been his style.

Though Mama's voice was controlled, she was no less angry than Charlie on our way home. "It's just monstrous, the way he behaved," she complained. "The dreadful things he said! Well, we'll just see about it."

"Mama, quit talking in riddles and tell me what happened!"

"When I told him that marriage was imperative, he

jumped up and got so wild I thought he was going to strike me. He kept saying 'Absolutely not!' He put all the blame on you and even on me. He even said . . ." She balked for a moment. "He even said that if you really *were* pregnant, we'd have to prove the baby is his—can you imagine? Your adoring Mr. Chaplin went so far as to suggest that he's not the only man you've been with, that someone else did this to you! What do you think of your lovely gentleman now?"

In agony, I asked, "What are you going to do?"

"I'm going to do nothing for a day, until he calms down. Then, if he's still stubborn and impossible, Grandpa will be told and he can take over."

"Oh, no . . ." I breathed, shuddering. "Grandpa will go crazy."

"You could've taken that into consideration some time ago," she said with a sniff. "What matters now, the only thing that matters, is that you be looked out for. Mr. Charlie Chaplin is responsible for what happened, and Mr. Charlie Chaplin and no one else is going to do what's right, either on his own or by force."

Charlie was somewhat calmer when he summoned Mama the next day. He had thought everything through very carefully, he explained. If she would bring him proof from my doctor that I was indeed pregnant, he would do the proper thing. He would pay for an abortion.

He made it as coldly simple as that. I was in the room, but he didn't look at me once.

Mama said an abortion was out of the question.

"What sort of blackmail have you got up your sleeve?" he said coldly. "I can't marry this child. You know that. I married a sixteen-year-old girl once before and the press crucified me. They'd have a heyday if it happened again. I'd be ruined! My whole career would go down the drain! Can't you understand that?" He was pacing about excitedly now. "I can't afford to be mixed up in another mess. And by the way, that's not all I can't afford! These fools who make me out to be a rich man don't know what they're blathering about. I don't have a hundredth of the money they say I—"

Mama quietly but firmly interrupted him. "Mr. Chaplin, we're not reaching each other. You are *not* being blackmailed. You *are* being reminded that my daughter is carrying your child. I will not let her have that child out of wedlock."

"Then have her get rid of it. I'll not only pay to have it done, I'll have my man make the arrangements. There's a doctor in the Valley who's expert at this kind of thing—"

"I'm not interested in 'this kind of thing,' " said Mama.

They argued back and forth, she softly, he in bitterly angry tones. They got nowhere until Mama rose to leave, making it clear that he would have to meet his obligation. He called her back and motioned for her to sit.

"Very well," he said wearily. "I have another solution, one that should satisfy everyone." He then proceeded to talk about me as if I were somewhere else. "She can be married, but not to me—definitely not to me. I'm prepared to give you ten thousand dollars in cash. Find her a young man to marry, a young man starting his climb up the ladder, someone who can benefit by that much money. It can be considered a dowry—Europeans do it all the time, and quite successfully. There should be no trouble in—"

"Stop it, both of you!" I cried. "Stop fighting about me! I'm not going to marry you, I'm not going to marry some man I don't know, I'm not going to marry anybody!" I shot up from the chair, sickened by being haggled over as though I were a piece of merchandise.

Charlie looked relieved, though for only a second. His hopeful expression vanished when Mama said to him, "I'll tell you once again—money is not an issue here."

"Then clear out of here!" he raged. "I've made two generous offers and you've rejected them both. I won't have you wasting another minute of my time!"

Mama started out, without another word. I wavered, looking unbelievingly at this gentlest of men, whose face was now contorted in such hatred. I went a little closer to him. "Please don't look so mad. You're the first and only man I've ever known. I love you. Please don't look at me like that—"

"Get out of my sight, you little whore!" he cried.

I was in the living room when Mama told my grandparents I was going to have Charlie's baby. Grandma Curry looked up, stunned.

We watched Grandpa and held our breaths in anticipation of the fury that was sure to descend upon us. But there was no fury. He simply left the room and went upstairs, and when he came down again he was carrying his shotgun. He clapped his hat on his head and started for the door. Both Mama and Grandma charged at him, clinging to him with hands and pleas, blocking his path. Suddenly he seemed very old.

"Let go of me! I'm going to kill that son of a bitch for what he did to this child!" he shouted in a voice that cracked with emotion.

Together they managed to restrain him and push him back into his easy chair, but he refused to let go of the gun. He demanded the entire story and sat ramrod straight as Mama gave it to him, ending with the last meeting in Charlie's office. Again Grandpa got up and again he was restrained. "I'm an old man," he snapped. "I don't have long to live anyway. What will they do to me if I kill the rotten son of a bitch? Execute me? No, by God, they'll hang a medal on me! I always knew he was called a tramp for a good reason, that dirty son of—"

"Dad, what we need now is a cool head, not these noisy conniptions," Mama said firmly. "Please quiet down."

He glowered at her, then nodded in agreement. "All right then, there's another way to go about this. The law in California about—ah—illicit relations between an adult and a minor is very strict. I'm sure it applies to Chaplin as much as to everybody else. Even with all his fancy attorneys he could rot behind bars till Doomsday, which is a pretty damned fine idea."

"Except that if he's punished Lillita will be, too," Mama reminded him. "They'd put her in all the newspapers. She'd never live it down."

"That's right, but then neither would Chaplin. I'll go see him myself and tell him what he already knows, I'm sure—that if he won't do right by my granddaughter I'll see him in the penitentiary."

Again no one was paying any attention to *me,* asking me *my* feelings. And what I resented most right now was being treated like a put-upon little angel who'd had no part in the seduction. "I want to say something," I began.

Grandma—my sweet Grandma, who in her entire lifetime had had only one opinion, that everyone on earth should be placid at all times—rocked back and forth, her feet not quite touching the floor, and prompted, "Will, Lillita wants to say something."

He frowned at me. "You've said enough, Miss, and you've done enough. If I'd thought for a second you didn't have the brains to stay out of trouble I'd never have let you anywhere near the picture business, much less a swine like Chaplin. Now you keep quiet."

Grandma gently criticized him. "Now, Will, that's not nice."

I'd had enough. I got up and left the room.

Just as I reached the stairs, the telephone in the hall rang and I answered it. It was Alf Reeves, who'd never called here before. "Lita, Charlie's shifting the shooting sequences again," he said, sounding ill at ease, like a man delivering an uncomfortable message. "He wants to experiment on some new bits with Mack Swain. So that means you and your mother won't have to check in at the lot for a couple of days, till we get back to you. That's why I'm phoning."

"Isn't everyone supposed to be on the lot on a shooting day, even if they're not in the scene? What's happening, Mr. Reeves?"

"Happening?" He cleared his throat. "What do you mean, happening?"

Quietly, so my family would have no chance of hearing, I asked, "Did Charlie tell you to call? Am I—Mr. Reeves, am I out of the movie for good?"

"Now where did you get a dumb idea like that? Why would you be out of the movie, for heaven's sake? I'm telling you exactly what Charlie said—he wants to work with Swain, and you don't have to report in till we call you."

"Thank you, Mr. Reeves."

Mama came into the hall to see who was on the phone. I told her, repeating the message. Then I climbed the stairs, plodded into the bathroom and brushed my teeth for what must have been a full minute.

Get out of my sight, you little whore! Charlie had said.

I didn't want to remember that; I wanted to recall the good things. But there were no good things now. Charlie had loved me, and now he hated me. There was a baby inside me, and I didn't want it because Charlie didn't want it. I didn't want to get married. I certainly didn't want to get married to someone who didn't want to be married to me. I detested loud voices, and there would be only loud voices from now on.

I got into my nightgown and into bed. Why had he called me a whore?

Although Grandpa had never had any use for my father, Robert McMurray, he had considerable respect for Daddy's brother Edwin, a successful San Francisco attorney. Rather than risk a long-distance telephone call that didn't guarantee privacy, he wrote Uncle Edwin a letter, detailing the situation and prevailing on him as "part of the family, someone I can trust implicitly," to take the necessary steps. Edwin McMurray wasted no time. He contacted Charlie and rattled a threatening sword, assuring him that statutory rape was a criminal offense, and that the state of California punished it severely.

Charlie gave in, on one condition: his own physician was to examine me to verify my condition. This was reasonable to everyone—everyone, that is, except me. I said that I wouldn't go through that again, no matter what happened. I didn't want Charlie this way. It was all so dirty, so unloving. It was holding a gun to his head. I didn't care what became of me; I wasn't going to force him into a loveless marriage.

I was told I had no say in the matter, that I didn't understand anything, that my family knew what was best for me. What did I want to do, have a bastard child? For what? For whom? For Charlie Chaplin, who'd had his fun and wanted none of the responsibility? How do you name a bastard child?

I submitted to the examination. The test was positive, of course.

Charlie tried persuasion again. He pointed out that I wouldn't be the first girl in the world to have an abortion. He would see to it I received the best of care, not only medically but financially, and he wouldn't even hold a grudge. He would still make the Napoleon and Josephine film and build me into one of Hollywood's most prominent stars.

That didn't work, so he repeated his suggestion that a man closer to my age be found to marry me, and said that instead of $10,000 he would bestow a "dowry" of $20,000. He was genuinely baffled when that offer was rejected, too, when he was told for the dozenth time that money was not an issue. "I'm showing perfectly good faith, and I'm being extremely practical, too," he maintained. "What kind of marriage would we have? Be realistic now, not emotional. On the other hand, what could be more ideal than having twenty thousand dollars and marrying a young chap who could use it to help him through a business or professional career? Why must everyone be so obstinate?"

Only then did I begin to realize how obstinate *he* was.

He still refused to talk to me or even look at me. Everything was my fault; he had no obligations. I suddenly began to see that my relatives weren't the only villains.

Charlie was stubborn by nature, but he knew when he was defeated. There would be a wedding, he conceded. There would also be a change in the *Gold Rush* cast. I would be replaced by Georgia Hale, the girl who'd played in Von Sternberg's *The Salvation Hunters* and who was similar to me in coloring and build. At first I thought he was making the replacement for revenge, but I soon learned that he wasn't. "I'm still a businessman," he explained. "We're so far into the picture, and we've shot so much footage of her"—referring to me in the third person, even though I was present—"that it would be imbecilic to replace her out of anger. But *Gold Rush* will take another six months or longer to finish, and her character appears in too many of the key scenes. By then she'll be big as a house."

Once he resigned himself to the fact that there was no way out, Charlie announced that the wedding would take place as soon as possible, but that he had no intention of its becoming a gigantic, hooplah affair attended by public and press. He devised a circuitous plan. We would go to Mexico by train, accompanied by a full technical crew. If anyone asked why, the explanation would be that we were going there to do some location shooting. Even I sensed that he was overdoing his ruse. Everyone knew he was doing a picture about the Klondike; then why location shots in Mexico? But Charlie would hear no arguments.

While Kono made the arrangements for the trip and Charlie went into seclusion, while Uncle Edwin returned to San Francisco, leaving Grandpa satisfied that he'd handled everything properly and Mama more and more convinced that things would turn out for the best, I quietly went to pieces. I couldn't eat, yet I vomited almost continually. I wasn't quite two months' pregnant, but my stomach felt as if it were about to burst. I was nervous and jumpy. I couldn't stand being alone, yet I couldn't bear it when anyone talked to me, even sympathetically.

The arrangements were completed. Kono arrived at the house with train tickets for Mama and me and instructions about meeting the next morning. He would be a member of the party, he said, to protect us from newspapermen. "It is of the utmost importance that neither of you talk to anyone," he instructed, and let himself out. I looked through the front window as he stepped onto the sidewalk. He appeared a little concerned to see a man in slouch hat and raincoat standing some yards from the house, but he walked on, quickly, in the opposite direction. The man stayed.

Kono met us on Platform Seven at eight the next morning, prepared to usher us to our quarters, but we were interrupted by two reporters who materialized from nowhere. "What's the story, Miss Grey?" one asked me. "Why this big exodus to Guaymas? Why are you going along?"

Deftly, Kono got in front of Mama and me. Sounding wholly unperturbed, he said, "Kindly excuse us. We're in a hurry," and hustled us onto the train and into our compartment.

We learned later that the reporters had boarded the train, too, and spent the onerous trip trying to get to me—without luck, for Kono saw that we stayed cooped up in the compartment; he even had all our meals delivered to us. They did reach Charlie, who gave them his friendliest grin and assured them that he only had one scoop—he was broadening the locale of *The Gold Rush* to include a number of scenes in Mexico. They considered that odd, and said so. Charlie chuckled. "I'm very odd when I make pictures. With luck, the finished product won't show it." He refused to explain further, and the reporters finally gave up and prowled the train in search of anyone else with information. They found no one.

Guaymas was an impossibly unattractive town, and the hotel made the one in Truckee seem lush by comparison.

A fishing craft was hired, and Charlie instructed the technical crew to sail it all day, every day, and make believe they were shooting Mexican sea scenes. This elaborate nonsense was kept up until the reporters who'd followed us —and the several other suspicious reporters who had popped up—put aside their bloodhound instincts at the nearest bar, which became a sort of second home for them as they gradually decided they'd come to Guaymas on a wild-goose chase.

This was what Charlie had been waiting for. The moment they relaxed their vigil, he bustled Mama, Chuck Riesner and me into a waiting car and we drove through the dusk, at breakneck speed, to Empalme, in Sonora, where a Justice of the Peace and an interpreter were waiting for us. Kono had been left behind to stall the newsmen if and when they realized they'd been given the slip.

Everything was moving with such slapstick speed that I found myself standing in front of the potbellied Justice, in his dreary, cramped, odorous living room, without entirely remembering how I'd got there. I was flanked by Mama and Charlie, and a grim-faced Chuck Riesner stood next to Charlie. The Justice was flanked by his equally potbellied wife and an old Mexican, serving as interpreter, who looked like Stan Laurel. Both Charlie and I were nervous, but he seemed frantically so. He was never much of a cigarette smoker, and certainly not on formal occasions, but during the ceremony he held a lighted cigarette between his fingers and even puffed on it nervously.

The Justice wheezed and mumbled in Spanish. I responded when nudged. Then it was over. Charlie blinked, cleared his throat, glanced awkwardly about and then, as awkwardly—and hastily—kissed my cheek. The Justice's wife blubbered, embraced me and chattered what must have been a string of congratulations and good wishes. She tried to embrace Charlie, as well, but he eluded her. Without looking around, he trotted out of the room through a side door, like an actor who knew the stage well and was making a carefully rehearsed exit.

Mama kissed me, and so did Chuck, who had tears in his eyes.

Empalme's single hotel was even more depressing than the one in Guaymas. Charlie and I were assigned a room, and Mama was given one down the hall. Once the manager had shown us to our rooms and departed, Charlie made it clear in a minimum of words that he would take Mama's room and she and I would share the bridal suite. He left us, marched down the hall and slammed the door behind him.

"Things will smooth themselves out, everything will be fine," Mama crooned serenely, sounding more like Pollyanna than Grandma did.

I was unstrung, but too drained to start crying again. The hotel room did nothing to put me even momentarily at ease. Its bareness was relieved only by a lopsided, antiquated iron bed, a wash basin and a chamberpot of cracked porcelain, a few blankets worn thin with use, and a pair of lumpy pillows covered with dingy white slips.

And when the nausea returned, I felt a total mess. Mama held me in her arms and sang to me, just as she'd done when I was a very little girl.

I'd needed a father then, too.

I have never understood what prompted Charlie to go to the extraordinarily melodramatic lengths he did, from the time we went to Mexico until the time we came back. The journey to a godforsaken setting, the elaborate business of taking along his technical crew in order to fool the press, the wild automobile ride over back roads to a gloomy wedding ceremony that could have been performed just as secretly and far more conveniently in countless less melancholy places—it all seemed like the peculiar inspiration of someone deranged. His explanation was that he wished to avoid the press, but that really explains nothing. He surely knew, whether he liked it or not, that in that November of 1924 he was the world's most publicized man, and that there was insatiable curiosity, especially among the press, about his every move. By the time we got back to Los Angeles, as he should have expected, everyone in America knew that he had married for a second time.

On the train back to California he sent word through Kono—who was again guarding me against all outsiders—that my mother should be shifted to his quarters. He would spend the night in the drawing room with me. I was confused and uncertain, but Mama was only too happy to oblige him. "He's mellowed, darling—don't you see? I predicted everything would smooth out. You have your husband now."

When Charlie finally entered the drawing room, more than an hour after Mama had left, he was anything but mellowed. "Riesner tells me one of those bastard reporters tracked us down to Empalme and wired his gawddam scoop on ahead to his paper. So for appearances' sake, the groom stays here with the bride," he said, locking the door.

"Please, let's talk," I pleaded.

He shucked off his jacket and wrinkled shirt without looking at me. "I don't talk," he said briskly. "I'm The Little Fellow, and The Little Fellow never talks, particularly with anyone for whom he has contempt, whom he knows to be beneath him. That's something about The Little Fellow you never understood, isn't it? Every intellectual and every illiterate all over the globe understands it, but you don't. The whole point of The Little Fellow is that no matter how down on his ass he is, no matter how well the jackals succeed in tearing him apart, he's still a man of dignity. He can still look down on you and your whole bloody bunch of money-hungry scum."

His tone of voice was the one he might have used to order dinner in an elegant resturant.

"Don't . . ." I begged.

"Don't what? Touch you? Don't worry, I shan't. I have as much interest in touching you as I'd have in making love to Attila the Hun—a gentleman I'm sure you've never heard of. You've heard of Valentino, and no doubt you know all the popular song rubbish of the day, and it's even possible—just possible—that you know how to spell your name and add two and two. Or is it?"

I closed my eyes. "All right, I'm terrible. Why wasn't I this terrible before?"

"You've always been terrible, from the instant you were conceived," he said, stepping into the adjoining bathroom, leaving the door open. Now he sounded like a teacher giving a monotonous lecture. "You had only one thing that wasn't terrible, and that was the thing between your legs. It didn't take you long to make the most of that one talent, did it?"

I could have taken his shouting at me, or hitting me, or even storming out. What I couldn't take was the soft way he was pouring out this vitriol, in a voice as smooth and sweet as syrup. I told him to stop—and he did.

Then there was quiet, except for the sounds of train wheels and tap water running in the metal sink. A terrible quiet.

Then I was asking for water, and he was asking if I wasn't afraid he would poison it. And then he was blithely engineering me into putting on a coat and getting some air on the observation platform, and once out there, behind me, he was asking why I didn't jump off—still in that silken, syrupy tone—and when I looked around to try to read his face in the darkness, it gave me no more answers than his voice had. The train gave one series of jerks after another, and the couplings beneath the metal platform we were standing on banged against the underpinnings of the car.

His expressionless eyes were hypnotic, and the clanking of the train seemed to grow louder, deafening. I wanted to bury myself somewhere, anywhere.

He walked away, off the platform, into the car.

I stayed where I was until the air got too penetrating, the chill inside me too acute. Then I walked numbly back to the drawing room. Charlie was in bed, lying on his side, lightly snoring.

Chapter Ten

Although I wasn't worried about my physical safety, I was hesitant to go alone with Charlie to the house in Beverly Hills. I wanted Mama with me, but she refused. "I'll go on to Grandma's and Grandpa's. Now don't act as if you're being deserted, darling. I won't be that far away. But your place is with him now."

At Shorb, a whistle stop just before Los Angeles, Kono proved himself a master of finger-snapping efficiency. He hopped off the train and beckoned to Frank the chauffeur, who had been alerted ahead of time to be there, to drive up as close as possible. He summoned a private taxi, ushered Mama and her luggage into it, gave the cabbie the address and paid him in advance. Then he gave the signal to Charlie and me, and as we hastened out of the train and into the limousine, Frank jumped out, fetched our bags, stuffed them in the trunk, and jumped back in. Kono stepped back on the train, prepared to go on with the rest of the company to Los Angeles, where a horde of reporters would doubtless be waiting.

Charlie drew the divider curtain and sat at the far end of the back seat. We didn't exchange a word throughout the whole of the long journey.

The car rolled up Cove Way, leaving clouds of dust in its wake. Rounding the curve at the top of the hill, we saw the gates, guarded by a battery of reporters and photographers.

Charlie yanked the side window shades down and barked, "Open that gate!" to Frank. Frank braked to a stop, bounded out and scurried through the crowd to the gate as the newsmen swarmed around us, trying to peer through the shade-drawn windows. Though it was only a matter of seconds before Frank flew back behind the wheel, bedlam reigned. "Drive straight through!" Charlie roared. The car lunged forward, charging at the opened gate, knocking cameras off their tripods, sending the crowd scampering for their lives. The powerful Locomobile roared through the melee and up the steep driveway.

Ralph, the Japanese houseboy, had the front door open for us and closed again the instant we were inside the house. Charlie, livid, strode straight for the stairs and climbed them two at a time until he was out of sight, leaving me alone with Ralph. Then Ralph disappeared up the stairs, evidently for the master's instructions, and I was left standing in the foyer, like a bundle of laundry waiting to be claimed.

I was home.

In a few moments there were angry noises from outside, and the doorbell began to ring insistently; the newsmen were demanding an audience with Charlie, and some were shouting that he'd broken their cameras and they were going to sue him for damaging their equipment. I stood motionless until Ralph reappeared, grinning at me. "Frank drive around side, he bring in suitcases when he sure newspaper all go home, and we bring suitcases upstairs."

He motioned for me to precede him up the stairs, and on the second floor he directed me to a room near the guest room in which Mama had slept. He opened the door and I went in. It was a comfortable enough room, larger than the guest room but not so large as Charlie's. This was to be my room, I was told. Instead of insisting on seeing my husband, I merely sat down, too tired and too frightened to move.

The luggage was brought in by Ralph and Frank, neither of whom looked at me. Then Ralph said that Mr. Chaplin would lunch downstairs in half an hour, before going to the studio: "He say you come down if you want lunch or cook bring you lunch here, maybe."

"Tell him I'll come down, please."

I showered, put on my brightest daytime clothes and went down to the dining room, where Charlie sat in his high-backed throne at the long table eating sausages and eggs. He knew I'd come in, but he did no more than glance up; his expression was as lifeless as the servants'. I sat opposite him, at the far end of the table, where dishes and silverware had been placed for me. Imu, another houseboy, served me and left.

After a few minutes of oppressive silence, Charlie finally spoke. Although we were separated by at least fifteen feet, he spoke normally. "Well, we've done it," he said, looking at his plate. "We're stuck with it. We might as well make the best of it."

Was I expected to apologize again? Was I supposed to gush that we'd not only make the best of it but that we would be the two happiest people in the world? I said nothing.

He didn't speak again until he had finished eating. Then he said, "I'm leaving for the studio. Kono should be here within the hour. He'll give you your instructions."

"Instructions?" I frowned. "Am I the new servant here?"

He realized the way it had sounded. "I didn't mean it that way. I mean I haven't the time to go into everything about the house. Kono will tell you all you need to know."

As he rose, I found the courage to ask, "Do you have to go? It's past noon now—the day's half over. Can't you stay—just today? I'd . . . appreciate it."

"I'm much too far behind now as it is," he said, and hurried out.

Kono was almost a stereotype of the Oriental villain in the movies. The other employees on the Cove Way staff— all Japanese—wore white jackets, soundless gum-soled shoes and a kind of collective grin that was annoyingly superficial, but Kono was different. He was a tall, straight man of indeterminate age, and he dressed in quiet business suits. He had a wife with whom he lived in a guest cottage not far away, but there was no doubt that nearly every one of his waking hours revolved solely around serving Charlie. I was to discover that in a number of ways I was more married to him than I was to Charlie.

My first encounter with him that afternoon was incredible. "Your needs will be furnished by the staff and by me," he said in flawless, toneless English. "The basic routines of running this house will not be changed because Mr. Chaplin does not like change. If you have any problems you are requested to come to me with them and not to Mr. Chaplin."

"What problems?"

"Of any trivial nature. We anticipate none. You will have a charge account at the drugstore only a block from here for anything you want or need in medicines and cosmetics. There should be no need at this time for you to make use of other stores. If you require something and it is necessary, I will see that you have it. Mr. Chaplin prefers quiet, so if you choose to entertain your family and friends, you will kindly do it when he is not here."

He impassively catalogued a list of rules and regulations, telling me what was expected of me and what was not.

He spoke in short, clipped tones and his voice was tediously flat, but his message was explicitly clear: I was not to be heard around the house, and as much as possible, not seen. At lunch I'd sarcastically asked Charlie if I was a new servant. Now I realized I was something even less appealing. I was an unwanted guest in my husband's house.

It was after midnight when I heard Charlie's steps reach the top of the stairs. I had spent the interminable day walking from one room to another in the house, rehearsing a hundred different speeches that would lower the hateful barrier between us. In spite of the waspish things he had said, in spite of having assigned someone else to introduce me to my responsibilities, I still couldn't believe he meant me to live like this. He was like Grandpa—British and stubborn. His plans for his career and his life had been drastically altered—and I had been the cause. I could understand his disappointment and frustration, even if my family couldn't, because I understood Charlie. But inside him he knew—he had to know, for there was nothing he didn't know—that I was constantly ready to be at his side, that I wasn't what he'd called me.

I tied the sash of my robe and went into the hall to meet him. He looked exhausted, in need of hot tea and possibly love. He saw me, and a flicker of recognition came over his face. I took a hopeful step or two forward, but stopped in my tracks when his shoulders sagged in weariness and sorrow.

"Can I get anything for you?" I asked softly.

Loosening his necktie, he yawned and nodded. "Yes," he answered, just as softly. "Get me a pistol. I feel like blowing my brains out."

He shuffled into his bedroom, but when he didn't close the door behind him, I followed and watched him slowly begin to undress. "You don't hate me," I said in a low voice. "You can't mean what you said. You couldn't have loved me so much just a little while ago and hate me as much as you say you do now. Please . . . let me stay here with you tonight. . . ."

"Don't be absurd."

"Please . . ." I repeated, trying not to cry.

"Just close the door as you leave," he said wearily, and his voice was a cold knife in my heart.

The telephones and the doorbell didn't stop ringing. At last, after an obstinate wait, Charlie's office officially confirmed what everyone knew—that he and I were married. There were no details, except for one additional, stark statement: "Mrs. Chaplin (*née* Lita Grey) has foregone her role as the Dance Hall Girl in *The Gold Rush,* now in production. 'I want to devote my every second to my husband,' she enthuses. The part in the photoplay will be portrayed by player Georgia Hale."

Reporters and columnists were clamoring for me to grant them interviews, but I was just as glad that they were kept from me, because I wouldn't have known what to say. Charlie, whose conduct with the press was erratic —he could be overly gruff or overly jovial—made a short public announcement explaining my seclusion: "My wife has not been in the best of health of late. It's nothing serious, but I wish for her to have as much rest as possible."

He was right on two counts. I was getting plenty of rest—there was nothing to do and no one to talk to—and I wasn't in the best of health. My morning sickness should have been over and done with by now, but I still woke up with cramps and nausea, and vomiting could leave me weak for hours. By Kono's arrangement I saw the doctor periodically. I was told that the pregnancy was progressing nicely, but that I should be careful not to exert myself.

Until Charlie decided when the time would be ripe for me to reappear in public, the trips to the doctor were the only ones I took away from the estate. Frank would call for me at the rear of the house and deliver me back there

147

so the press would have no chance to see me. Mama would go along, and more often than not, she would come back to Cove Way and spend the rest of the afternoon with me, to keep me company. In the beginning I was full of tears and recriminations against Charlie, and Mama patiently heard me out. But after a while the topic became pointless, because there was nowhere for either of us to go with it. Mama was still certain the admittedly unnatural marriage would improve, that in time the roadblocks would wear down and fade away. I had little faith in her optimism.

I was pleased that she was looking well and, she swore, feeling fine. She was putting off her operation, to be sure, but she claimed that the medication she was taking was making her fit as a fiddle. There hadn't been a speck of discomfort since the night she'd stayed here, she said, and she was positive there wouldn't be, ever again.

If anything amusing happened to relieve those first long weeks of being a lonely bride in a lonely setting, it was having the Los Angeles school system catch up with the fact that I was still of school age. Charlie, or his lieutenants, was purposely confusing the nosy public by surreptitiously passing the word around that I was seventeen or eighteen or—so it seemed from some of the baffling newspaper and magazine items I read about myself—both. But the school system had my records and insisted I be educated. As a result, it was arranged that a tutor, Hildur Petersen, come to Cove Way for several hours a day and teach the high school curriculum to Mrs. Charlie Chaplin.

Curiously enough, though I'd been an indifferent student before, I now started to take a more than passing interest in my studies. I began to want to learn, to read all the books on Charlie's shelves and to know as much as he—to make him proud of me, when and if he ever came out of his black mood.

Books were the only objects in the rambling house that didn't have a specific place for themselves. Numbering in the thousands, they were to be found in almost every room, and most of them had been well-thumbed. I was to learn

that Charlie was a fantastic reader. I still have no idea
where he found the time to read as much as he did, but
he did read voraciously, and as I saw from my own brows-
ing, on just about every imaginable subject. When Kono
or the servants weren't about, I would inspect the books
as though at a library and help myself to those I thought
I could cope with.

After a week of this I was shocked to realize that, of all
the books from which I had to choose, the only ones I
could really get through—and with breathless relish—
were the ones that dealt with sex. I was fascinated by a
pompously written medical manual that managed to discuss copulation for chapter after chapter after chapter, and
I was intrigued that the sections underlined in pencil by
Charlie were those detailing dozens of ways of having intercourse in addition to what was persistently referred to
as "normal intercourse." Comically enough, the manual
insisted that perversions were beneath moral contempt,
but at the same time it missed no opportunity to describe,
in meticulous detail, acts that would have awed a savage,
not to mention positions that would have bewildered a
contortionist.

With the help of the medical dictionary, I mastered that
book in a manner that would have amazed my tutor. I
also tackled a fat novel called *Memoirs of a Woman of
Pleasure,* which I later learned was much better known
as *Fanny Hill.* I was drawn to the passages that Charlie
had underlined—the sex scenes—and I wished all the
harder that Charlie would call a truce and come to me.

But if anything, Charlie seemed to be pushing himself
even deeper into *The Gold Rush,* ignoring me all the
more. When he was home he was locked in his room,
either working or sleeping. He tried to keep the work days
on the lot pretty uniform in terms of hours, if only because
he hated to see his company being paid for just standing
around, but he wasn't in a routine as far as his own hours
were concerned. Sometimes he would work in his bedroom
till dawn, catch a short nap, then hustle on to the studio.

Other times he would sleep late through sheer exhaustion, leaving a note for Kono that under no circumstances was he to be disturbed. For all the estate's many rooms—most of which he was only passingly aware of—Charlie had no home office as such. He used an old desk near the window in his bedroom, kept plenty of yellow pads and pencils on it, and once he came home—at six, or nine, or later—he rarely stirred from it.

My queer existence as unacknowledged boarder in this great house was broken in the middle of a gloriously bright Sunday afternoon. I was sitting by the pool, deep in—of all incongruous things—the homework my tutor had given me, when Charlie appeared in his bathing suit. His curly hair was rumpled and his mood seemed less grim than usual. He had just come awake for the day, and Ralph brought him a glass of orange juice.

I had stopped chasing after him, and I dug my nose deeper into my book, pretending he wasn't there.

But he was, and he sat down and asked, as if there had never been a trace of tension between us, "What's that you're reading?"

"American history."

"Oh? Where are you up to?"

"Teapot Dome."

He chuckled, and from the corner of my eye I could see him nodding. "Yes, Teapot Dome. What a pretty name for such an unpretty scandal . . . all those pious, sanctimonious pillars of the community robbing widows and orphans. Have you ever noticed that the prettier-sounding the name, the crueler, or at least the duller, the people are who're associated with it?"

He sounded chatty now, in the mood for conversation, for the first time since well before Empalme. I didn't close my book, but I did look at him, holding myself in check for the moment when he might tell me, or show me in some way, that we needn't live like enemies any longer.

"It's an interesting idea," he went on, lounging back and raising his face to the unshaded sun. "In England, the loveliest-sounding places were inhabited by the slimiest cutthroats. And there's a village in some part of New York called Far Rockaway that's supposed to have breathtaking views of the ocean, but I'm told the dreary cretins who live there or vacation there face their chairs inland. And in Pennsylvania, a small town with the beautiful name of Pleasant Unity is said to be full of thieves and murderers. And what better proof of my theory, come to think of it, than to just mention the name"—he made a frame of his fingers in the air—"Hollywood? Is there a prettier name, and are there more thieves and murderers per square inch anywhere else on the planet?"

He was served fish and toast and coffee, and I sensed his discomfort as I refused to unfasten my eyes from what I was pretending to be reading. "We're going to have a very small dinner party tomorrow evening," he said. "Rob Wagner and his wife will be here. Rob is a painter and writer, about my age, very talented, very quiet and thoughtful. It should be a pleasant evening. He—ah— knows about . . ."

I knew what he was fumbling to get out, and I looked at him angrily. "He knows what? That I'm having a baby?"

Charlie's eyebrows shot up at my uncustomary sharpness. "Yes. Rob is a true confidante, and so is his wife. We needn't pose with them."

"We don't have to pose with anybody," I snapped.

"What's all this—"

"Have you told these friends of yours all about me? That I tied you up and forced you to sleep with me and made my family make you marry me?"

"*Shhhhh-hh!* The servants . . ."

The floodgates of anger had opened at last—and I couldn't close them. "Have you told your friends that I'm a little whore, and that since we've been living under the same roof you've wanted me to be your wife because you're oh-so-wonderful and forgiving but that I won't let you touch me? Tell me! Tell me what you've told these friends

151

of yours, so I'll know how to behave at dinner tomorrow and not make you ashamed of me!"

Charlie was even more disturbed to hear the speech than I was to make it. He threw his knife and fork onto the tray and got up, his face dark. "You're cheap, incredibly cheap, and I'll never know how I got mixed up with you!"

He stalked back into the house and I didn't see him for the rest of the day.

The Wagners arrived the next evening at half-past six on the dot. They were sweet and unaffected, and though much of the dinner conversation was over my head, they didn't treat me like an utter sap. I stayed quiet until the conversation got around to books that they and Charlie were reading. To show off, I remarked, "I've just finished reading *Memoirs of a Woman of Pleasure*."

There was stunned silence for a moment, and then I learned why. *Fanny Hill,* though considered literature, was banned in this country then, and it wasn't the kind of book read by refined ladies, particularly sixteen-year-old refined ladies. Charlie exclaimed, "Well, this is news to me. I had no idea that was your cup of tea, Lita!" He grinned sheepishly at the Wagners. "My bride appears to be quite the emancipated young woman."

I suspected I'd committed an unforgivable *faux pas,* but a few hours later, after the Wagners had said good night, Charlie looked at me approvingly. "You were a charming hostess tonight. I congratulate you."

I couldn't tell whether he was being sarcastic or not. I decided he wasn't. "What did you think I'd do," I said, "suck my thumb and play with my dolls?"

He laughed. Then: "Let's go to bed, Lita."

This about-face startled me. Did it mean the siege was over? The thought thrilled me, but I forced myself not to show it. "You've said some terrible things to me. And anyway, I've gotten used to my own bed." Blushing at the

Grandfather William Edward Curry was born at sea on a British ship —but he and London-born Chaplin were oceans apart. In fact, Curry greeted the news of Lita's pregnancy by brandishing his gun

—not for a shotgun marriage; he merely wanted to kill Charlie. Grandmother Louisa Semourfina Carrillo Curry was proud of being descended from prominent Spanish settlers.

Lita's father, Robert Earl McMurray, dropped out of her life after a two-year marriage to her mother, Lillian. Shown here at the age of

24, Lillian was to remarry twice more—to Hal Parker, assistant director to Cecil B. De Mille, and to an engineer from Alabama.

The birthplace of Lillita Louise McMurray as it looked fifty-eight years ago. The house, which stood on the corner of Cahuenga and Highland, was torn down for freeway construction. The family resettled in Grandpa's new apartment house, The Navarro.

When Lillita was four months old, her parents' marriage was already shaky. Her lifelong attachment to her mother was strengthened by the lack of paternal affection.

Lita at five, a year before her first meeting with Chaplin. That encounter was just a chance introduction in a restaurant. The seduction did not take place until ten years later. ▶

In one of his most flattering gestures, Chaplin had Lita sit for a portrait emulating the famous "Age of Innocence" painting. This photograph of Lita posing for the artist was made on the set of The Kid *in 1920. Lita was 12 years old.*

In that same year, Charles Chaplin was 31 and already a living legend. The Kid *was his sixty-eighth picture. Numerous one- and two-reelers preceded his feature films.* ▶

Cast, crew and studio tourists gather for a group picture during the
shooting of The Kid. Four-year-
old Jackie Coogan is perched
above The Little Tramp's left
shoulder. Lita nestles in his lap.
Edna Purviance, female lead, does
not appear in the photograph.

This old and blurred frame from
The Kid shows Lita in her role as
The Flirting Angel teasing The
Tramp during the famous dream
sequence.

In this classic silent still from The Idle Class, *Lita and her mother are cast as maids, Chaplin plays both a fop and a tramp; and Edna Purviance is the wife.*

During a rare real Hollywood snowfall in the early twenties, the picturesque Chaplin Studios on La Brea and Sunset look like a Christmas card.

Miles of Gold Rush *footage, including this collector's item scene, were junked when Lita became pregnant in mid-1924. Georgia Hale took over the lead role.* ▶

The star, at his most Chaplinesque, amuses his leading lady, costumed for her abortive role as dance hall girl ◀ *in* The Gold Rush, *1923.*

UNITED PRESS INTERNATIONAL

After a quick screen test, Chaplin made a decision resented by his staff: Lita would star with him in The Gold Rush. *In this publicity shot at contract-signing are, from the left, Eddie Manson, Chuck Reisner, Mama Lillian, Chaplin, Jim Tully, Lita, Henry Bergman, Eddie Sutherland and Alfred Reeves.*

At the time of her romance with Chaplin, Lita imitates the pose of a femme fatale; actually, at 15 she was anything but a sophisticate, though the following year she was to become a wife and mother all at once.

Chaplin's Cove Way, where Charles, Jr. and Sydney were born, was a Georgian-style mansion set on a plateau overlooking Beverly Hills. The Pacific lay beyond the rose gardens.

In November, 1926, Chaplin sent Lita and Chaplin, Jr. off to Hawaii with Mama. This was the first calculated separation— and the beginning of the end.

Merna Kennedy stars with Chaplin in The Circus. *Lita meant only to advance her friend's film future—not her husband's extramarital career.* ▶

The beach house in Santa Monica was one of Hearst's "little" gifts to Marion Davies, his adored mistress for thirty years. She and Lita often spent long visits together before the storm of scandal broke.

WIDE
WORLD

CULVER PICTURES, INC.

William Randolph Hearst's castle, San Simeon, was the scene of Lita's first lesson in social polish and sexual realities. At one spectacular costume party, Lita and Charlie came as Napoleon and Josephine; Hearst appropriately posed as Henry the Eighth.

UNITED PRESS INTERNATIONAL

Lita and her mother, flanked by four lawyers who handled the divorce action. Chief attorney was Lita's uncle, center, the tough and tenacious Edwin McMurray. In November, 1926, Lita wanted $10,000. In August, 1927, she got close to a million.

During the two years of their marriage, Chaplin's name was often linked with assorted Hollywood beauties. Here is a modest gallery of five.

POLA NEGRI

CLAIRE WINDSOR

PEGGY HOPKINS JOYCE

EDNA PURVIANCE

MARION DAVIES

Because Chaplin's wives were all nubile cinema hopefuls, it was common to find their mothers close at hand. Here is his first bride, 16-year-old Mildred Harris, and her mother in a homey pose.

Lita and her mother, Lillian, by now divorced from her third husband, were more inseparable than ever once the Chaplin marriage began to founder. Chaplin's attitude toward Mama alternated between tolerance and scorn.

Paulette Goddard, her mother and Chaplin wave from shipboard as they arrive in Honolulu for a spring vacation in 1936. Paulette, Chaplin's third wife, was fond of Lita and adored both boys. It was mutual.

In 1929, when Charles, Jr. was four and Sydney was three, the Chaplin children were as alike in appearance as identical twins. During these early years they spent weekends with their father.

Charles, Jr., left, and Sydney pose playfully for publicity photographs in 1932 when Warner Brothers offered them and Lita a contract. Chaplin objected, intervened and won in court.

The news photographs of Chaplin, right, and Lita, below, on the witness stand before Judge H. P. Wood put the family back on the front pages. In August, 1932, Chaplin succeeded in preventing the children from appearing in films.

New York STAR

THE NATIONAL AMUSEMENT WEEKLY—EDITED BY ROLAND BURKE HENNESSY

Vol. XXI. No. 6   FEBRUARY 1, 1930   10c a Copy: $5 a Year

LITA GREY CHAPLIN
THE BEAUTIFUL RKO STAR
Who returns to the New York Palace the week of Feb. 1st. Direction: Harry Weber—Simon Agency

By 1929, Lita had made a huge dent in her million dollar divorce settlement. She signed with the Keith Circuit for $2,500 per week as a vaudeville singer, partly in an effort to supplement her income but mostly to establish herself as a personality in her own right.

*Perched on Irving Actman's piano, Lita rehearses with him
and Jack Harris for her London debut in January, 1936.*

*Chaplin wooed Lita, among others, with promises of
starring her as Josephine in his never-to-be-produced
epic film of Napoleon. Here Lita models the Napo-
leonic jewels in a promotion photograph.*

*Georges Carpentier, former box-
ing champion, former war pilot
and former friend of Chaplin,
was for five years the most important man in Lita's life, although he was already married.*

*Henry Aguirre became Lita's
second husband in November,
1936. He had been an understanding companion after her
nervous breakdown, but both
agreed that this had been an
insufficient basis for a happy
marriage.*

*With Charles, Jr., left, and Syd-
ney, Lita and her third husband, Arthur Day, pose at their
wedding on July 5, 1938. The
couple ended their marriage
after eight years.*

As an internationally successful chanteuse, *Lita toured nightclubs and theaters from the Palace in New York to London's Café de Paree. She was hailed by the Detroit Evening News as "A stormy beauty with a really phenomenal voice."*

Lita went back to California in 1943. Buoyed by a
talk with Charlie, she entered a sanitarium. Soon
after, she opened the Lita Grey Talent Agency in
Los Angeles.

Paulette Goddard dines at the Coconut Grove with Chaplin and sons.
Lita was grateful for Paulette's attention to and concern for the boys.

Today, Lita looks upon her life "with little bitterness and much under-standing." In the early 1950's, Chaplin helped her through personal tragedy. She, in turn, rallied to his defense in a legal attack by Immigra-tion Authorities. She will always remember that Chaplin once told her, during the early days of his marriage to Oona O'Neill, "I've really loved only two women—you and the girl who is my wife now."

hed in Report of Romance

FILM COMEDY KING FINALLY SUCCUMBS TO CUPID'S DARTS

MEDIAN REPORTED
N WAY TO GUAYMAS
TO MARRY LITA GREY

Charlie Chaplin,
Leading Lady Wed

COMEDY KIN
'S WED IN
MEXICO

LITA GREY MARRIE
CHAPLIE CHAPLIN

ita Chaplin Likes
Nother Role Best,

Mother and Dad Chaplin

CHARLIE, JR., MAKES HIS PREMIER SHOW

SECOND CHAPLIN HEIR RUMOR

Divorce? No! Says Chaplin's Wife

Stork Said to be Contemplating

LITA CHAPLIN
ASKS DIVORCE
IN STARTLING
ALLEGATIONS

corns Huge
by Chaplin;
nsel for Wife
ts Her in Huf

Only in S. F. for Brief Visit

She's Sorry to
Disappoint
Gossips

NOT A SLIP-KNO
MRS. CHARL

, who
says
—no

LITA ON WITNE

Miss Grey Ge
Up Actor's

ITA WINS DIVORCE
AND $625,000
PLIN BOYS

ARREST OF
CHAPLIN IS
THREATENS
ON ALIMO

MRS. CHAPLIN WINS
AND $82

Files Su

silliness of that prim speech, I stalked off. And as I left I heard him chuckle.

Minutes later I was in his bed and in his arms.

He hadn't forgotten how to get me quickly aroused. Between kisses, he whispered references to some of *Fanny Hill's* episodes, then paused for my reaction. I obliged by shivering in sensuous delight. Encouraged, he acted out the passages, teasing me so unbearably that I begged him not to hold off a second longer. Wild with desire, I was sure that this night, of all nights, I was going to experience the climax I had been denied for so long. It didn't happen for me, not the first, second or third time Charlie had his, but I still had no complaints. I had Charlie back again.

Except that I didn't. Before he left for the studio the next morning, he told me the time had come for me to be interviewed by "the newspaper pests." He said he was satisfied that I didn't show any signs of pregnancy yet, and that he would have Jim Tully coach me in what to say. I waited for him to display a fraction of the love he'd shown the night before—a kiss, a kind word, a glance of approval. But he left the house without even a good-by, as though there had been no night before.

Tully spent an entire afternoon coaching me in the ways of newspaper interviews. He taught me how to field embarrassing questions, how not to get trapped, how to be perfectly innocuous and yet give reporters the impression that they weren't being short-changed. I was amazed at the obviousness of the ploys he suggested, but I listened and learned.

A mass interview with reporters from the papers and wire services had been set up, and I approached the day with considerable misgivings. Luckily, however, my fears proved unfounded, for the interview turned out fine; fortunately, in those days journalists' questions weren't nearly so probingly personal as they can be today. I handled myself well. I used all the gushing clichés—"Charlie swept me off my feet!" and "What girl would turn down a marriage proposal from the dearest man in the world?"—and found that the reporters were quite content to hear them. And I realized how wise it was of Charlie to stay away from the mass confrontation; his absence made him much more the focus of attention than he would have been if he'd been present. He read the stories when they were published and he was satisfied.

Just before my figure began to give our secret away, Charlie let it be announced that "The Chaplins Are Expecting!" He played the role of the jubilant expectant father for the public but to me he was cold again. Sometimes he would come home in time for dinner and surprise me by suggesting that we eat together. On such occasions we would eat at a bridge table near the fireplace in the living room. Invariably I would rekindle the hope that he would truly see me as his wife, and invariably we would eat our dinner as strangers. Somewhere between the soup and the meat dish, I could count on him to inquire, "How are your studies coming along?" I would say they were coming along well, and he would reply, "Good, good. No one can be too educated." Once in a while he would remark, more to himself than to me, "I've got this vague idea for part of a scene. It could be awfully funny, but I can't work it through." I would invite him to talk about it, on the chance that somehow I might be able to come up with a thought that could trigger the idea. He would then either abruptly change the subject or prop the evening paper in front of him and read for the rest of the meal.

On the nights Charlie summoned me to his bedroom I went, feeling increasingly like the whore he'd called me. I went to him, after all, as a girl on call. Sometimes he made love to me, Lita Chaplin, but more often than not, during that period, he simply expended his passion in me and dismissed me, explaining that he had work that had to get done.

Being brushed off like that always devastated me for a time, and I would try with everything I had to make him see me as something besides an albatross around his neck.

"Do you know I have a pretty good brain?" I said once.

He glanced at me, mocking. "Has anyone denied that?"

"It needs polishing, but it isn't asleep," I continued. "I learn things very fast, if there's a reason to. I wasn't just talking when I told those reporters I love you. I'd like very much to learn everything I can and be of whatever kind of help to you I can." I paused. "Why won't you let me come into your life?"

Quietly he asked, "What would you do there?"

He saw the hurt in my eyes and said, "All right, that sounded cruel. But jollying you along would be much crueler in the long run. There's no way we can be compatible, except in bed. I realize that you're probably lonely, that you mightn't have enough to do to occupy your time—"

"I could spend it doing things for you," I pleaded. "Can't I answer your fan letters, or read things that might give you ideas for pictures and put them in a scrapbook for you, or—I don't know, do *something* to be part of you?"

"Lita," he said softly, "how many times must I repeat it? My life is very well organized. I hire dozens of people to do things for me, and they do them the way I want them done because they've been trained to do them the way I want them done. But I've been thinking . . . why don't you have your mother move here? She'd do it like a shot, I'm sure, and it would be good for you."

Mama moved in only after I urged her, and when I assured her that the idea had been Charlie's; she believed that mothers shouldn't live with married daughters and sons-in-law. Frank brought her and her belongings to the house, where Kono, though impassive as always, informed her that she was welcome and that this home was her home.

The moment she arrived I felt less like a stranger to the outside world. And then, to my tremendous surprise, Charlie came home for dinner and welcomed Mama royally. At the table, and until he excused himself to go to his room, he treated her like an honored guest. He was effusive and charming, and he regaled her with funny stories of incidents on the set. He conducted himself with her, in fact, the way one might have expected him to conduct himself with his wife. And one would never have thought that he and my mother had been at each other's throats just a few months before; they were altogether friendly now. Charlie seemed relieved that his unwanted child bride had someone to take care of her.

Now he could go off by himself without guilt.

Chapter Eleven

Party invitations kept pouring in, but Charlie declined them, not only because he felt he wasn't caught up with *The Gold Rush,* but because, generally, parties for their own sake bored him. I was surprised, then, when he suddenly told me that we were going to attend one at Pickfair, the home of Mary Pickford and Douglas Fairbanks. I learned eventually that they had insisted we come; they were not only business associates of Charlie's—all three of them were partners in a company they'd formed, United Artists—they were long-time friends, and they'd taken him aside and told him it was criminal that he wasn't letting his friends meet his wife.

Charlie relented, but seemed genuinely appalled when I said I literally had no decent clothes to wear. "Why haven't you gone to Kono?" he asked.

"I have, lots of times," I answered. "He said I have a satisfactory wardrobe. Maybe I do. I don't really care all that much about clothes. But if we're going to Pickfair, and I wear something shabby, won't that look bad for you?"

It worked. I was driven to a department store to pick out an evening gown, one I could wear for months after my belly expanded. Discreet instructions were given that the gown be nice but inexpensive; I was beginning to see how hard it was for Charlie to part with a penny more than he absolutely had to.

Pickfair matched Cove Way in opulence, but it seemed warmer and cozier, perhaps because the touch of women servants was obvious, while Cove Way was completely staffed by men. And though Pickfair's lord and lady appeared as mismated as Charlie and I on the surface—Doug was a great big jolly kid while Mary was a dignified lady who decidedly belonged in the Age of Innocence—it didn't take long to see that they were splendidly matched. Mary was more than America's Sweetheart, she was Doug's—and he clearly adored her.

Charlie was in a festive mood until John Barrymore arrived; then, suddenly, he was subdued, and he restrained his high spirits the rest of the evening. I was to see Charlie and John together on a number of occasions, and I was intrigued by the indisputable fact that my husband, who rarely felt uneasy in the company of people he admired, invariably grew quiet and withdrawn when The Great Profile was about. To my knowledge, the exquisitely handsome John Barrymore didn't have a jealous or competitive bone in his body; he was an expansive man with artists he respected, and it was obvious that he thought Charlie was unique, a genius. Charlie wasn't a jealous or petty man when it came to art, either, but John's very presence unfailingly drove him into a strange retreat, as if he felt that the actor automatically overshadowed him.

John arrived a little drunk, but he was gracious to his hosts and he lit up when he saw Charlie. "Well, how's the foremost ballet dancer?" he boomed. This, I found out later, referred to a crack his friend, W. C. Fields, had made. Fields had watched as much as he could bear of an early Chaplin short, *Easy Street,* in which Charlie had weaved, trotted, leaped and run with eloquent grace. Asked what he'd thought of Charlie's performance, the jealous Fields had snarled, "He's the world's greatest ballet dancer, and if I ever meet the son of a bitch I'll murder him!"

A subdued Charlie replied that he was well, and introduced me to the actor. "Ah, she walks in beauty like the night!" John exclaimed, in mellifluous tones. Then, lightly tapping my stomach, he declared, "I am informed by my international network of spies that you have a cake in the oven, my flawless pigeon. Will you do something for me? If you have a squirrel, will you name it after me?"

Although Charlie was not the type who frolicked about at a party with a lampshade on his head, I think he felt threatened to the point of sullen immobility by the fact that Barrymore was. John could take over a gathering as a cutup and do it with spirit and spontaneity, and he was in dynamic form that night. Both before and after dinner he jumped over chairs and about the room, shadow-fencing an imaginary opponent to show how Doug Fairbanks had won fame. His impersonation was ludicrously overdone, but there was nothing mean in it. Doug nearly collapsed laughing, but Charlie, who could do a funny impersonation of our host, too, merely sat back in his seat and watched. He laughed from time to time, but the sound was a bit tinny.

I got the feeling that Mary didn't approve of this horseplay, but she didn't go out of her way to show her displeasure. And when she finally had a chance to get a word in, she asked advice on a personal dilemma. After years of film success as the little girl with the golden curls, she had recently made a picture—*Rosita,* directed by Ernst Lubitsch—in which she'd made a serious stab at maturing her characterization, at least to the point of adolescence.

The public hadn't approved, yet she was wise enough to know she couldn't stay a professional tot forever. Charlie suggested that she hold onto her child's characterization for as long as possible: "You're not trying to fool anyone. You're not one of those old character actresses who try to convince the public that they're half their age. Everyone knows you're an adult and no one cares. What they care about is that you play the part better than anybody else ever could. You're giving them a beautiful illusion, not a lie. That's the difference. Don't listen to the bullies."

John suggested that she immediately liven up the motion picture screen: "In your next film play a hoochie-koochie dancer who takes dope, smokes nine-inch cigars and sleeps with sailors on a cut-rate basis. I guarantee you, you'll leave your mark in the film firmament for all time to come!"

Mary winced. Doug roared. And Charlie, in spite of himself, laughed.

I couldn't help noticing that Charlie became more attentive toward me at the party as it became clear to him that the others appeared to like me. The Fairbankses were charming to me, although I had little to say. And with all his joking, cavorting and drinking, John was very attentive and sweet. None of this was lost on Charlie, who patted my arm as though to convey the idea that I'd passed a crucial test.

Although Charlie had no use for most religious festivals, he could get quite sentimental about the Christmas season. At Christmas in 1924—with our baby due in about four and a half months—he made preparations, through Kono, for a tree, dinner in the afternoon, and a gift for Mama and one for me. When I asked Charlie if my grandparents might come for dinner, he looked at me sharply, as if I'd asked the impossible, but answered, "Very well, if they'd like to—and as long as it's understood there's to be no religious folderol and none of those insufferable carols."

At first, Grandpa raged. Under no conditions would he set foot in That Man's home. But Mama and Grandma went to work on him, and the Currys arrived at Cove Way on time.

Charlie and Grandpa shook hands gravely and circled each other as warily as cavemen, each of whom is convinced that the other is hiding an ax. But after a glass or two of sherry the two men seemed to get along reasonably well if not famously; both having come from Britain, and both having certain characteristics in common, found they had enough of a meeting ground to lessen the tension. When we sat down at the table, Charlie began paying extravagant court to Grandma, who was overwhelmed. He carved the turkey himself, with precision and skill, and then, when everyone was served and just before we began to eat, he befuddled me thoroughly by inquiring, "Would someone like to say grace? I think it would be fitting." Grandpa obliged.

The day was not the easiest one for any of us to get through, but I must say for Grandpa that he behaved civilly and for Charlie that he sat through the stilted after-dinner conversation with a minimum of squirming.

Shortly after New Year's we received an invitation to a spectacular fancy-dress ball to be given by the sometime actress, Marion Davies. It was to be held in the Grand Ballroom at the Ambassador Hotel and attended by a thousand or more of the elite—movie stars, society leaders and other celebrities—and no expense would be spared. Charlie vowed we would go, he said, because of his fondness for Marion. It was to take me a while to discover just how fond of her he was.

Deciding that we would go as Napoleon and Josephine, he immediately—and personally—ordered the costumes. When they arrived, just before the ball, I was concerned that my pregnancy would alter the graceful lines of the Empire gown, but he showed me how the lines of a period costume were such that the bulge wouldn't matter. Then, smiling in self-satisfaction, he said, "Anyway, you don't know how lucky you are. The other Napoleon could never make his Josephine pregnant."

This was one of the precious few times he had referred even fleetingly to his impending fatherhood, and I had to make some comment. "What about you? Do you feel lucky?"

The smile vanished. "Oh, extremely!" he said with a sarcastic bite to his voice, and turning, marched out of the room.

Even my disappointment at Charlie's coldness couldn't dim the enthusiasm I felt for my costume. The gown was magnificent. It was a pale blue velvet, with artificial pearls and diamonds embroidered lavishly over the upper part of the bodice, and it was high-waisted and shockingly décolleté. Mama, whose excitement was equal to mine, brought out the velvet wrap, gloves and gem-encrusted tiara that completed the ensemble, and helped me dress. The long, deep folds of the skirt hung on me in a way that more than concealed my pregnancy. Mama placed the tiara on my head, turned me around so I could see myself in the mirror and asserted, "You're gorgeous, Lillita. Grandpa would have screaming fits if he could see how low that bodice is cut, but you're an absolute dream!"

I kissed her and hurried to Charlie's room, to stand framed in the doorway in all my imperial aplomb. Charlie, fully dressed in his Napoleon costume, was standing in front of his own mirror, examining himself with great care and trying to decide whether to wear his Legion of Honor medal on the right or left side of his chest. When I mentioned remembering a photograph of my grandfather in which he'd worn his ribbon on the left side, Charlie nodded and took the suggestion. Then, backing away from the mirror to get a better perspective, he placed the wide hat on his head with utter precision, inserted his right hand through the opening of the coat and thoughtfully studied his reflection for another second or two. Then he glanced at me, said, "You look nice—let's go now," and strode imperiously out of the room.

The ball was dazzling. From the great hall's high ceiling hung revolving crystal chandeliers that cast glints of color onto the costumed galaxy of celebrities below and caused brilliants, diamonds and pearls to sparkle in constant flashes of light. The bar provided a vast selection of drinks, though champagne seemed to be the rule of the evening, and the buffet table that extended the entire length of the Grand Ballroom contained everything from a wide variety of canapés to crepes suzette in flaming chafing dishes. Images in ice, surrounded by mint leaves, ferns, and papier-mâché decorations in matching and contrasting hues, made glittering centerpieces. The bustling waiters were dressed in knee-length satin breeches, black slippers with silver buckles, white wigs and all the other paraphernalia of the French Court in its heyday. Earl Burtnett and his Biltmore Orchestra, hired from the Ambassador Hotel's competitor, played without pause, and the ballroom rang with gaiety.

Even the thunder of a thousand voices, the din of the music and the clatter of plates and glasses failed to shake my Emperor in his composed and austere bearing as he stood at the entrance, our engraved invitation in his hand. We were confronted by a sea of faces, some totally obscured under heavy makeup and incredibly overfussed hairdos, but most of them instantly recognizable. Near us were a sheik and an Arabian dancing girl—Rudolph Valentino and Natacha Rambova. Behind them were Lillian and Dorothy Gish, dressed as Orphans of the Storm, talking with John Gilbert as Prince Danilo. Beyond them I recognized the Duncan Sisters, Vivian and Rosetta, as Topsy and Eva, and the Ernst Lubitsches as Romeo and Juliet—a comic sight, for Lubitsch had done nothing to corset his tubby stomach and was genially munching on a long cigar. And not far away, chatting with a circle of friends, was William Randolph Hearst, America's outstanding newspaper tycoon, dressed as Henry the Eighth.

It didn't take Charlie long to gather some worshippers, and as soon as we had our own small but attentive following he seemed to relax. I was again puzzled by what seemed like an uncharacteristic side of him, for he normally was the opposite of the attention-seeking celebrity. What I didn't understand then was that Charlie was impatient with adulation only when he was the sole true artist on the premises. When there were others on hand—and there certainly were that night—he became anxious lest he be overlooked.

Marion Davies, dressed in a lovely white crinolined antebellum gown, crossed the dance floor, came over to us and embraced Charlie. Although we were to get to know each other well, to the point of sharing intimate confidences, she all but ignored me at this first meeting. I didn't mind. I enjoyed looking at her. She was so pretty and full of life, with a stutter about which she was so blithely unconcerned that it was appealing, and she had such a charmingly feminine way of attaching herself to Charlie that somehow I was flattered rather than upset.

I was flattered, too, that men wanted to dance with me, and I did dance with one after another, though each time I signaled to Charlie for permission and he nodded. Each man in turn complimented me on how I looked, and though I fluttered my eyes and blushed, I must admit that for a long time that evening I felt like the most beautiful woman in the ballroom, which to me meant the whole world. I liked myself; for the first time in ever so long I felt clean and even secure within myself, and I had an identity. For these wonderful hours I *was* Josephine, and I was captivating everyone with my beauty and my cool sophistication.

At the buffet table I suddenly heard, "Hyah, Queenie!" I turned and saw John Barrymore, swaying from side to side like a slow pendulum and holding a plate on which sat a mountain of beef and pickles and olives. Extending the plate to me, he said grandly, "A morsel of simple foodstuffs for my morsel of enchanting empress."

He was dressed as Hamlet, and he was outrageously drunk. When I smiled and shook my head, he put the plate on the table and said sleepily, "Can't blame you. This slop was brought to these shores from France by our brave doughboys in 1918. It's all been sitting here, waiting for this ball. Nobody remembered to stick it in the icebox. A hell of a note. Our brave doughboys do our dying and fighting for us, and we don't even put the slop in the icebox. Come on, I'll teach you a fancy fandango, taught to me when I was a mere youth by a luxuriously bearded madame of a luxuriously bawdy cathouse. Can't recall her name, but she was one of our brave doughboys."

He steered me away from the buffet table, but it was obvious that he was in no condition to dance. Fortunately he realized this before long and let me steer him to the nearest empty divan. "Sit with me," he said, and I did. As I refused the cigarette he offered me, a waiter in satin breeches approached with a tray of drinks, and John kept waving until he was handed a cocktail. "Bless you, brave doughboy," he declared. "You wear your uniform with distinction. Would this were a steadier day, for I wouldst rise and salute you."

The waiter grinned and went away.

"Don't let this get around," said John, and paused to take several noisy gulps, "but that young Nubian waiter who just left us is my son. I had his intelligence tested and he has a 201 IQ, which is in the unheard-of-genius class. I made him give me his solemn oath that when he dies he'll leave his brain to a first-rate waiter college." He drank again. His eyes, over the rim of his glass, were fixed on the low cut of my gown.

"You're very funny," I said a little nervously.

"And you're very full in front, mine empress," he said with a leer so extreme that it had to be harmless. "I am a firm believer in breasts. I believe in firm breasts. In fact, I am the mandarin of mammaries, the titan of tits."

Embarrassed, I hastened to change the subject. I couldn't remember if he was married or single, so I asked, "Who'd you come with tonight?"

"A fetching young lady. But someone fetched my young

lady away while I was watching my hat and coat." He sighed. "The brave doughboy truth is that she called me a drunk and an uncouth undesirable and a number of names reflecting on my parents' marital status, and left me."

"I'm sorry."

"Well, she was correct. I *am* uncouth." He winked at me. "I'll prove it. How about if we turn on the heat, Queenie? We'll have to find a can opener to pry me out of these tights, but once that's done—"

I wasn't insulted—he was doing everything to assure me he was clowning, not passionate—but I got to my feet, anyway, because this sad wit was too much for me. "I'd better find my husband," I said. "He'll probably be wondering where I am."

"The ballet dancer? He's with Maid Marion, isn't he? These Scotch and watery eyes of mine saw him with dear Marion. Dear Marion's a barracuda. She won't deliver him back to you safely till she's properly devoured him."

Drunk or not, he spoke with a conviction that suggested he knew something more than just rumors about my husband and Marion Davies. But I was too flustered to stay with him another minute. "Excuse me," I said weakly.

"Mine empress," he declared, "I'm told that when Peggy Hopkins Joyce first met the ballet dancer, she twittered, 'Charlie, is it true what all the girls say, that you're hung like a horse?' Could you furnish me with the answer? My friends in the pool halls are curious to know."

I bolted away and went in shameless search of Charlie. John Barrymore was a drunken, dirty man with his mind in the gutter. It was inconceivable that Charlie would be having an affair with Marion Davies, or anyone—and certainly not tonight, at a ball like this. . . .

No, not really, I told myself. It's not inconceivable at all. Very few things about Charlie are beyond belief. He just might be doing it with her, even though I'm pregnant. Or maybe because I'm pregnant. Or maybe for no reason except that he wants to.

Someone asked me to dance. I shook my head and pushed on through the crowd of guests and waiters. I was perspiring, yet I felt chilled. I needed to find Charlie. Maybe he didn't have any love, any feeling for me, but I couldn't believe, I didn't want to believe, that he would make love to anyone else.

William Randolph Hearst, a tremendous man with a startlingly high-pitched voice, suddenly materialized in front of me in his Henry the Eighth costume. "Pardon me, but you're Mrs. Chaplin, are you not?"

I said I was, and he introduced himself, unnecessarily. "Ah—would you happen to know where Charlie is now? I—ah—haven't had an opportunity to say hello."

I knew he was worried, too. I managed to smile. "I'm sure he's around somewhere, Mr. Hearst. This is a big place. When I see him I'll tell him you were looking for him."

"Thank you. I just want the opportunity to say hello."

Ten minutes or so later, in another part of the ballroom, Marion Davies entered from one of the many side doors, fluffing her hair with her fingers and smiling, and immediately joined a small knot of guests. I stayed where I was, and soon I saw Charlie enter from the same door. He glanced all around, straightened his shoulders—I could almost hear him sigh with relief—and then looked with what seemed to be sudden desperation for someone to be with.

Not liking myself now, I got to him before anyone else did. Oddly, he brightened on seeing me. "There you are!" he exclaimed. "I was looking all over for you!"

Purposely deadpan, I said, "I was with John Barrymore."

He walked, one short step ahead of me. "That's fine. When John's not too far in his cups, he can be quite entertaining. He has a very quick, very brillant mind."

"He asked me to go to bed with him."

Charlie's head snapped around. "You're joking!"

"About what?"

"He's a total knave, but he's my friend and he has integrity. Did he actually ask you or is that what you surmised? Barrymore's not a complete lecher unless he's absolutely drunk, and then he's incapable. He must be *very* drunk."

I baited him. "What are you saying? That no sober man would find me attractive?"

"Oh, stop that. Just because you had a chat with Barrymore, don't get delusions of grandeur about yourself."

"I met some other people, too," I said innocently. "I met William Randolph Hearst. And we had a talk."

Charlie stopped in his tracks. "About what?"

"He asked me if you and Marion Davies were making love here tonight."

Turning white, he grabbed my arms. "Say that again!"

I wasn't frightened. "You *were* doing it with her, weren't you? Everybody in the whole ballroom knows it. Mr. Hearst knows it. Even your stupid wife knows it."

I never saw Charlie so anguished, before or after. His eyes seared mine and his slender fingers were steel clamps on my arms. Then, letting me go, he stalked away, and I saw him greet Mr. Hearst and Mr. Hearst greet him. They were long-lost brothers, and their conversation seemed friendly and animated. Eventually Marion Davies hove into view, and the three of them were all embracing and smiling as they bantered. If there was any problem, the show of camaraderie revealed not a whisper of it.

We left well before the ball was over because, according to Charlie, he saw too many other couples in Napoleon and Josephine costumes, and this disturbed him.

On the way home, Charlie sat back and shut himself off behind a barrier of silence. Once I mentioned Marion Davies, and he said, "Preposterous, preposterous. Be still now." And I was still for the rest of the ride.

Chapter Twelve

My baby was kicking with such force that there seemed no question I would have a boy. The doctor agreed and went even a step further; he couldn't be certain, but he thought, during one routine examination, that he heard two heartbeats. It was around this time, incidentally, that the Los Angeles school system had second thoughts about the compulsory education of a mother-to-be and withdrew my tutor.

As I began to expand, Charlie began going through periods when he withdrew from me even more. One evening, when we had his half brother Sydney and Sydney's wife Minnie over for dinner, I noticed that Charlie could sit quietly for only a few seconds at a time. He was genuinely fond of his brother, who worked for him now in an all-around capacity at the studio but who had been his first business manager, even before the formation of the Chaplin Film Corporation. It was Sydney who had worked out Charlie's initial million-dollar deal, a fact that never ceased to impress Charlie. "I was amazed that Sydney knew so much about stocks and bonds and investments," he told me once. "If it hadn't been for him I'd never have made any real money."

Sydney was several years older than Charlie, six inches taller, and possessed of a great depth of sensitivity. He noticed Charlie's immense nervousness that evening, and later, when he and I were alone for a few minutes he said, "Be as patient as you can with Charlie, because he's undergoing more of a strain than you can imagine. He's very fearful about the baby."

"Fearful?"

He nodded. "We've talked about it. When his first baby died after three days, he went into a terrible depression, and after all this time I don't think he's entirely come out of it. He believes it was his fault that the baby was born deformed and died. Now, with another baby on the way, he's sure the whole thing is going to be repeated."

"He told you all this?" I asked, and Sydney nodded again. "Why wouldn't he have said it to me?"

"Because that's the way Charlie is. I'm sure you don't have the easiest life, Lita, living with him. But do try to be as understanding as possible. Most of Charlie's instincts are good. It's just that he doesn't understand himself very well."

Some of the tension surrounding *The Gold Rush* eased when the bulk of my scenes were reshot to Charlie's satisfaction. He came home for dinner one night unusually cheerful, and explained that a great load was off his shoulders now that he was getting back on schedule. He even invited Mama and me to visit the lot, something he hadn't done since before the wedding. And that same night he let me know he wanted me to come to his bedroom. I hesitated, chiefly because of the specter of Marion Davies, but I went, and he was uncommonly loving. My shape was bulky and cumbersome now, but he made no mention of it, either in criticism or teasing. I didn't feel especially receptive, but I pretended I was, and this pleased him.

On the lot the next day I met Georgia Hale. There was a natural wrench in seeing my replacement, in seeing her in my dressing room and on the set where I had held forth, in seeing her being given the star treatment by members of the company who had given it to me not so long before. But she appeared so eager to be friendly that I could hardly be haughty with her. I was pleasant, in spite of my suspicion—one that refused to go away—that it wasn't only in the picture that she was Charlie's girl friend. I was ashamed of myself, for I had no evidence of this, but after the Ambassador Hotel ball my faith in Charlie was less than firm.

As it happened, Georgia did no work that day. Charlie had shot and reshot the cabin scenes with Mack Swain, but because he considered those sequences the visual spine of the movie, he insisted on repeating them. One of the scenes with Mack was the famous one in which Charlie, on the brink of starvation, cooks his shoe. Months earlier I had watched him do the scene over and over for several days running, and had assumed—as had everyone else—that it was finished and forgotten. But that day he got it into his head to do the scene again.

Striving for perfection, he cooked the enormous black shoe in a tureen, stirred it, brought it out, placed it on a dish, garnished it and began delicately to carve it as Mack watched in fascination. (This fascination, I learned later, was tinged with true revulsion. Poor Mack had struggled with the shoe-eating scene for five consecutive days a couple of months earlier. The shoe and the laces were made of licorice, which he—and Charlie, too, for that matter—abhorred. So for five days, in retake after retake, he'd been kept on a steady diet of licorice, and for days after was too queasy to eat. So was Charlie. And they both were going to be sick again.) Charlie served a portion of the shoe to Mack and they began dinner. Such was the master's brilliance that the disgusting-looking shoe became appetizing; Charlie cut it as though he were cutting guinea hen, wrapped one lace around his fork like spaghetti, and from the way he feasted, you were sure he'd concocted an entree fit for royalty.

Everyone—and Mack in particular—was relieved when he announced, "All right, I think we've got it this time." Then he remembered that I was on the set, and feeling most expansive, he called for a break and escorted me around to be greeted by the company. He was even courtly with Mama, and he seemed so proud of me. What I couldn't understand was how he could switch off this feeling of pride as easily as one switches off a light.

To pass the time I began to learn to sew, with Mama's help. After some disastrous starts, I made some dresses that won Charlie's enthusiastic approval. "Lita, these are pure art!" he exclaimed. "They're as good as anything we could find in Paris!" They weren't all that splendid, of course, but they had the very great virtue of being inexpensive.

One of the many curious things about Charlie Chaplin was his bewildering attitude toward spending money. I am aware that his grinding poverty in childhood, his seldom knowing for certain when he would have his next meal, contributed a lot to the penny-pinching that sometimes reached the point of foolishness. I recall, too, the many times he would point to people obviously down on their luck and say, "Do you see So-and-so? Once upon a time he just about owned Hollywood. But he thought the gravy train would keep rolling forever so he spent his money faster than it came in, didn't make a single investment, didn't tuck away a penny. Now he's looking for handouts. That shan't happen to me." Still, nothing explains his inconsistency. Charlie could be impossible about money; he could throw great amounts away on lavish parties while he kept using the same tennis ball long after it had lost its last fuzz and the bounce was gone. No one knew how he was going to deal with his well-deserved fortune from one day to the next, least of all Charlie himself. He would say, "We're going to the Goldwyns' for dinner next Thursday," or "We've been invited to the De Milles'," without realizing that, although I had no great urge to be a clotheshorse, the fact that I wore the same few dresses time after time at gathering after gathering was a reflection on him. I said so to Kono, who promised to bring it to Charlie's attention. He didn't, of course, but before our next evening out I brought it to Charlie's attention myself.

He told Kono to open a charge account for me at a medium-priced department store.

There were nights when Charlie came home very late, and even though he probably was the hardest-working man in motion pictures, I couldn't believe he could put sixteen and eighteen hours into the studio day after day after day. Too timid to come right out and accuse him of seeing other women, I began testing him in a rather crude though seemingly logical way. I would steal into his bed and surprise him. If he indicated he was too tired for sex, I would presume I knew what had made him tired. If he was happy I was there and made love to me, I would tell myself I had misjudged him.

Usually he was happy I was there and made love to me. But what took me a while to comprehend, even though he had proudly admitted it many months earlier, was that he was the kind of sexual prodigy most women can only dream about. He was a human sex machine who, even in his middle thirties, could make love half a dozen times in the course of a night, and his sixth time could be as vigorous as his first. As far as the possibility of adultery was concerned, therefore, I was back where I'd started.

A little private research showed me that Marion Davies was the least of my worries. That the two of them were intermittently sleeping together was a fact I was to have proved to me later, but at that time it seemed clear that the fundamentally free-and-easy Marion wasn't serious about anyone except William Randolph Hearst, if only for reasons of financial security. She maintained a home in Beverly Hills and Hearst spent most of his time at his private nation, San Simeon. But he was crazy about her, showering nine-tenths of the lavish world on her, and she was not about to endanger that fine situation by getting seriously involved with Charlie Chaplin or anyone else.

What bothered me were the newspaper rumors that he was seeing exotic temptresses like Pola Negri. Pola Negri was a richly beautiful German-Polish feline, and her specialty in movies was the ultra-sophisticated femme fatale who used sex as a device to destroy. I took this specialty seriously, especially when I remembered that Charlie had once told me quite a lot about her. He'd called her the most sensual animal he'd ever met.

I prayed I'd never have to come face to face with her, but when we were asked to the Ernst Lubitsches to dine and see a screening of *Forbidden Paradise,* I learned that she had also been invited. I flatly refused to go. Charlie demanded to know why. "What are you afraid of?" he snapped. "You know Ernst and Vivian, who've been very civil to you. You know some of the other guests who'll be there. Why are you suddenly giving me an ultimatum?"

"I don't want to meet your—friend."

"What friend, damn it? What in hell are you being so mysterious about?"

"Pola Negri. I don't want to meet her."

"Pola? Why not, for God's sake?"

"Because I think you're still having an affair with her, and I'd die if we were all in the same room together."

Charlie was momentarily struck dumb. Then: "What must I do, telephone the lunatic asylum to come and collect you? What *are* you babbling about, Lita? I'm having an affair with no one except a mistress named *The Gold Rush,* who takes up every second of my time. Now stop this idiocy and get dressed!"

It was no accident that Pola Negri was 1925's most popular screen vamp. At Paramount executives and junior executives who had to deal with her privately called her

The Polish Situation because of her titanic fits of temper and incredible demands. (One limousine wasn't enough for her, she complained; she needed two, the second to follow the one she rode in.) But this took nothing away from her powerful magnetism. From the moment we stepped into the Lubitsch home that evening she took over, even when she hadn't a word to say. She was sitting in a French chair, her diamonds sparkling, her bodice cut scandalously low. She was the most stunning woman I have ever seen.

I had heard that her language was salty to the point of being shocking, and she now proved the rumor was true. Smiling a blinding smile at Charlie, she called, "Sharrlie, how nice to see you again, you old son of a beetch!" and kissed him extravagantly. Rather uncomfortable introductions were made, and she nodded to me, but it was clear she had eyes only for Charlie.

Cocktails were served to everyone but me. Though the Lubitsches tried to start any number of conversations, Pola was not going to allow a minute to pass that didn't center on her—her or Charlie. She was playing the regal role for all it was worth, and Charlie was obviously captivated, despite his normal aversion to women who cursed. She sipped her Martini delicately, while lacing her chatter with four-letter words. Then, setting the glass down on a marble-topped table, she leaned forward, revealing what little bosom had remained covered. She picked up a cigarette from the coffee table, settled back in her chair and held the cigarette imperiously until Charlie leaped across the room to light it for her. She thanked him softly and blew the smoke out through her nose. Every move she made struck me as calculated. It was all terribly transparent, yet it worked; Charlie didn't seem to know there was anyone else in the room. Even the Lubitsches appeared to be feeling a bit in the way. I was miserable.

At dinner she rasped vulgarities in a guttural voice. Little if anything she said was meaningful or witty, but you couldn't take your eyes from her. The contrast of jet black hair and pure alabaster skin was electrifying. Her eyes, set very far apart, were large and dark and almond-shaped, and she used her voluptuous body as if it were a weapon.

Just before dessert and coffee, two men from Mr. Lubitsch's studio arrived and began to set up the equipment for the screening. Charlie and Mr. Lubitsch took a short walk to talk shop, and a moment later Vivian Lubitsch excused herself. I found myself alone with Pola. She glanced at me—for the first time, it seemed. "So you are Mrs. Sharrlie," she said, scanning me up and down. "Tell me—how did you snare dat elusive but sharming bastard?"

Priggishly I said, "Don't call him names like that."

She thought that was funny, and throwing her marvelous head back, laughed. "Don't mind me. It's joos' my vay. I've been plenty criticized for my language, but I really don't geef a damn vat people sink, you understand?" I forced a feeble nod, and she said, "Sharrlie is so vunderful. You're lucky to get him—any girl vould be. He's so zexy."

Seeing I was shocked, she got up and strolled toward the garden, leaving the topic in midair. Vivian Lubitsch returned and said, "I do hope Pola hasn't disturbed you, dear. She has a frank way about her, and it's often misunderstood. Of course, we understand her—you know how those things are. And she's just divine for Ernst to work with."

The picture *Forbidden Paradise,* directed by Ernst Lubitsch and starring Pola Negri, was ready to be shown. We all took our places, and for an hour and a half there was mercifully no need for anyone to talk. I was able to forget that I found Pola's personality so obnoxious. The movie was excellent, and so was she.

I was thankful that this was to be a short evening for all. Pola had an early morning call, Lubitsch had arranged a tight shooting schedule on his current picture and wanted to be at the studio before nine in the morning, and Charlie, just finishing the last touches of *The Gold Rush,* was getting ready to begin cutting the negative. We said our good nights about eleven o'clock, and as we walked down the garden path in front of the house, we could still hear Pola's guttural laugh, her words tumbling forth in their rasping tones. In the car, Charlie sighed. "An amazing woman. A real paradox. Very blunt, and very talented."

The blood rushed to my cheeks. "And very good in bed," I added.

"Oh, that again!" He frowned. "Do you intend to turn green every time you see a female between eight and eighty?"

"Would it do any good if I did?" I asked.

It was after we arrived home that Charlie proved himself to be an atrocious actor. "Oh, I meant to tell you," he said. "I'm going to spend a little time with my old friend, Georges Carpentier, the boxer. He's appearing at the Pantages Theatre this week. I'll show him the sights. It'll be best if I'm alone with him—'man talk,' you know. Ah—then, too, I have a deadline with the exhibitors. I'll be staying at the studio for a while, perhaps until I'm finished with cutting *The Gold Rush*. You'll be all right."

"Yes. I'll be fine."

The weeks before the birth of a baby are supposed to be an expectant mother's most exciting time, but as the day drew near I was overcome with a lassitude I couldn't shake off. By now Dr. Kayser, a new doctor Charlie had acquired, was making regular trips to the house, checking me in a routine way and assuring Mama and me that there was nothing to worry about. The only thing that bothered me was the fact that I couldn't seem to stay awake. I would sleep ten or twelve hours at night, rise and have juice and toast—the only things I could keep down—and then feel the oppressive need to go back to sleep again. Exercise was necessary, both Mama and the doctor told me, but I had no energy for it.

Charlie wasn't with me. He kept in touch with my progress through Dr. Kayser and Kono, but he couldn't or wouldn't find the time to look in on me. At least, not until the day he learned I had been approached by the Los Angeles *Times* reporter, Harrison Carroll, who'd somehow come onto the estate without having been spotted and who had waited to catch me in the garden.

The young and personable Harrison Carroll and I weren't exactly strangers, but when I saw him my first impulse was to run; I'd been warned over and over against talking with anyone from the press. But Kono was away, Mama was inside and the servants were at their chores. I had the feeling that Carroll was different from other reporters, and I was sorely in need of a sympathetic friend.

He knew I was frightened, so he began with a casual smile. "I just got married, Mrs. Chaplin—I'm a bridegroom," he said. "That ought to convince you I have some respect for womanhood." The remark was disarming, and I laughed. He explained that he had been assigned to get a Chaplin story for his paper, and that he'd gone several times to the studio. Charlie had never been available. Alf Reeves had been affable and offered to show him around the lot, but that wasn't the story his paper wanted.

"Are you and Chaplin separated?" he asked, point-blank.

"No, of course not," I answered. "What—what makes you think that?"

"Just a rumor that's making the rounds." When I got up nervously to leave, he said hurriedly, "Wait a minute, Mrs. Chaplin. I'd like to explain something. I want you to understand a reporter's position. I'd like to write a story that won't hurt anyone—even your husband, if that's possible. The other reporters around town aren't that considerate. They have strong hunches about your . . . well, we all suspect you didn't conceive a baby after your wedding in Mexico—"

I just gaped. I hadn't imagined our secret was so public.

"—but the other fellows are itching to get the facts and turn the story into a circus. You can't really blame them. When a man smashes cameras, avoids the press, shows no gratitude for the public's interest in him, it's only human for reporters to want to see him get the worst of it. But it doesn't have to be that way. What I'm saying is that a news story should tell the truth, but it doesn't necessarily have to be slanted to hurt the party it's written about. Your husband should've been cooperative with everyone from the beginning, but it still isn't too late."

He was getting me in deep, and I tried to turn away from him. "Excuse me now," I pleaded.

"Wait," he said. "I'd really like to be your friend, before the others get to you and chop you up. If there's anything you'd like to tell me—on or off the record—you can count on me to be discreet."

"There's nothing to tell," I said, walking quickly into the house, not daring to glance back.

The garden conference hadn't passed unnoticed. Kono came home and phoned Charlie at the studio, and Charlie was home within the hour.

"How did Carroll get here? What did he want? What did he ask you? What did you tell him?"

I repeated Carroll's most withering implication: that he knew I'd been pregnant before the trip to Mexico. "Oh, he knows, does he?" Charlie sneered, eyes ablaze. "Then why hasn't he put it in his newspaper?"

"Maybe he was afraid it might hurt me."

Charlie went into a rage. "Hurt *you*—what about *me?* You have nothing to lose! What have you ever done? What have you ever accomplished? I have a career! The whole world is watching me!"

He began to spend more time at home.

Apparently Harrison Carroll had decided to spend most of his honeymoon in his car at the foot of Cove Way, with binoculars in hand and his bride seated beside him. If any newspaper stories about the premature arrival of the Chaplin baby were to appear he was determined to be the reporter to send them in.

Charlie was aware that Carroll was sticking like glue,

that he had even bought a telescope, and a war of nerves ensued between the tenacious reporter and the anxiety-ridden Chaplin. Night after night Charlie would crouch in the dark at an upstairs window, peering down at the car and muttering to himself like a man deranged. One night I came in and found him aiming a revolver at the window. The sight of the gun upset me, but the thought of the melodramatic Charlie actually squeezing a trigger was so preposterous that it was almost funny. What wasn't funny was his agitated state, his ridiculous mutterings. "I have the right to shoot any prowler foolish enough to step on my property," he said excitedly, not realizing that it was exactly the sort of nonsensical talk that in more lucid moments he would have brushed off as childish.

As soon as the delivery was just a few weeks away, I was kept practically under lock and key. My lassitude gave way to intermittent waves of panic. I wasn't afraid of pain, but I *was* afraid of having Charlie's baby without Charlie's love.

In my eighth month of pregnancy my anxieties became so acute that the problem of staying awake reversed itself. As I paced the floors sleeplessly, the house I could never truly call mine became a jail, and the very knowledge of Kono's presence became almost unendurable. Dr. Kayser went to Charlie with a suggestion: in the best interests of easy delivery of the coming baby, I should go somewhere where there could be uninterrupted peace and quiet until the child's birth.

To my astonishment, Charlie had a small house rented for Mama and me in Whitley Heights, not far from where I'd been born. With it, he supplied an Oriental couple—Tomi and Todah—to care for me. This towering generosity left me thunderstruck. I wasn't to learn till months later that Charlie had got it in his head that I might die.

We were bustled off to the rented house in the dead of night, and almost at once I was free of the great pressure

I'd felt—there was no Harrison Carroll keeping vigil. Best of all there was no Kono to bedevil me with watchful silence. The two new servants were not made from the Cove Way pattern; they were talkative, friendly and helpful, and they were doing everything within their power to make life as pleasant as possible for my mother and me. Todah was a genius of a cook, and Tomi was not only a capable maid but an absolutely inspired hairdresser.

Perversely, Charlie now came to see me every day! He brought a gift each time—candy, fruit, flowers—and for the first time it seemed as though I was being courted. He would seldom phone ahead of time, but when he arrived he would stay sometimes for hours, talking animatedly, asking me countless questions about how I was feeling and about the movements of the baby, as if he had just come to be aware of what the fuss was all about. Mama once again regained her faith that the marriage had a splendid chance, and I reveled shamelessly in the attention being paid me. I was sewing attractive maternity housecoats, feeling infinitely better and enjoying Charlie's enjoyment of me.

This enjoyment, as I should have expected from the world's least predictable man, soon became a physical one; the more misshapen I was, the more irresistible I seemed to become. On his third visit, Mama was barely out of the bedroom before he was undressed and diving into the bed. At first I was shocked, but only because I thought I was supposed to be. I accepted him that day and in the days that followed, and I no longer felt alone.

I still couldn't entirely forget that he'd called me a "little whore" the October before in his office, but the words had lost their sting. If that's what I was, then so be it, as long as I wouldn't have to have my baby with only my mother to comfort and love me.

Dr. Kayser called to see me, often when Charlie was at the house. There was the usual examination and the usual advice: exercise, no emotional upsets, lots of rest. During one of the doctor's visits he and Charlie held a long consultation in the hall. I could hear only a word here and there, but I could tell they were having a disagreement. Charlie seemed to be rejecting something Dr. Kayser kept insisting on. The discussion went on and on, and as it neared its end I got the idea that the doctor had finally resigned himself to Charlie's point of view. I had no idea what they'd talked about, but I should have realized that, with the baby due any day, it was imperative to Charlie that the public and press think the birth was still some six to ten weeks off. If the Chaplin baby were to appear, big and bouncing and full term in all respects, it would take a genius to explain away the phenomenon. Charlie was desperate for a way to conceal the truth.

At dawn on the morning of May 4, 1925, I awoke with pain that I immediately knew was the beginning of labor.

Mama left me in Tomi's care while she ran to phone Charlie and tell him it looked as if I was ready to deliver. She scurried back to inform me that the Locomobile would be sent instantly, that Charlie had decided he wanted the baby born in the big house, not in this impersonal, rented place.

Mama and Tomi packed a small suitcase and dressed me in a heavy topcoat. When the limousine arrived in thirty minutes, they helped me down the stairs. The three of us went out into the otherwise deserted street, with Todah trailing behind, assuring me that he would take good care of the house and that I would have a son, maybe two.

The drive to Cove Way seemed to take forever. My pains came and went, but I was drenched with perspiration and an intermittent terror. Mama squeezed my hand, and Tomi kept mopping my brow and neck with a handkerchief. At last we reached the driveway entrance to the house. We were relieved as the car swung in between the opened gates, gates that one of the houseboys was poised to lock behind us.

Charlie himself was in front of the house to open the door and help me out. He took me through the entrance hall toward the stairway, whispering reassurance. "Everything's under control, Lita. Dr. Kayser's been alerted and he's on his way over." Halfway up the stairs I had to stop once, for the pain across the small of my back was excruciating. Charlie turned white. When the pain eased I forced a smile to reassure him.

He guided me to the bedroom at the northeast corner of the house, which had been equipped for a delivery; there were surgical instruments, porcelain pans, a special, professional-looking light, boxes of sterile dressings, a two-burner gas stove, a baby's bathinette, and even a pulmotor. As Mama and Tomi worked to make me as comfortable as possible, Charlie picked up the bedside clock and began timing my pains. They were coming at intervals of about every fifteen minutes, and Charlie looked profoundly relieved when the doctor appeared.

Dr. Kayser sent Charlie out of the room and examined me. "We're going to have a long wait," he said to Mama. "I don't think she'll deliver for another twelve to fifteen hours yet." He asked me, "Hurt?" although he obviously knew the answer. I nodded. He gave me a pain-killing injection in each leg and showed me how to breathe each time the contractions came. Then he and Mama tied some bedsheets to the footboard of the bed so that I could pull against the contractions when and if it was necessary. Finally he said, "She'll be all day and then some, but the injections will help. I advise you to go and have some breakfast, Mrs. Spicer." He left the room.

The shots weren't helping much. Every quarter of an hour a pain came, and with each I writhed and pulled hard on the sheets. Mama and Tomi took turns at drying the rivulets of sweat that poured off me and trying to soothe me. Charlie kept coming in, looking worried and helpless, and assuring me that I would be all right, that it would be over soon, that I was brave, that I was very pretty. They were platitudes, but I welcomed them. He would hold my hand for a time, then disappear, then return to hold my hand and talk to me, then disappear again. Late in the afternoon the doctor gave me more injections against pain. They didn't help. If anything, the contractions grew more agonizing.

By eleven o'clock that night, the pains were five minutes apart, but even then Dr. Kayser said I had hours to go. Charlie was collapsed in a chair, prepared to wait out the ordeal. Tomi padded in and out. Mama sat beside me, squeezing my hand, grimacing every time I groaned.

When the time for the beginning of delivery finally approached, Dr. Kayser again sent my now-haggard husband from the room, gave me another series of shots and spoke to me firmly. "Bear down when the pain starts, Lita. Keep on bearing down until it subsides. Save your strength between so you'll have the energy for the next one."

The pains were now so terrible that I couldn't understand how I could still be alive. My mother became panicky; when I needed her most she cried, "I can't take any more of her suffering!" and fled into the hall. The contractions were getting closer and closer together—five minutes apart, then four, then three, and within the endless hour there was only one minute between. I could scarcely catch my breath. Finished with one back-splitting moment of agony, I found another one upon me. I writhed, and I screamed.

The doctor put on rubber gloves and fixed a cone-shaped object with gauze over my nose. "Breathe in, Lita, just keep breathing in," he kept repeating. I drank in the ether fumes and the next few minutes were blessedly hazy. I could hear voices and I could feel a dull pain, but I could experience nothing of what he was doing to help me. Mama had come back, and I could feel her holding my hand tightly.

And then I blinked and saw my baby.

Something in the doctor's face alarmed me in spite of the ether. He slapped my baby vigorously on the buttocks, cleaned out its mouth and nose, and dipped it first in hot water, then in cold, then hot, then cold . . . I forced myself to rise up on my elbows. Weren't babies supposed to be born crying, or didn't they always cry when they were spanked into breathing? I heard a fearful whimpering, and I realized it was coming from me.

My baby was a boy. And he was ashen-colored.

And he wasn't breathing.

Mama and Tomi held me back as the doctor quickly placed a piece of gauze over the swollen little mouth and blew his own breath into my baby's lungs.

There was still no response. He tried again . . . inhale, exhale, inhale, exhale . . . there was no response. "Mama, he's dead," I gasped. "My baby's dead!"

Again. And again and again and again. Inhale, exhale, inhale, exhale, inhale.

Suddenly there was a choking bleat. And then a cry.

My baby was breathing. And crying.

I giggled idiotically in relief and thankfulness, then leaned forward to look at the tiny face. The eyes were puffed and the little body was contorted in its fight to live, and I wept and I laughed and I fell back into the pillows fatigued and grateful.

Once more I became only fuzzily conscious. The doctor's voice was far away, but I could hear him tell Mama, "Here, take him, wrap him in this blanket. I'll tend to the cord." Then I was given something to drink and I felt the doctor's hands pressing on my abdomen. Then I was out.

I awoke at two in the afternoon. Mama was standing near me, holding my baby in her arms. I could tell from her smile that he was all right. "Here, dear," she said. "Nurse your beautiful son."

I fed him, delighting in my baby. I asked if Charlie had been here. "Yes, he was here at noon," Mama said. "He looked in, and then went downstairs to have some lunch. He told Tomi he was going to get some sleep. I guess he's in his room."

"Mama, did he seem . . . happy?"

"Now why on earth wouldn't he be?" she said. I didn't even realize that she hadn't given me an answer.

For all his genuine pleasure at being a father of a healthy baby, Charlie was determined to be practical, too. He and Dr. Kayser had spent much of the past twenty-four hours in argument. "You're the only one who can help me," he'd persisted. "A six-month baby would put an end to my career."

They argued back and forth, and at last the doctor gave in. He had a cabin in the San Bernardino mountains where I could stay in hiding.

And, for a fee, he would falsify the birth certificate. He would record my baby's birth as June 28, 1925, instead of May 5.

Chapter Thirteen

What possessed us to agree to go into hiding as though we were criminals? My mother agreed because her relationship with Charlie had reached the point where he could talk her into anything. I agreed because I had no choice. I was still unable to talk back to Charlie on any subject of importance. We agreed to leave for the cabin as soon as the baby and I could safely travel.

But one thing that warmed me toward him was the absorbed attention he paid the baby. He was afraid to pick it up or even to touch it, but he would stand by the crib and cluck almost unbelievingly, "Isn't this marvelous . . . this is my son!" I wanted the baby to be named after him. He didn't think it was a good idea, reasoning that children who carried the names of famous parents were given a cross to bear at birth. "In any case, we've plenty of time to concern ourselves with names. This baby won't be born officially for another six to ten weeks yet."

On the ninth of May, four days after the delivery, Kono reported that Harrison Carroll was still tenaciously camped at the foot of the driveway. Charlie went into action. He summoned Dr. Kayser by phone and came back to give Mama and me instructions: "Pack your essential things. Once you're at the cabin, don't communicate with anyone except me or the doctor. I'll get up to see you if I can. Hurry now!"

Because it was too risky to have the chauffeur drive us, Charlie had worked out another of his elaborate schemes. Dr. Kayser would drive to the cabin, and Mama, the baby and I would follow him in Mama's Studebaker. At the "go" signal we emerged from the house by a side door, where the doctor was waiting in his car. As we followed him down the steep driveway in Mama's car, I held the baby tight and crouched over, as instructed, so that if Carroll happened to be at his post, he wouldn't see me.

"Why are we doing this, Mama?" I asked. "We're acting like two nuts."

"No, we're not," Mama said blithely. "We're going on an adventure. Think of it as going camping."

I stared at her as if she had really gone mad.

The trip to San Bernardino took two hours through traffic and then another hour of bouncing along over the unpaved roads into the mountains. Dr. Kayser guided us to a dismal log cabin with its door and windows boarded up with pieces of rotting wood, as if it had barely weathered the hard winter. I snuggled the baby close to my body and waited as the doctor got out of his car and Mama stepped out of ours. The day was cold, and heavy dew had settled on the ground and on all the foliage. From the looks of the shack it wasn't any warmer than the outdoors, but it couldn't be any colder, so, wrapping the baby securely in his blanket, I got out of the car and walked to the front door, where the boards now hung off to the side on one or two rusty nails.

The doctor's tone was apologetic. "My friends and I use this for hunting and fishing, but only in the summer season," he explained. "It must be pretty dirty and damp right now, but nothing that can't be remedied. Let's go in and take a look." He pulled the boards away and opened the door.

The inside was certainly dirty and damp, and incredibly dreary. Until Mama and the doctor started a fire in the fireplace, the only light in the main room came from a crude fixture suspended from the ceiling by a corroded chain. The doctor seemed restless, as though he wanted to leave as soon as possible, and acted like a man ashamed of what he'd agreed to do for money. "The place isn't much, I know," he said, "but it's well stocked, and the baby will be perfectly all right. There's a good supply of canned goods and plenty of pots and pans and dishes and things like that. Cleaning stuff, logs and newspapers are all on the back porch. If you have trouble making a fire you can use the oven to keep the place warm. There's—uh—no telephone, but you won't need anything. I'll be back Friday night for sure, and I'll bring some things."

He went out, and after a minute or so the hum of the car motor grew fainter and fainter, and then there was silence outside.

The log crackled in the grate. The baby began to cry.

The mountain cabin had no hot water, no rugs on the floor and very little kitchen equipment, but it did have comfortable beds, enough blankets and a phonograph with plenty of records. And I had to concede, once I got over the insulting feeling that I had been swept out of the sight of civilization, that the landscape was beautiful. Spring had brought fresh green shoots to all the trees and shrubs, and wildflowers grew in profusion, their color streaking the green of the sloping, wooded hillsides.

We settled down to a steady routine. While the baby slept, which was most of the time, we would tackle the housework, soak up the delightful sunshine, play the phonograph and retire early. I felt fine. For the first time in over a year I was able to go for long periods without even thinking of Charlie. This surprised me, and rather pleased me, because I found that not dwelling on him—either in adoration or hate or fear—didn't make me disintegrate. I could be myself. I could give myself to the baby—to *my* baby.

Dr. Kayser drove up on Friday, bringing with him a baby scale and some more supplies. He examined me, weighed the baby, pronounced both of us in robust health, said the baby was gaining weight normally and made ready to leave. I asked him if he'd seen Charlie, if Charlie had sent any message.

"He's busy and he may not get a chance to get up here, but he sends his best wishes," the doctor answered, and was off again, leaving us to our hermitlike limbo. Sometimes I just played records over and over. Sometimes, when Mama took the baby in for his bath in the sink, I lay outside on a blanket and watched the insects building their summer homes, then turned over on my back to watch the birds soaring high over the treetops. In my torpor, it was easy to make believe that what I was doing here wasn't demeaning, that I should do my husband's bidding without question.

Near the end of the second week, after complaining that we were running low on groceries, Mama drove off down that road. She returned some time later with food and the news that there had been some curiosity about her in the little market she'd found. Dr. Kayser arrived on the second Friday with more supplies and more examinations that verified we were well, but no news about Charlie except that he sent his regards. His *regards*. Embarrassed, he went briskly on his way again.

On the following Wednesday, a man knocked at the door and asked pleasantly for Dr. Kayser; he'd played poker with him the preceding summer and had seen smoke coming from the chimney while driving by. He just wanted to say hello. Not identifying herself, Mama explained that the doctor wasn't expected for a couple of days. Then, as soon as the man left and she was fairly sure he wouldn't come back, she drove to the country grocery store, placed a call to Charlie and told him what had happened. She was ordered to pack our things and wait for Kono and Frank to come for us. He hadn't asked about the baby. Or me.

Kono and the chauffeur came the next morning and preceded us—Mama, the baby and me in the Studebaker—to a two-story house in Manhattan Beach that Alf Reeves's wife Amy had rented for us, under an assumed name, in a matter of hours. This new place still wasn't home, but it was a big improvement over the enforced rustic life. It faced the sea, and only the main boulevard along the seacoast separated it from the sandy beach. The sound of the breakers rolling and crashing into explosions of white foam was a welcome relief from the silence of the mountains.

Amy Reeves was a fine woman, eager to do anything for Charlie, who'd brought Alf to California from England to manage the studio. Charlie had lawyers and banking houses to keep his personal funds in order, and his brother Sydney handled his investments, but it was Alf who actually signed the company payrolls, paid all the bills and accounted for every penny. Amy moved into the house with us, and she was jolly and efficient. I was being pampered now, and my baby was thriving, but I was deeply hurt that Charlie stayed away, and for that matter, didn't even telephone. He'd announced in a formal press release that the baby was due on June 28, and he was apparently determined that no boat be rocked, even inadvertently, until then.

On the twenty-fourth of June I suddenly developed a fever, and a hard lump was noticeable on my left breast. I started to hemorrhage, and the soreness in the entire area surrounding the lump was so acute that I couldn't bear anything to touch it. The baby was immediately put on the bottle.

By two in the morning, my inexplicable condition was so much worse that Amy called Charlie and commanded him to come right away with the doctor. She described my symptoms, and Charlie promised to call back.

He did, in about half an hour. "It should take us at least an hour and a half to get there, but I'm leaving this minute. I'll have to stop at the doctor's house to pick him up."

They arrived at four, and Dr. Kayser went to work instantly to stop the hemorrhage. I had been in agony during labor, but only at intervals; my pain now was racking and constant. The doctor put a thermometer in my mouth and examined the angry-looking purplish spot on my breast. "She has caked breast, too much milk," he announced, and took a breast pump from his bag. "This and massage should help."

Charlie's eyes widened when the doctor read the thermometer: "A hundred and four. This is a sick girl. The fever won't drop till we get rid of this inflammation." Removing his jacket, he rolled up his sleeves and told my equally wide-eyed mother, "Bring me some oil, preferably olive oil."

Unwilling or unable to look at me, Charlie asked how serious the condition was.

"That breast is so full of milk I'll have to remove it as fast as it forms so the breast can be manipulated," he answered. "The lump will have to be massaged out."

By the time Mama returned with the oil. Dr. Kayser was working with the pump and I was screaming with pain. After getting as much milk out of the breast as he could, he began rubbing the oil around the sore spot, pinching the hard lump with his fingertips and making my eyes water, and perspiration break out all over my body. I grabbed at the sides of the mattress and held on tightly.

192

"Just a little more now," he was saying, "just a lit-tle bit more, and we'll be finished for a while."

At dawn my fever was down to ninety-nine and there was every indication that I would continue to get better. It had been a terrible night. The doctor had massaged and massaged until his hand had become limp, and I had shivered, sweated and cried through most of the treatment. But the lump was gone and the hemorrhaging was under control.

I slept most of the day, and woke at dusk to find Mama and Amy sitting in near darkness at the window; neither had bothered to turn a light on. Mama came to me. "Well, you're finally awake," she said, relieved. Her face seemed drawn.

Amy slipped out, and a minute or two later Charlie came into the room carrying some broth and crackers on a tray. He nodded to Mama, who left. Then, sitting on the edge of the bed, he began to feed me.

"This will help make you strong," he said, and his small, weary smile bordered on compassion.

"How long have you been here?" I asked.

"I haven't left. The doctor did, some time ago. He's satisfied everything's shipshape. I didn't want to leave till you woke. I wanted to see for myself that you're all right. And you are."

When I could find words, I said, "Then you don't hate me . . ."

"Hate? I've never hated you!"

Passively, gratefully, I let him feed me the broth. Finally I dared to ask, "When can we go home?"

"Tomorrow, if you're up to it," he said. "You and my son have been away long enough."

Home meant a whole new experience with the mercurial Charlie; it was as if there hadn't been a moment's discord between us from the day we'd met. He became so solicitous and considerate—and so consistently so—that I was overwhelmed. *The Gold Rush* was still being edited for August release, but he spent a great deal of time at home, seeing that my every need and desire were filled and basking in the wonder of his son. I was additionally overwhelmed when, on June 28, he announced to the press the birth of his son, Charles Chaplin, Jr. He had vetoed the name when I'd suggested it, and I'd never mentioned it again, but obviously he'd come to consider the name a suitable one. He clearly loved the baby, even though he was still afraid to pick it up, and every morning before he left for the studio he came in and viewed it with a mixture of rapture and awe. He seemed particularly taken with the similarity of the baby's head to his. "Look at his ears— flat to his head, just like mine," he would exclaim. "Even the back of his neck is like mine!"

On one of those mornings, he came in wearing a new light suit and bent over the bed to inspect Charles junior, who was naked, wriggling and happily kicking his legs. Suddenly a forceful gush of urine splattered Charlie's new suit, and Charlie leaped back in shock. But the shock lasted less than a second. Charlie burst out laughing, so spontaneously and uncontrollably that he collapsed onto the bed, holding me in one arm and our son—for the first time—in the other. He laughed and laughed, and I laughed with him. We would slow and stop, gasping, and then one of us would start again and the other would join in. At last he got up, buttoned his jacket and announced with a mammoth smile, "I don't know what can top this today, but I'm going to work."

I pointed to his stained suit. "You're going to change first, aren't you?"

"Change?" he thundered, beaming. "My son *peed* on this suit! I'm going to show it off to everyone I meet!"

No pictures of Charlie junior were released to the public, although Jim Tully fed the papers and wire services reams of material about the jubilant Chaplin family. And in view of the new way Charlie was acting toward me, there was no doubt in my mind that he *was* jubilant. He was tender again. He began to talk to me as warmly and as considerately as he'd done in the earlier days, before our marriage.

Then something unexpected happened to me, too, and I became almost consumed by it: I wanted sex with Charlie, lots of it.

There had been surges of heat and waves of lust for him in the past, to be sure, times when the mere anticipation of his making love to me had turned me heady and breathless. But this was different. My desire for him in the past had been laced liberally with thoughts of girlish romance and solemn, childlike love. Now I wanted his body and I wanted him to have mine; it was as absurdly simple as that. When I wasn't tending to and loving my baby, I spent an embarrassing number of waking hours experiencing clamorous urges of passion in my still-swollen body, and they were far more animalistic and persistent than I'd ever allowed them to be before. I had heard that such naked urges can invade and overtake women who've just given birth. I didn't know about other women; all I knew was that, mad or not, I couldn't wait to know him—and myself—in new ways.

Charlie was a completely willing partner, and he was obviously impressed by my hunger. I still balked at one kind of oral foreplay, in spite of the fact that it was the one in which he especially wanted me to participate, but beyond that there were no limits. I surprised him—and occasionally even myself—by my inventiveness, and by the aggressive ways in which I was inventive. I dreamed up lascivious games for us to play, delighting Charlie and making him say, with dazzled sincerity, "You're the damnedest girl who's ever lived, Lita. No one was ever like this."

At any other time I wouldn't have taken pride in the compliment. But now although their names weren't mentioned, I felt I had surpassed Pola Negri and the other human sex symbols Charlie had known. And winning the contest exhilarated me.

I won another contest—with myself. After the birth of Charlie junior I finally began to reach once unattainable climaxes, and the bliss they brought me propelled me all the more. The bed we now shared each night became an arena, and Charlie remarked repeatedly that he couldn't get over my transformation from a docile bed partner to an insatiable one.

For weeks we were ecstatic when we were together and restless for each other when we were apart. It was more than a year since we'd first touched, but it was as if we'd just discovered how wonderful sex could be. I was turning, irrationally but joyously, into what must have been almost a caricature of a sex-obsessed nymphet. It did cross my fevered mind, I'll admit, that the more erotically fulfilled I kept Charlie the less his eye would be likely to rove elsewhere, but I was never that consciously calculating about it. I was genuinely enjoying my husband, and I was all the more stimulated by his enjoyment of me.

As for Charlie, I have no way of knowing—except from gossip—what his techniques were like with other women, but I know he followed certain rather unwavering rules with me. The things that can excite many men were to him commonplace and therefore to be avoided. Except for that one night when he'd quoted *Fanny Hill* to me, he never used four-letter words or obscene images before or during the act of love. And once, when I brazenly attempted to arouse him with a few choice words and suggestions of my own, he told me a bit pompously that it was unbecoming and that I should stop. Out-and-out pornographic pictures and writings for the purpose of sexual stimulation generally bored him, and he was not a fetishist. Men friends who remarked to him that they were particularly intrigued by female legs or hips or bosoms disappointed him, not only because of their coarseness, but because of what he termed "their pathetic parochialism." Charlie was a sensualist; nearly anything connected with the senses could stir him—a subtle perfume, the rustle of taffeta, a certain gaze.

As soon as I could fit into a size twelve dress again, he was eager to take me out in public. Mama was all for this; it would allow her to spend more and more of her time in the nursery fussing over the baby. In a single week Charlie took me to a Wagner concert at the Hollywood Bowl, to a movie premiere at Grauman's Chinese and to dinner in the Rendezvous Room of the Biltmore Hotel. He was even having corsages delivered to me!

On the evening of the Biltmore dinner we were waiting at our front door for the car when Kono materialized with an envelope. Charlie pulled out a card and read aloud, "Mr. William Randolph Hearst requests the pleasure of your company, August 20, for a weekend outing at San Simeon. It is suggested that you bring riding togs, bathing suit and casual clothes."

He seemed elated, and put on his straw hat at a jaunty angle. "Well, this'll be something! I've always wanted to see San Simeon."

When we got to the Biltmore we found that the Rendezvous Room was packed with celebrities, but Charlie insisted on a table on the lower level, away from the dance floor. He was still in excellent spirits while he ordered dinner, but his face was nearly crimson with controlled rage by the time the waiter left. "Who are you looking at?" he demanded.

I'd been watching the people dancing, and his abruptness startled me. "Looking at?" I repeated. "I'm not looking at anything in particular."

"Come on now, you're looking at that fellow dancing with Jane Peters."

I wondered how he could see that far—I couldn't. I recognized Jane Peters, the comedienne whose professional name was soon to be changed to Carole Lombard, only after he angrily pointed her out. I didn't recognize the man she was dancing with, nor could I detect anything about him that made him especially worth looking at, and I said so. "What are you accusing me of?" I asked. "Why are you doing it?"

"Why are you denying that you were looking at him?"

He was acting so peculiarly that I couldn't tell whether or not I should be angry. "This is stupid," I said sharply. "And if you keep it up, I want you to take me home."

"That's all right with me," he said coldly. "But I intend to have my dinner first."

The dinner was eaten in strained silence. After he paid the check—leaving a tip of exactly ten per cent, as was his custom—he rose from the table, gathered my gloves and bag and handed them to me, and took my arm to walk me out through the plushly-hung archway of the entrance. I thought he was through with his bewildering nonsense, but once in the car he started it all over again.

"I want to know why you were looking at Jane Peters' dancing partner."

Too furious to say anything, I grabbed his straw hat, threw it on the floor of the car, and drove my high heel through it.

Strangely, Charlie didn't look angry, or even unhappy. He looked excited. He circled my waist with his arm, nuzzled his mouth up against my cheek and whispered, "Kiss me, Lita. Kiss me the way I taught you . . ." His mouth was so warm and his touch so remarkably gentle that I turned my face to him before I had time to figure out what was happening. Our parted lips came together and we gripped each other in irresistible hunger. He murmured something to me that I couldn't make out, but I understood his tone of voice and nodded vehemently. He reached over and closed the divider curtain.

He'd made that silly accusation in the Biltmore for the bald purpose of getting me mad, because my anger aroused him. Now that I saw through the trick, I should really have become angry. But I didn't. By then we were making love in the back seat of the car, and it was the best ever. . . .

As we prepared to go to San Simeon for the weekend, I had a few private misgivings because I knew Marion Davies would be there.

What I didn't know was that I was pregnant again. Nor did I know that, largely because of this second pregnancy, our marriage was now doomed.

Chapter Fourteen

You weren't exactly forbidden to drive your own car to San Simeon, but Mr. Hearst preferred that things be done his way. To keep him happy, you and the other weekend guests assembled at a prescribed time at the Ambassador Hotel in Los Angeles, where a pride of black Cadillac limousines would be waiting. You would be assigned your chauffeured limousine, the others would be assigned theirs, and then you all would ride in a long line to the north of the city, up the coastline and to the castle. It was like being in a wedding or funeral party. It was also very impressive.

To call San Simeon impressive is to use an absurdly inadequate word. The castle was then on 240,000 acres of land, and it had an ocean frontage of over fifty miles. As we approached the base of the hill, we saw a pile of huge packing crates spread over an area the size of a city block; we were told later that they contained pieces of Italian churches and small castles, to be uncrated and reassembled when the always busy workmen on the premises could get around to them. I was excited as we neared the driveway, of course, but Charlie seemed to be in a trance. Normally intolerant of ostentation, he was goggling through the car window like a pauper about to cavort with a prince.

Oddly, William Randolph Hearst greeted us all with a manner less like a prince than a mild-mannered caretaker who was rather embarrassed at his employer's fabulous display of wealth. We entered by way of the main building, called The Dining Hall, and then were shown to our quarters in guest houses that overlooked the Pacific, with the promise that those of us who were here for the first time would, if we liked, be taken on a tour after lunch.

The bungalow I shared with Charlie had a ceiling paneled in squares inlaid with hammered gold leaf. A thick tapestry-like coverlet was draped over the enormous bed, and cheerful French paintings lined the walls. The view of the ocean was panoramic. While one of the corps of houseboys who had brought us here unpacked our bags with swift efficiency, an awestruck Charlie called me to inspect our private bathroom, which was done in black marble with a sink of solid gold. "Have you ever seen anything like this in your wildest dreams?"

He was even more awed when he learned what the two buttons he had discovered in the bedroom were for. If you wanted valet service, such as having your clothes cleaned, you pressed one button; if you wanted a drink or snack, you pressed the other. He pressed both, and within three or four minutes a valet and a maid were at the door. He gave the valet some clothes to be pressed and asked the maid for a Scotch and soda. While waiting for them to come back, he strutted about on a cloud of plutocratic joy. "This is the way to live!" he said. It seemed incredible that this was the man who sincerely grieved for the world's starving millions and who frequently displayed great and positive interest in socialist experiments that would destroy the greedy grasping of the land barons. Conversely, it seemed even harder to believe that this man, who was a millionaire many times over and who could well afford nonstop luxury if he chose, was behaving in these surroundings like a gaping hick.

The drink arrived scant minutes after the maid had scurried away to fetch it. When I came out of the shower the glass had barely been touched, but that didn't matter; my husband had proved whatever it was he'd wanted to prove.

We dressed casually for lunch and were escorted to a comparatively small dining area where a refectory table had been set up for fifteen—fourteen weekend guests and Mr. Hearst. At the Santa Monica Swimming Club and elsewhere I had met Greta Garbo and John Gilbert, and of course I had met Marion Davies, who breezed into the room with the certainty of a guest who is in reality the hostess. I was introduced to the others—among them Norma Talmadge, one of the day's highest paid film stars; Donald Ogden Stewart, the writer; and Robert Millikan, the physicist, who seemed rather lonely in a party of people loosely linked together by their mutual involvement in the arts and mass communication.

The table could have accommodated fifty people, and there was something vaguely eerie about seeing thirty-five empty chairs. A butler-waiter stood at either end of the table, and in spite of our casual clothes and the promise of a casual lunch, I felt about as relaxed as if I were at Buckingham Palace—which, incidentally, is unassuming compared to San Simeon. Mr. Hearst seated us all where he wanted us, with Marion at his right. He placed Charlie and me close to the opposite end, which, I couldn't help noticing, didn't please Charlie at all.

Throughout the lunch our host remained the mild-mannered caretaker, listening more than talking, and listening as though he were grateful he'd been permitted to attend. This once again struck me as strange behavior for a powerful man whose very name, in 1925, could induce terrified chills in so many hearts. I remembered that his voice was high-pitched and carried poorly, and maybe he was embarrassed by it, but I felt somehow that that alone couldn't be the reason he appeared to be on the periphery —and voluntarily so—of the gathering.

Charlie, growing more relaxed, divided his time between talking books with Donald Ogden Stewart and taking sidelong glances at the quiet Greta Garbo. I couldn't blame him; everything about her added up to beauty, and every man there was bewitched. Even the waiters gravitated toward her, and John Gilbert, whom gossip claimed to be her lover, was staring at her with pleading, mooncalf eyes—but Charlie was the only man I was concerned about. If he was Marion Davies' sometimes boy friend, San Simeon was certainly the last place they would select for a rendezvous this weekend—and anyway, she was huddling close to Hearst. I didn't see the pretty Norma Talmadge as competition, if only because her husband, Joseph Schenck—who wasn't along this weekend—had had a falling out with Charlie over Schenck's recent ascension to the presidency of United Artists, and she had vigorously taken her husband's side. The other women were either terribly plain or terribly proper, or both. If there was any female to fear, it was the mysterious Greta Garbo.

My jealousy faded when it became evident to me that she intended to ignore Charlie. She appeared to be ignoring Gilbert, too, but with a difference. She knew the love-struck Gilbert existed, and she was playing a torturing game with him, a game of being remote. If she knew Charlie existed, it didn't seem to matter.

Lunch done, the towering, sixty-two-year-old William Randolph Hearst clapped his hands like a prissy librarian and squeaked in an eager voice, "All right, those who want a tour of the ranch, let's go!" San Simeon, officially called La Casa Grande, was casually referred to as "the ranch" by its potentate.

I found his eagerness to show us his home appealing, and I found just about everything we saw unbelievable. Eight of us—Garbo, Dr. Millikan, Charlie and I, along with two Hearst executives and their wives—went on the personally conducted tour, and none of us tried to be blasé, because that would have been ridiculous.

Mr. Hearst had begun furnishing his empire in earnest only three years before—by 1949 he was to have lavished thirty million dollars on it—but even now nothing seemed to be missing; there were treasures of painting and sculpture and architecture from all over the world, and every object bespoke riches. The interiors of the vast buildings contained representations from every conceivable culture. Mr. Hearst took us into the building he himself occupied most, and we took an elevator—which, incidentally, had once been a confessional in an old Catholic church in Europe—to the library on the second floor. This library held countless thousands of fine old books, most of them first editions and all of them, he confided, his most prized possessions. He had insured none of them, he added wistfully, for no money could begin to cover their loss.

We were guided through a dozen or so of the fifty-three bedrooms in the main house, each one unique and individually constructed. Mr. Hearst showed us an array of fine tapestries and pointed to one, his newest acquisition. "I paid a hundred thousand for that, but it's hard to judge what it's really worth," he said. "One of these days I'll get around to having it appraised." We were taken to the main dining room, which boasted a solid gold mace from Ireland and a sixteenth-century ceiling from Italy. We saw the tremendous kitchen, with a chef for almost every course, and the gigantic walk-in refrigerators in which hung frozen game and fowl by the thousand, much of it grown and killed on the premises. We were shown Mr. Hearst's own bedroom. "This bed was Cardinal Richelieu's," he said with a grin, "but I've had a somewhat more modern mattress put on it." We saw the system of telephonic trunk lines, connected to all his far-flung publication centers, that allowed him to talk with any of his employees within a matter of seconds.

Then, outdoors, there were the gardens, the immense zoo, the private airport, the herds of cattle, the stables, the —well, the everything. We were shown a swimming pool. "This was built from the Greek colonnades, and it's laid in mosaic tile. It cost a hundred thousand," said Mr. Hearst, and then directed our attention to a summerhouse: "The hand-chiseled alabaster plaque you see over that group of columns came from the Dora Palace in Italy. Now I'll show you the other swimming pool."

Charlie, half-dazed, came to long enough to joke, "Two swimming pools? What's the second one for—rinsing?"

The second one was huge. "This one cost a million dollars," explained Mr. Hearst. "I had Italian artisans work on it for more than two years. See the lapis lazuli mosaics?"

Charlie, the hungry kid from the London slums, gave a low, reverent and uncharacteristic whistle.

Some of us spent most of the afternoon in and near the pool—the million-dollar one, naturally. I was thinking— perhaps almost gloating—about how much better I looked in a bathing suit than Greta Garbo. This was cruel of me, granted, but I envied her great beauty, and I had nothing with which to compete except a good figure. She was talking in soft, apparently serious tones with John Gilbert, who obviously idolized her, and she seemed ill at ease that her wide shoulders and solid legs were exposed.

Charlie and Marion were still steering clear of each other. He was deep in conversation with Dr. Millikan, and she was gaily chatting for a minute or two at a time with everyone and no one in particular. Eventually she sat beside me and said, "We haven't really had a chance to talk with each other, have we?"

Glancing furtively about, she took a metal container and a paper cup from the beach bag strapped over her shoulder. She poured a colorless liquid into the cup and winked at me. "Champagne," she confided. "It's mother's milk to me. I adore it. W. R.'d kill me if he was here—he's in his study, working—but you won't squeal on me, will you?"

I shook my head. She offered the cup to me, and I shook my head again. Grinning slyly, she drank and settled back. "Well, now, speaking of mother's milk, you're a mother, aren't you?" she remarked with that disarming stutter. "That night we met at the Ambassador I wouldn't have believed you were expecting a baby. You looked terrific. I was jealous of you, do you know that? I thought I was the belle of the ball, and then you came along and stole my thunder."

But you stole my husband, I wanted to say. I didn't, though, because this woman I barely knew was too warm and pleasant to make me angry. Pola Negri, yes; I would have been only too ready to explode at a Pola Negri. But there was something so open and unthreatening about Marion, so immediately likeable, that I suspected I wouldn't be shatteringly upset if she were to admit to me, then and there, that she and Charlie had been lovers.

"That's nice of you to say, Miss Davies. Actually I—"

"Oh, call me Marion," she broke in. "Let's be friends, okay?"

"Sure."

"I meet so many stuffed shirts here most weekends that it's a pleasure to come across somebody who's home folks, like me. Not that I mind all of the stuffed shirts." She chuckled. "W. R.'s the biggest stuffed shirt that ever lived, and I'm crazy about him. And good old Charlie, your fella, he's sort of a stuffed shirt when he isn't watching, and I'm crazy about him, too."

Quickly, though not defensively, she amended what she'd just said. "You know what I mean. I don't mean crazy about him that way. I mean he's a hell of a good friend and I'd hate not knowing him." She glanced around again and took another drink. "No, I shouldn't call your fella a stuffed shirt. You're dippy over him. I can see that."

I was getting more and more comfortable with her. "You're right, I love him," I said, "but I'm not blind. He's just—well, he can be pretty formal when he sets his mind to it."

"Can he ever! You know something I can't get over about Charlie, though? When you least expect it, when he's at his most stuffed-shirtiest—is that a word?—he can fool you and turn around all of a sudden and have one beaut of a sense of humor about himself. You notice that?"

"Yes," I lied. I seldom noticed Charlie, the world's funniest man, exercising his sense of humor on himself.

"Not like those two," said Marion, lowering her voice and jerking her chin in the direction of the sad-eyed Garbo and Gilbert, who were sitting a good fifty feet from us. "They've got a swell thing going, but they act like mourners at a wake. Look at them. Did you ever see two more beautiful faces and two sadder-looking people? Johnny's a great guy, all man, everything going for him except the Swede. He's been at my house in Santa Monica twice in the past month, and both times he flung himself down and busted into tears because the Swede wouldn't marry him!" She shook her head in wonder as though to say, What good is life without a sense of humor? As time went on I was to see that Marion met most of her responsibilities with maturity, but she believed that life was meant for good times and made no bones about it.

Marion hastily hid her portable bar, and I saw why: Mr. Hearst was lumbering up to us. He was cordial toward me, and solicitous with Marion. "Now, Marion, how many times do you have to be told you shouldn't be out in this breeze if you're not dressed warmly?" he chided.

There was no breeze. The sun was strong. She was even wearing a light shawl.

She sounded very calm and very patient, as though she went through this kind of thing with him regularly.

"W. R., if it was any hotter we'd all melt. You be a good boy and go act nice to the company."

"Not until you have a sweater. I'll find one of the boys to fetch it for you."

Marion sighed, got up and stood on her tiptoes to peck at his chin with her lips. "All right, I'll go. I tell you, you're worse than a pack of grannies." She winked at me and left.

He watched her go, clearly entranced by her. Though he was to live another twenty-six years, he was never to marry Marion Davies. But she was to be at his bedside when he died. Counting the Ambassador Hotel ball and this weekend, I was to meet William Randolph Hearst no more than half a dozen times. I heard dreadful stories about the heartless uses he often made of his fantastic power, and I'm sure all those rumors can't be lies. Yet I was sincerely fond of him, in spite of the fact that I always found him a little frightening. The Hearst I knew was completely without arrogance or cruelty. Despite San Simeon, he was one of the least pretentious men I ever met. When he said he'd paid hundreds of thousands of dollars for this and a million dollars for that, he seemed to be simply making a statement of fact, not trying to prop up his ego with his wealth.

Freedom of movement was the motto at San Simeon, and there was only one rule that every guest was expected to obey: dinner was served in the main dining room at seven, and not a minute later.

Mr. Hearst had a rotation system that seated us at different places at different meals, which put Charlie and me closer to the head of the table than we had been at lunch; I was given the honor of being seated at Mr. Hearst's right. Dinner was so incredibly plush that it made the elaborate lunch we had had that afternoon seem like a hasty snack. There was a wide selection of wines from the vast wine cellar that had been the pride and joy of

Mr. Hearst's mother, Phoebe. Butlers came around with rolling trays containing almost every imaginable kind of meat and game, vegetable and salad. The service was perfect, the food superb.

Charlie and Dr. Millikan, who had been huddled in intense discussion through much of the afternoon, were still at it at the table. I was able to follow very little of their friendly argument, but I was truly impressed by Charlie's ability to hold his own with the foremost American physicist of the day, the man who was later to be credited with having most successfully proved Einstein's Theory of Relativity. Dr. Millikan was stating with quiet pride that man was close to dealing with nature's energy more usefully than ever before, while Charlie kept expressing apprehension.

Dr. Millikan argued: "Mr. Chaplin, certainly there's risk in every undertaking of progress. You're the finest in your line, for instance—no doubt of it. But your film making is a young, still growing art, isn't it? If films are to improve, technically and artistically, won't some changes have to be made—by you, as well as others? Won't they entail risks?"

Clearly the doctor was referring to the approaching advent of talkies, an area that had started to make Charlie increasingly touchy over the past months.

"I don't deny that there's a great deal of room for technical and artistic improvements in motion pictures," conceded Charlie, "but I do insist that change for its own sake —in my field and in yours—can do only damage, more often than not."

Then, either because he believed he was being attacked personally, or because he felt that the threat of talking pictures was too delicate a subject for him to stomach at dinner, Charlie maneuvered the discussion on to less controversial topics.

After dinner we were all shepherded to the castle theater to watch a movie—Mr. Hearst enjoyed movies and had a different one shown every evening—and after the film, although it was still early, Mr. Hearst announced he was going to bed. He sternly warned Marion against drinking any more champagne, bade everyone good night and left. Marion giggled and drank champagne happily. "It's a game we play," she explained. "W. R. knows I love this stuff and he tells the help not to serve me any after a certain hour, but he knows I can wrap the help around my pinkie."

Before we all retired, we sat in one of the gargantuan gardens and listened to a mellowed Charlie's views on the oncoming reality of talkies. "I'm worried about talking pictures—naturally I'm worried—but not for my sake. My work can't be affected one way or another. What worries me is that sound can become a plaything that will enslave talented producers and writers and directors. As it is, with little enough real art in motion pictures as a whole, there are signs already that sound is intriguing everyone in the industry for all the wrong reasons. They're already thinking in terms of scrapping their equipment to make way for this new toy, and consequently their minds aren't on their work."

"You're pessimistic, Charlie. Talkies could be the shot in the arm that pictures need," said John Gilbert, whose career would eventually be ruined in part because of sound.

Charlie nodded. "I'm pessimistic only if sound pictures constitute the bulk of commercial film output. Then art will really be dead as a dodo in pictures, because in every art there must be a lot left to the imagination."

The weekend flew. The three or four times I saw Charlie and Marion chatting, I saw that Mr. Hearst was also not too far away, smiling tentatively, as if he suspected something between his mistress and his friend yet hadn't the evidence to confront them. My own suspicions were undiminishing. But Marion had been so genuinely nice to me that I would need indisputable proof of their intimacy before I turned on her.

When I learned I was pregnant again, I thought Charlie would go out of his head with rage. Again I was to blame, he charged, although he wouldn't explain how it was my fault that he refused to take precautions—not on moral grounds but on the ground that contraceptives were esthetically hideous. I met the news that I had conceived a second baby, so soon after delivering the first, with some shock of my own. The responsibilities of taking care of one baby in a rickety marriage were more than enough to handle, even though the baby gave me so much joy; the anticipation of having to double the responsibilities left me temporarily numb. I waited for Charlie to demand that I have an abortion—and in spite of my mixed feelings about becoming a mother for the second time inside of a year, I was primed to tell him No.

He made his demand. I said No. He ranted, for surely the dozenth time, that I was conscientiously plotting to ruin his career, his life. I still held firm to my decision.

After a few concentrated days of roaring at me—so steadily and abusively that Mama raised her own voice and complained that he was acting like a madman—he finally quieted down and never brought the subject up again. This surprised me, for he'd been so ferociously insistent that I'd tricked him, that all I lived for was to see him destroyed. I never did know why he dropped his demand so abruptly. Maybe, secretly, he wanted another child. But most likely he was too caught up in his work schedule to follow his rage through. *The Gold Rush* was done and being hailed as a major success, and he was deep in preparation for his next picture, *The Circus*. One of the details he had to iron out was the selection of a leading lady; he had been satisfied with Georgia Hale in *The Gold Rush,* but he didn't believe she would be right for the part of the petite bareback rider in *The Circus*.

Less than a week after he was told he was once more to be a father, he and Kono took a train to New York, where he was to confer with motion picture exhibitors.

With Charlie away for two weeks—and with no Kono around to shadow me—I felt a bit less shackled. Mary Pickford impulsively came to the house one noon, loaded down with presents for Charlie junior, and took me to lunch at a restaurant in Hollywood. And one day, hungry for the company of youngsters my age, I invited two girls with whom I'd gone to the Cummnock School of Dramatics, and whom I'd especially liked, to the house for lunch and a swim in the pool. That turned out to be a sad mistake. At school we'd all been equals and now we weren't, and no matter how hard I tried to be one of the gang, I wasn't—and never could be again. For better or for worse, I was Mrs. Charlie Chaplin, not Lillita Mc-Murray or even Lita Grey. I lived in a big house, and I had servants. And I was a mother. The girls were ill at ease, and their eyes popped. I couldn't reach them.

Strangely, the one person whose company I enjoyed was Marion Davies. I spent many afternoons at her house in Santa Monica. She liked me, I'm sure, or she wouldn't have kept inviting me back—but I never fooled myself into believing she saw me as a bosom buddy. For all her laughter and vivaciousness at San Simeon, she was fundamentally a lonely young woman, and I think she regarded me as an immature but equally lonely girl for whom she wasn't expected to put on an act.

Marion was probably not an alcoholic—in those days, at any rate—yet she usually had a glass of champagne in her hand and a bottle or two nearby. I accepted some, out of curiosity, but the dizziness scared me back to soda pop. Generally we sat out on the terrace, and she would start out being as bubbly as her champagne, telling jokes and harmless gossip, giving me good-humored advice about marriage and motherhood, although she had experienced neither. She would talk about Charlie, but always as a friend, not as an artist and certainly not as a lover. I still couldn't bring myself to ask her when they'd last made love.

Gradually, particularly on days when the wine really

got to her, she would unburden herself to me—not because she wanted or needed my help, surely, but I guess because she somehow knew I could keep her confidences.

"Being Charlie's wife must be the toughest job in the world," she said late one afternoon, her smile gone.

"Why do you say that?"

She shrugged. "Why not? He's the biggest, he's the greatest thing in pictures, right, sugar? Even if he wasn't so great, even if he had a twentieth of the talent he does have, he still couldn't stay normal with all those hands clapping for him. Nobody could. But that doesn't make him a prize package to live with, I bet. Mildred Harris was no saint, but she wasn't really a bad kid, and Charlie, God bless him, loused her up good."

Carefully I asked, "How did he do it, Marion?"

"Hasn't Charlie told you all about her—from his point of view, naturally?"

"Charlie doesn't—tell me very much about anything. You'd be surprised how little I know about him . . . or the people in his life."

"Umm. Well, nobody can say Mildred smelled sweet as a rose before Charlie married her. Maybe she loved him, but it's for sure she figured he was her ticket to the high life in the movies. Is that wrong? I don't know—maybe it is, but I do know that once she climbed on board she tried to be a good wife to him, and when he kicked her out after a couple of years he treated her like she was dirt. She got some dough out of him, but only after things got mighty messy. So she got some money, so fine, so what's it done for her? She's still a kid, and I hear she's a hopeless drunk."

It all sounded ugly—and it all sounded true.

"I feel like a traitor, talking about Charlie like this, because I like him so much," Marion said. "But you look out for yourself, Lita, and that baby, and that other baby you're hatching, because leopards don't change their spots, and Charlie's a leopard. I got no inside information about anything, mind you, but I know all about lovable bastards.

Charlie's going to try to hurt you some day, sugar—when or how I don't know—but you better keep your guard up. Or should I just shut my trap?"

Instead of listening to the painfully true things she was saying, I picked that moment to ask, "Marion, are you and Charlie sleeping together?"

She flushed. "Now where did a question like that come from?"

"Are you?"

"No," she replied. Then, measuredly, she said, "We had ourselves a fling, yes, but that was before you and he latched onto each other. Uh—why are you asking? What's he been telling you? Or where'd you get that sort of idea in your head?"

I was satisfied she was telling the truth. "I apologize," I said. "I shouldn't be so dumb. You wouldn't be treating me like a friend and having an affair with my husband at the same time. I say a lot of dumb things sometimes."

"No harm done." She smiled. "Look, sugar, even if I was all for getting fixed up, what good would your fella do me? I've already spoken my piece about him—a great guy, sure, but nobody any dame in her right mind should get a hot case on because it couldn't lead anywhere except the junkheap. And as for calling on him for a quick lay —hell, I'd be a candidate for the booby hatch. W. R. would find out. And I can assure you, a hundred of the best quick lays wouldn't be worth getting W. R. mad."

The next time I saw Marion she drank an alarming amount and talked about herself and William Randolph Hearst.

"God, I'd give everything I have to marry that silly old man," she began slowly, reflectively. "Not for the money and security—he's given me more than I'll ever need. Not because he's such cozy company, either. Most times, when he starts jawing, he bores me stiff. And certainly not because he's so wonderful behind the barn. Why, I could find a million better lays any Wednesday. No, you know what he gives me, sugar? He gives me the feeling I'm

214

worth something to him. A whole lot of what we have, or don't have, I don't like. He's got a wife who'll never give him a divorce. She knows about me, but it's still understood that when she decides to go to the ranch for a week or a weekend, I've got to vamoose. And he snores, and he can be petty, and he has sons about as old as me. But he's kind and he's good to me, and I'd never walk out on him."

Marion spoke often of the practical side of the relationship. She told about the time she'd heard that Hearst was nursing a brief interest in a pretty blonde from New York. Although she wasn't jealous, she claimed, she went to him and told him bluntly that she had no intention of giving her prime years to him if she had no security. She had seen too many girls lose their hearts and looks and youth in affairs, only to be cast out without a cushion to fall on. Hearst immediately understood. He gave her the house in Santa Monica, a fortune in jewelry, a hotel in New York City and other investments that would guarantee her a life of luxurious solvency.

"Tell me something, Marion," I said. "Would you love him as much if he hadn't provided for you so well?"

She looked at me as if I were insane. "*Love* him!" she cried. "With all the drawbacks I mentioned? I wouldn't even give him the time of day! Girls get *old*, sugar, and they either have to be looked out for or look out for themselves when they're tied up with our kind of men. That's what I was trying to tell you. The sooner you learn that, the less likely you are to get hurt."

Chapter Fifteen

A day before Charlie was due back from New York I got a phone call from Merna Kennedy, who'd just returned to Los Angeles after nearly two years of touring in vaudeville. I insisted that she come to the house and stay for dinner.

We fell into each other's arms like long-lost sisters, which in a way we were. Merna had changed, and much for the better. Her talk was still a little salty, but all the rough edges had been worn off her manner and the way she dressed. She embraced Mama as though she were greeting her own mother, and she was intrigued by the baby.

Before and during dinner we brought each other up to date on what had been happening to us. Merna had been a big hit in vaudeville, she said, and she'd seen a giant chunk of the country. I played down my own past couple of years, although I answered most of her questions—not very honestly—about what it was like to be married to a movie star. If she knew Charlie junior's real age she did nothing to give herself away.

I was taken by Merna's bouncy good looks, and I suspected that Charlie would be too. I suddenly envisioned her playing the bareback rider in *The Circus,* but I didn't dare tell her and build up hopes that could be so easily dashed. She had freshness and verve, a figure that would look good in the bareback rider's brief costume, and a gingery personality that just might come across perfectly on the screen. I decided to try playing talent scout—but for the moment I was glad simply to be with a friend my age.

Charlie came home in a slightly better mood than when he'd left, but only slightly. He gave me a rather formal nod, said hello gravely to Mama, looked in on the baby, then went to his room and locked the door. Although he was still stiff and remote at breakfast the next morning, he talked a little about his New York trip, the cold he'd caught there and how spent it had left him for nearly a week, what an interesting but expensive city New York was, what remarkable business *The Gold Rush* was doing there at the Strand Theatre and how he would love nothing better than to take to his bed for a month and do nothing but sleep.

"Why don't you?" I asked. "You do look tired. You don't ever seem to stop working. A long rest would do you a world of good."

"Can't. There are a million things to do, and everything falls on me. The exhibitors are clamoring to show *The Circus,* and I haven't even started the bloody picture yet. I haven't even found my leading lady."

"Could I make a suggestion for one?"

He peered at me. "Who, pray? You?"

"No. Merna Kennedy. Do you remember her?"

He repeated her name twice. "Vaguely. That playmate

of yours, right? Rather pretty if innocuous face? Red hair?"

"You wouldn't call her innocuous if you saw her now," I said, hoping I wasn't overdoing my enthusiasm. "She was here the night before last, and she looks just stunning. She's been touring in vaudeville."

He nodded. "I see. She wants to be in the flicks, and you guaranteed her that your famous and influential husband has a part made to order for her, and all you need do is snap your fingers and wave your wand and the part's hers. Is that about how the evening went?"

"No. I'm sorry I brought it up."

"Well, I should think so," Charlie said, and finished his breakfast in silence. But before leaving he said, "That Kennedy girl might be worth testing. Have her get in touch with Alf Reeves."

I phoned Merna, who was living in Glendale. Two weeks later she was signed for the part.

Merna came to me, full of effusive thanks, as though I had gotten her the part rather than merely suggested her. We had a nice hour together, and I invited her to visit more often. She promised she would, but it was months before she called me on her own. She was pleasant each time I phoned her, and each time she had excuses why she was too busy to see me; she was just on her way to an acting lesson, a dancing lesson, this appointment or that appointment.

Unfortunately I had more than enough time to sit and count my wounds, for I rarely saw Charlie at all any more, except on the formal occasions when he took me to evening parties or to premieres or concerts. We started going to the Hollywood Bowl one night a week, partly because he enjoyed classical music, but chiefly, I discovered, because music that was heavy, moving and sad invariably instilled in him a deep sense of pathos, which in turn enhanced his own creativity. Somehow he needed the aura of melancholy while he was building ideas. But only the aura; actual news of the death of someone he knew, or even someone he didn't know but simply admired, could hurl him abruptly into the depths of depression. Instead of enriching his work, as did solemn music, such news could immobilize him, brooding, in his quarters for days and nights at a time. These were the times when he would call the studio and order, "Send everyone home—I don't feel funny today."

During the early months of my second pregnancy he grew more distant, more withdrawn; he became less aware not only of me but of Charlie junior. He had always been an avid bather, but now he was taking as many as eight and ten baths and showers a day. He was developing into an inveterate insomniac who stole about the grounds in the middle of the night, carrying a pistol and searching for prowlers. I became worried, of course, and in spite of his growing detachment from me I would seek him out and show my concern. He would tell me to mind my own business and send me away.

My two main concerns now were Charlie junior and the baby on the way. Physically I was feeling well, not at all as I had in the first pregnancy. Morning sickness was almost nonexistent, and I was suffering from none of the nausea or queasiness that had been so much a part of my previous experience.

Emotionally, however, I was in somewhat worse shape. I was more sure of myself socially than I'd been a year earlier—by some sort of osmosis, perhaps, I had taught myself to be not nearly so uncomfortable in company—but I was striving harder than ever to find some strand of continuity in my marriage. There had to be an answer to our problems somewhere. But where? What was driving Charlie, and why was it driving him so far away from me?

With the baby due in a only a few months, my feeling of futility grew. There was Marion to visit, but that was hardly a life. There was Charlie junior to love, but Mama was giving every possible waking hour to him, leaving me with a bare minimum of motherly responsibilities. I went to the studio several times to see how *The Circus* was shaping up, but Charlie was never really available to me except when he supposed he should impress others with his husbandly concern, and Merna was cordial to me but too busy with the myriad tasks of being a leading lady to give me much time.

I was ready to tear my hair because two things were abundantly clear: my second baby would be born into a home that was no happier than the one my first baby had joined and our marriage could only go either of two ways —it would end or it would continue to drift. As it turned out there was a third way—an ugly deterioration of the little that was left of our relationship.

It started on the Sunday afternoon Charlie came home with Dr. Albert Einstein, a guest he treated with pious reverence. I was awed, too, for I knew this was one of the greatest men of the century, even if I had no more than an inkling of why he was great. He stayed for dinner, preferring to talk music rather than physics. He was a shy, almost demurely modest man whose deep-set eyes looked quizzically out from beneath bushes of eyebrows and whose hair, a pepper-and-salt mixture of black and gray, fell over his collar at the back. His clothes were loose-fitting and without style. He spoke in a soft, heavily accented voice that was not easy to follow, but it was obvious that Charlie was completely charmed by him.

Though I tried to follow the conversation, I'm afraid I saw little more than an unkempt, very old man, and when he left and Charlie came from the door, exhilarated, I couldn't keep from saying as much. "I'm sure that Dr. Einstein is a great man, but can't you understand that I'm starved for friends my age?" I asked.

To my surprise, Charlie listened. He wanted no teenagers cluttering up his house with their empty-headed songs and chatter, he declared, but if they were all that important to me, he supposed he couldn't see any great harm in my getting together with them on the outside—as long as I didn't make a career of it. Thinking it over, he summoned me about an hour later and said, "You might like to give a little party—not here, but perhaps somewhere in town. Nothing fancy, nothing expensive, but if it'll give you something to do, I guess I can see my way clear to paying for a small party. I shan't attend, of course —I haven't the time or the desire—but if you want to play hostess, tell Kono I said it's all right."

I told him I appreciated this unexpected offer. I wanted to tell him more, but he waved me away, saying he had a ton of studio work to tackle.

The first guest I phoned was Merna. "Oh, gee, Lillita, any other time, swell, but for the next couple of months all I can do is eat, drink and sleep the picture," she apologized. "I've got so much to learn, so much to do, that any time I took away from work'd make me feel like a royal rat. But thanks anyway, and have a swell time, okay? Give my best to everybody!"

Click.

I was bewildered by the peculiar way I felt she was acting toward me, but I was determined not to be thrown by it or to read anything especially unusual into it; this was her big chance in the movies, after all.

Merna's turn-down didn't dampen my feeling of excited anticipation. Kono, who had been sent on a tour of comparison shopping, found a caterer and a private dining room at a reasonable rate at the Biltmore Hotel. He informed me I could have a maximum of eight guests. Enthusiastically, I began working out the guest list—and soon discovered I didn't know a single boy well enough to invite. Still undaunted, I got in touch with four girls from the old days, girls I could call friends without stretching the word too far beyond its meaning, got them to accept and suggested they bring dates.

But for all my planning and ardent anticipation, the party was an embarrassing bust. The kids who came, like the two girls from school I'd had to the house, wanted to be as spontaneous as I did, but it just couldn't be done. I was their age, but I also was Mrs. Charlie Chaplin—and

I was not only a mother, I was about to be a mother *again*. The evening was a polite one—and endlessly long.

At ten o'clock, as the party, defeated, wavered on its last legs, I became desperate. This couldn't be *all* I'd have left to savor! In a burst of grown-up bravura, I called out, "Listen, everybody! How about if we all go to my house and I'll show you around!"

Instantly, everybody came to life.

I gave them the address and we agreed to meet there. I got to the house first, wishing I hadn't be so impulsive yet simultaneously glad I had been. What was I doing wrong? This was my home, too, wasn't it? And these were nice kids, not roughnecks.

The houseboy admitted me, and gawked at the cars driving up the hill in single file. He seemed a trifle horrified and said, frowning, "Meesa Chapleen, he no home yet from studio." But I told him it was all right, that my friends were coming in for a few minutes. The four girls and four boys reassembled and came inside, the houseboy took their coats to hang up in the cloakroom under the stairs, and Mama appeared to greet me and my friends for a few minutes before returning to the baby.

I saw how my guests' eyes were bugging out and I began to tell myself with a swelling, showoff pride that finally I—I, myself—was impressing others, that this whole place belonged to me, that I had a perfect right to have anybody here I pleased, and if Charlie didn't like it he could lump it.

Holding myself erect, I took them through the rooms I knew would interest them most, starting with the big room where Charlie kept his own screen and projector. I heard whistles and awed murmurs. Next I took them to the music room, and after that to the living room, where I was eager to show off the extensive jade collection. They were only passingly attentive now, for they were so agog at everything at once that there enthusiasm began to get out of hand, at first imperceptibly and then to the point where they were on the verge of rowdiness.

All eight were chasing around the large room, scattering like marbles. One of the boys found the phonograph, opened the cabinet doors and pulled out some records. Instantly the other seven were clustered about him, reading off the Beethoven and Verdi and Bach titles and groaning in unison until they came to a recording of the Charleston. A whoop of recognition went up. I could just as well have not been there at all.

Before I could mobilize myself to stop them or to ask them at least not to get too carried away, the record was on the turntable and four couples were happily dancing. There were no partners as such. Each of the boys grabbed me for a few moments' quick spin and then grabbed the nearest girl to continue. It all began so fast that I still hadn't found the words to order them to stop, but an instant later I could summon up no earthly reason why they should. The setting was an austere one, to be sure—certainly this ultra-dignified living room had never seen anything approximating abandon like this—but so what? My guests were having fun. And I, I had to admit, was enjoying myself more than at any other time I could remember.

The record began again. I saw the houseboy come from the pantry and head down the hall toward the front door, and I supposed the doorbell had rung.

I followed him, worried, and saw I was right. Charlie came through the door, looked from the wildly gesticulating houseboy to the direction the music was coming from and back to the houseboy again. He stalked up to me, past me and into the living room, shouting, "What's going on here?"

Every kid froze except the one who switched the phonograph off. Quickly, I started to explain that we'd left the Biltmore at a little past ten to come here and see the house and we'd all arrived just a short time before and—

"Get that crowd of bloody drunks out of my house at once!" Charlie bellowed, and stalked toward the stairs. "At *once, I said!*"

As the kids began heading sheepishly for their coats, Charlie marched halfway up the steps. Then he stopped, glared directly at me, and in a roar that no one in the house could miss hearing, demanded, "Is this what happens when I leave you in my house, that you turn it into a whorehouse for all your gawddam dirty-necked drunken playmates?"

I was speechless, unable to move. The kids were scrambling for their wraps, but a beet-red Charlie wasn't finished. "What would've happened if I'd come home ten minutes later? You pack of whores and pimps would've all been at one another all over my furniture, all over my home! Not *her* home, *my* home!" And to me: "Get this filth out of here! You can get out with them if you think you're too high class to waste your time milking me any more!"

He charged to the top of the stairs and slammed his door.

I didn't watch the eight teen-agers scurry out. I was too blind with rage.

Charlie's voice had been so deafening that even Mama, who had moved happily into the background since coming to Cove Way, emerged from the nursery with a worried look. I shook my head, motioning for her to go back in, and stormed into Charlie's room, slamming the door behind me. I was furious. And I wasn't afraid of him.

"If you'd bawled me out in private that would be one thing," I raged. "But you embarrassed me more than I've ever been embarrassed in my life! What about *you?* What are they going to go home thinking of *you?*"

He peered at me as if he were trying to figure out whether I was serious. "What *they* think of *me?* Is that your great problem in life? What that scum thinks of *me?*"

"Why did you make that terrible scene? Why did you embarrass me so?"

He was still livid. "It won't work, Lita! We can't live together! God knows I've always meant only good to everyone on this earth—I've never been conniving, I've always been connived against. But you ruined me, you forced me to marry you with one baby and now you're trying to finish me completely with another one. I don't want it, I don't want you, I don't want anything except to be left alone to do my work. I despise you, I despise the day you came into my life, I despise those hoodlum friends of yours, I—"

Softly I said, "And Charlie junior? Do you despise him, too?"

"Ah, now we pluck at the heartstrings, don't we?" he snapped. "Damn it, what does it take to convince you that I find everything about you intolerable?"

He was pacing, his face so red and the vein in his temple pulsating so fiercely that he seemed almost apoplectic. I was less furious now than troubled, and I said quietly, "Then maybe we'd better start talking about getting a divorce."

Wheeling on me, he cried, "Yes, that's what you've been leading up to—divorce. Tap the money tree for all he's worth and spend the rest of your days living in the lap of luxury with that bunch of Mexicans you come from! I was wondering how long it was going to take you to speak it out!"

Then my husband, who abhorred any kind of physical violence, sprang over to his desk, opened a drawer and pulled out a revolver. It shook in his beautiful hand, but he pointed it at me.

He was ranting absurdities now, and I was terrified, though not at the thought of being murdered. I couldn't conceive of his pulling that trigger. I was frightened for him, for the wild things he was saying and for his irrational melodramatics.

I stood perfectly still as he waved the gun and roared his insane charges and threats. He stopped only when someone began rapping frantically on the door and we heard Mama demanding to be let in. At once Charlie blinked, gazed at the revolver in his hand, and apparently realizing how loud he'd been, quickly turned and placed the gun back in the drawer. Squaring his shoulders, he opened the door and admitted my mother, who stood blinking at us in confusion.

"I lost my temper for a moment, that's all," he said blandly, as though it was of no importance that he'd just been shrieking at me. "Nothing to be concerned about. Now you two get yourselves some rest." He gently ushered us out, closing the door after us, evidently convinced, somehow, that I wouldn't tell Mama about the gun.

Remarkably, I didn't. I told her we'd had a short fight, but I gave no details. I'd long before stopped confiding in Mama, mainly because she'd repeated too often that it wasn't proper for her ever to be brought in on our spats.

Sydney Earle Chaplin was born on March 30, 1926, five weeks prematurely. His birth was as easy as Charlie junior's had been difficult.

Later, as they were growing up, Charlie was to show both boys genuine, if inconsistent, affection, but in 1926 no paternal instincts were evident; he seemed to be dividing his energies between developing *The Circus* and cursing me with increasing fervor. The subject of divorce now was a matter of fanaticism with him, and he would come to me or summon me and rant about nothing else. I was no goddam good as anything but a millstone, and he wanted me off his neck and out of his life, he said. I had been clever in trapping him, but he would show me how he could handle Mexican tramps, he said.

These tirades became such an obsession with him that I could expect hysterical recountings of my sins against him every night he came home. But in spite of his barrages of abuse, in spite of how successful he was in hurting me, it gradually became apparent to me that even if I were as treacherous as he claimed, I still couldn't be completely responsible for the violent and increasingly unbalanced way he was acting. Why was he picking on me, railing at me, so violently and so continually? Why, when I was determined to sit silently and not egg him on, were his eyes so wild and his rantings so brutal? Had the pressure of fame and the responsibilities of his work finally caught up with him? Was he breaking down? I couldn't really believe that I was the whole reason for his behavior.

At last, nearly ready to break down myself, I again suggested that perhaps we'd better divorce.

"I'll divorce you when I'm good and ready, and strictly on my terms," he declared. "Oh, I'll pay you off, all right, but when it's convenient to me. Don't get funny ideas about running out and talking to the newspapers or anyone at all. I can have you killed, you know. I have contacts who can do the job quickly and quietly and not think twice about it. How would you like to be killed quickly and quietly?"

Once more, Charlie was being so overly melodramatic that I couldn't take his threats seriously. I could, and did, take *him* seriously, though, and as calmly as possible, I said as much. "What do you mean, pay me off?" I asked. "You're all agitated now and I know you don't mean those other crazy things you're saying . . . but what makes you suppose I'm thinking about being paid off? That's a terrible thing to say. I don't care how many times you keep repeating it—I'm not some gold digger you've had over a weekend. I'm your wife. I've given you two sons. How can—"

He nodded. "That's right, you've given me two sons. I only wish I could find out if I'm really their father."

I had worked hard to keep myself from crying in front of him ever again, but now I couldn't help it. I was deeply stung, and I wept. Unfazed, he resumed his maniacal threats. He knew what I was. He would unload me when the picture was finished, and not before. If I were to get uppity and leave him, he would pay anything necessary to damage my reputation so that even my riffraff family would have nothing to do with me. He knew I wanted his money, but if I was thinking about calling lawyers, I shouldn't bother with such thoughts; his income and property were so tied up that I would never get a cent through the courts. He warned me that he was far from crazy when he talked about having me killed. I knew William Randolph Hearst, didn't I? Did I know that Hearst was so powerful that all Charlie would have to do would be to go to him and Hearst would have me put away for good?

I awoke the next morning, and on subsequent mornings, almost convinced that this lunatic side of my husband was nothing more than part of a horrid dream I'd had. Charlie's movies reflected him as a man of compassion, as a sworn enemy of anything violent. Then I would remember that no dream had been uglier than reality; he did hate me, and he did want to get rid of me. He became so intense about it, in fact, that, as I discovered some months later, he had an electrical eavesdropping system installed and hidden in my bedroom. His plan was an ingenious one: when Mama and I were there alone, he had the servants take turns listening in on our conversations over the receiving set in the basement of the house. They were to monitor our plot against him and furnish him with daily reports. When and if I ever dared to take him to court, he would be prepared to offer evidence that my mother and I had been conspiring for a long while. Eventually, I learned, the servants were released from the task. They were unable to bring him any significant information, simply because there was no information to bring.

Spring dragged into summer. I had, little by little, given up any hope that our marriage had even the slimmest chance of survival. We still went out to dinner parties and premieres—"for appearances' sake," he would remind me —but by now I merely went through the motions of being Mrs. Charlie Chaplin. I wasn't totally lost—there were the babies, and Mama, and those wonderful servants Tomi and Todah, who had come back to the house to cook and help Mama and me with the children. And I still saw Marion,

228

in whom I had started to confide. She rarely had anything to offer in the way of advice, but I valued her friendship.

What I couldn't resign myself to, what drained and constantly disappointed me, was Charlie's indifference to his sons. He would look in on them from time to time, strictly as an afterthought, but their ups and downs, their ailments or their progress, were of no real concern to him; they were duties, obligations to be supported, and beyond that he was uninvolved.

I don't mean that he couldn't take emotional responsibility for anyone close to him. He had sent for his mother, Hannah, and she had come over from England. He placed her in a pleasant, comfortable little house in the San Fernando Valley, hired a married couple to care for her and took trips—at first, at every free opportunity—to see her, and for a time he was a touchingly devoted son. Soon he began to take me, and the boys, to visit.

It was obvious that Hannah Chaplin had once been a very beautiful woman; remnants of that beauty were still evident. She had had a history of confinements in mental institutions in England, and now, with advancing age, she shuttled between moments of lucidity and lapses into a haze of senility. One minute she would play in a perfectly natural way with the grandchildren she adored; then the next minute she would be convinced that it was more than thirty years earlier and that they were her own two sons. Charlie became very restless and nervous at these times, and before long he had me bring the boys to the Valley while he stayed behind. "I'm so thrown off when I go to see her that I can't create, I can't function, for days," he explained. "I know she's not in pain, but when I look at her, when I remember how beautiful and gay she once was, when I see how her mind's not working, I get too upset. It's best that I keep away from her unless it's absolutely necessary that I go to her." Hannah died in 1928, and Charlie, I was informed, grieved for many months.

With the approach of fall, *The Circus* was well under way. Charlie's personal tirades had decreased in number and volume, but they didn't stop entirely. I could now recognize a pattern: the more stress he was under while he was away from the house, the more he strove to tear me to ribbons when he came home, almost as if he could unwind by digging into me. He seemed to find some sort of malevolent joy in expressing, at length, his hatred of me and in threatening what he would do or have done if I ever tried to take his money away from him. Often the words and charges he spewed out were so cruel and obnoxious that an outsider would have suspected he was drunk. Ironically, he came home staggeringly drunk once and only once during our life together, and that was very late at night in September of 1926. I say ironically because on this, the one night when one might expect liquor to loosen his tongue and make it nastier than ever, he went straight to bed without a word.

I kept the details of these vicious scenes from Mama, partly because she had grown fond of Charlie and partly because I felt—and here I admit my reasoning was queer —that if I told her everything she would find fault with me instead of with him. And I couldn't bear having them both against me. I took my woes to Marion, wailing, "Why does he hate me so? Why does he have to talk with such contempt?"

Marion shrugged. "If you want a bed of roses, sugar, go marry a drugstore clerk. If you want Charlie, put up with him."

If you want Charlie . . . All right, did I want Charlie? I still loved him, but he despised me, and more than that, *enjoyed* despising me. Till now, when I was at my lowest, I had been able to tell myself that the babies needed a father.

But what kind of father was Charlie? He ignored his children. He had told me countless times that they bored him, that all babies bored him. If we were to stay together, where was the assurance, even the vaguest sign, that he would go on being anything other than an indifferent father?

For more than six months—from before Sydney's birth in March through September—there was no sex between Charlie and me. While I regretted this, because every woman is convinced, often rightly, that a marital rift can be settled most speedily and most effectively in bed, it was my decision not to resume relations. Several times during this, his most hateful period, Charlie let it wordlessly be known that he had an appetite for me, that he felt we could somehow go to bed together and enjoy each other, even though he detested me.

But I let him know—also wordlessly—that I wasn't going to be an instrument for his pleasure until he changed his impossible attitude toward me. Charlie could totally separate sex from affection, but I would not let myself be used by night and abused by day.

During this period we spent several weekends at San Simeon, and during one of them, while Charlie and I were sharing a guest house in cold civility, Elinor Glyn introduced us to a girl named Andrea Gatesbry, whom she expansively called her protégée. Andrea, in her late twenties, was unpainted, angular and singularly plain until you really looked at her slate-colored eyes and saw how alert they were. She was a writer who had recently translated a number of books of German and French poetry into English and who, with Miss Glyn's generous help, was just beginning to make a small name for herself as a poet in America. I found her pleasant, if rather colorless, and I thought no more about her till Charlie and I were in our bungalow, getting ready to go to sleep.

"How did you size up that Gatesbry girl?" he asked.

"I really don't know. She wasn't mannish or anything like that, but she wasn't feminine, either. I guess she's just a cold fish."

He laughed. "That's where you'd lose a bet. I would've, too, because that's the way she appeared to me—all career and no gender. But Jack Gilbert and Marion took me aside and told me quite a different story."

"Oh?" I said, pretending I could barely muster interest enough to answer.

"Yes," he said, getting into his pajamas. "It seems this plain Jane is really a pretty hot article. She likes sex and she's ready for it any time and anywhere—although she's discreet, I understand. She goes in for perversions, any and all types. She's evidently a bit of a connoisseur, a collector. She'll try anything if it's creative enough."

"What is she, a Lesbian?" I asked, compelled to show off, in spite of my coolness, the fact that I knew what a Lesbian was. I'd read about such people, in fascinated revulsion, in one of the books in Charlie's library.

"No, no, nothing like that—not as a full-time commitment, at any rate. . . ."

Charlie continued to detail what Marion and John Gilbert had confided to him about Andrea Gatesbry, and he spoke with such enthusiasm that I had to look at him. Why was he telling me—and telling me so much?

Minutes later I discovered why: "I'd never have anything to do with her myself, of course," he said, "but—well, somebody that erotically free and inquisitive naturally fascinates me. Frankly, I spent most of the time at dinner and afterwards playing a little game. I imagined that there's a contest going on, that the person who can come up with the boldest and most inventive way to make love to her will win a prize. It sounds like an exciting game, doesn't it?"

"Oh, very exciting," I said flatly.

Another minute passed. Then: "Lita?"

"Yes?"

"You're a good sport when you want to be. We could invite this girl to the house and have some fun with her. You, she and I. The three of us in a great, wide bed. What do you say?"

Somehow I had suspected that he was leading up to something like this, so I reacted in anger rather than shock. "I say no! Definitely no!" I was seething. "Go with her, if you like. Go do anything with her or anybody else you feel like. You're the big genius, you can do anything you want to do. Just don't try to get me mixed up in that nuthouse stuff!"

He frowned at me, but he didn't answer. Nor did he come near me that night, even though we were sharing one bed. I turned on my side, away from him, and feigned sleep, wondering on and off for hours what my answer might have been if we were getting along well. A year before, at the limitless height of my love for Charlie, we had begun to make love and he'd remarked, from out of the blue, "Wouldn't it be interesting if we had an audience right now, watching us doing this?" I had whispered, "Yes," automatically, because I'd wanted at that particular moment to please him. If he had taken my answer seriously, if he had left at that moment to come back with a hundred people to serve as an audience, it's possible that I would have taken an active and shameless part in the charade, because then I'd loved him so desperately and so completely.

Now, though, I was disgusted that this hostile stranger had offered me such a dirty proposition.

Throughout the remainder of the weekend, I observed Andrea Gatesbry as she moved easily about the grounds, saying little, taking in everything—and looking sexless. I didn't know whether her reputation was earned, or whether the whole story was an attempt to trick Charlie. But I had learned something about Charlie's exotic—and cruel —desires.

Merna Kennedy phoned me.

"Hi, Lita! How's everything? Long time no see."

"Long time is right," I said coolly. I certainly didn't expect Merna to be undyingly grateful to me for having helped her, but she surely could have called before now out of simple friendship.

We made a date to meet for lunch at a café in Hollywood. I got there first, and scarcely recognized her when she breezed in. We were the same age, and we'd known each other since we were eight years old, but she bore almost no resemblance to the Merna I remembered. She was sophisticated and chic now, in an outfit of brown wool, with hat, shoes and gloves to match, an obviously expensive fur piece and a dazzling diamond bracelet on her wrist. My first thought was that she must have struck oil, but not at the Charles Chaplin Film Corporation; Charlie paid all his employees, from messenger boys to featured players, notoriously small salaries.

Merna fired a volley of questions about me and Mama and the babies, and then began babbling exuberantly about all the wonderful things that had been happening to her. She felt awfully guilty about not having called me sooner, she said, but she just hadn't had a minute to breathe over the past half year, what with acting and dancing lessons, interviews and working so hard in the picture. She was immersed in herself, and I was more than tolerant, for I'd had my own taste of the star treatment and could understand her perpetual excitement.

After I had congratulated her, I said, "You're sitting on top of the world. And it looks like you've got a generous boyfriend. That bracelet is beautiful."

Letting my remark pass, she jabbered on through the meal, all joy and vivaciousness—but I sensed she was eager to tell me something and was waiting for the precise moment.

It arrived over coffee. "Charlie gave me this bracelet," she said suddenly.

I bit my lip. Charlie simply didn't buy gifts, certainly not gifts that cost more than a few dollars. One and one were two, and night followed day, and B came after A, and there could be only one reason why he had bought the bracelet.

Aware of my silence, Merna put her hand—the braceleted one—over both my unbraceleted hands. "Wait a second, Lita," she said hurriedly. "I didn't do anything wrong. Is that what you're thinking? Believe me, I didn't do anything that was wrong."

I said nothing. I just sat and looked at her. And watched the chic and sophisticated leading lady start to squirm.

"You know I wouldn't let Charlie fool around with me," she said. "After all, you're my best friend. If it hadn't been for you I wouldn't've gotten the part. Charlie . . . well, he gave me this because, like he said, I'm going to be a big movie star some day, and he figured I should be in the right frame of mind before I get really famous and I should wear nice things like I'm famous already. He's got big plans for me. He's talked to you about the plans he's got for me, hasn't he?"

I shook my head, still not saying a word.

"Oh, it's all so wonderful. You know what he's going to do, Lita? He's going to make the story of Napoleon and Josephine when we're done with *The Circus,* and he says I can play Josephine!"

Josephine!

She babbled on for a few more minutes, and then stunned me by the extent of her gall. It turned out that she'd invited me to lunch because she wanted to ask a favor of me. Charlie had talked a lot about the Napoleon and Josephine movie, but he hadn't mentioned it lately, and she was a little afraid to go to him and bring it up. Would I discuss it with him and sell him on the idea that she'd be a perfect Josephine?

When I was able to collect my outraged wits, I said, "Merna, I want to ask you a question. Why did you wear that bracelet today? He gave it to you—isn't that enough? Why come and dangle it in front of me?"

She blinked as though she didn't understand. "You sound sore. How come? I told you I didn't do anything wrong."

Half rising, I slapped her across the face. Then I ran out of the café, not looking at the other people, who must have been almost as surprised as Merna.

I confronted Charlie.

I expected him to bluster and deny everything, but he didn't. Of course he'd bedded Merna down, he admitted defiantly. And there had been others since November 24, 1924, and he ticked them off just as defiantly. They were all names I recognized . . . Edna Purviance . . . Peggy Hopkins Joyce . . . and Marion Davies!

"What business is it of yours anyway?" he snapped.

"I'm divorcing you," I announced crisply. I had said it before, but with none of the conviction I gave it now.

Charlie began to call me the vile names I'd almost become used to. Now, though, they just bounced off, and I shouted at him for the first time in my life. "*Shut up!* I'm finished with you, I'm through with you. I'm done being your whipping girl, I'm done having you pour your garbage over me and making me feel small and worthless. You're not going to scare me or threaten me again, do you hear? I'm leaving you and divorcing you, and I'll curse every day I ever spent with you!"

He heard me out with frightening calm. When I couldn't find another word to say, he said with quiet finality, "You can't leave me. You'd be ruined. Not only you, but the children, too. You'd all be ruined for good."

It seemed he had planned meticulously for this showdown. If I dared to take any legal action against him, he explained, there were several unappetizing things I could be certain he would do. The servants were loyal to him, not to me, and would say anything he told them to say. They would testify that on numerous occasions they had seen me so drunk they had had to carry me to bed. They would testify that I ignored my children, that I had brazenly brought lovers to the house, that I held wild orgies. He would hire a number of young men, coach them in lines he would write, have them subpoenaed and then testify to my dozens of adulteries. He, the beloved Charlie Chaplin, would be awarded the sympathy of the world—and the children.

Furthermore he had paid the good Dr. Kayser twenty-five thousand dollars to falsify the date on Charlie junior's birth certificate and he would make this public if necessary; not only would the doctor automatically lose his license to practice medicine, but Charlie junior would be marked forever as the reason for his parents' marriage, and Sydney would suffer in the public eye as well. This would hurt him too, of course, but he would bear it gladly to make things unpleasant for me.

"If you're a smart girl you'll wait before making a rash decision," he said, and then smiled. "I'll tell you what I'll do. I'll give you enough money for a nice trip. Go to Mexico, Hawaii, anywhere you like. Have a good time and think it over. You may decide that life with me isn't so bad after all."

Chapter Sixteen

Tomi and Todah took doting care of Sydney, who was much too young to be taken on an ocean voyage, and Mama and Charlie junior sailed with me to Hawaii.

Mama annoyed me. Once we were out at sea I related to her all the despicable threats my husband had made, expecting her wholehearted sympathy. Instead, although she didn't come right out and defend Charlie, she found ways of painting him as less of a monster than I was positive he was. *If* he'd committed adultery with all those women, then that was dreadful, of course, she agreed. And granted, he shouldn't have spoken so crudely to me. But she would never in a million years believe he seriously meant any of those silly things he'd said. He was a difficult man, no doubt about it, but I was his wife and the mother of his children, and she wouldn't hear any more of this nonsense about divorcing him. She knew about marriage, she reminded me. She'd had three husbands and she'd learned her mistakes as a wife too late. Her biggest mistake was that she'd refused to recognize the fact that men need a fantastic amount of pampering. Maybe I wasn't nice enough to Charlie. If I were nicer when we got back home, all our little problems would smooth themselves out.

I hadn't told her about the revolver he'd waved at me. I did now.

Even that left her unfazed. "Charlie is an actor, darling," she said. "Other husbands wave their fingers. Charlie waves a gun—an unloaded gun, by the way, I'm sure. I can't imagine him as a gangster. That's plain laughable."

I give up, I sighed to myself. The only way she'll believe me is if I get murdered.

In Honolulu we checked into the Moana Hotel. I swam and surfed at Waikiki Beach, and I was terribly restless. The long holiday from Beverly Hills was giving me plenty of time to think, as Charlie had predicted. The situation was hopeless, the marriage beyond repair, and the longer we stayed away the more real the parade of indignities became. I wondered if marriage with him could be endured by any other woman.

Woman, I though glumly. A woman was something I wasn't. Maybe that accounted for much of the problem; I had done a great deal of growing up within the past two years, but I still wasn't a woman.

Each time I caught myself mellowing slightly, ready to face the fact that I truly loved him, thinking that things *could* somehow smooth themselves out if only I made some radical changes within myself, I catalogued that list of cruelties and lapsed back into hopelessness. Charlie had become sadistic in a variety of ways, perhaps too much so to be forgiven by even the world's wisest and most understanding wife. He had threatened to damage not only my name, but his own children's future. He'd arrogantly boasted of his adulteries after I'd become his wife, and he'd sneered that his love life was none of my business.

I was hurt most of all, not by Charlie, but by Marion Davies—and that to a numbing degree. It was possible that he had lied about her, but I didn't think so. And yet Marion had been my only true friend and confidante since I'd moved to Cove Way. She'd looked directly at me and told me there had been nothing between her and Charlie since we were married. Merna's sleeping with him shocked but didn't shatter me. Marion's did both.

By the time we returned to Los Angeles three weeks later, I was on the verge of another flipflop. Partly because of Mama's bland insistence that any marriage can be saved, partly because of my own gnawing desire to try again, I approached the house eager to do anything—everything—possible to keep us all together.

I was in for a rude reawakening. My first stop, naturally, was the nursery, where I held and kissed my husky, gurgling Sydney. I was able to relish the reunion with my baby for barely a minute before Tomi closed the nursery door conspiratorially and tiptoed back to me. "I hear what Todah tell me, what he hear servants say," she confided in little more than a whisper. "Servants say you got fight with Mister Chapleen, that if you leave him he going keep Sydney here, not let you take. Servants, they know. They say you not supposed be told, but they tell Todah, he tell me. I tell you so you be careful. Bad thing, bad, if he use tiny baby like that."

It was two o'clock in the afternoon. I didn't wait for Charlie to come home. Holding Sydney, not letting him go, I told Mama we wouldn't stay under that roof a second longer than necessary, that Charlie meant business and I wasn't going to allow him to use my baby as a pawn. I told Tomi to pack some of the baby's clothes quickly, and I urged Mama to telephone Grandpa and have him come for us.

Mama balked, calling me rash and impulsive, telling me

it was a mistake to plunge headlong into a decision I hadn't taken the time to think through.

"Then you stay here with Charlie," I snapped, at that moment hating her. "I'll do everything myself. I'll make the call, and I'll take the children. Keep playing your game of make-believe. You stay here and rock in your rocking chair and bask in how wonderful it is to be Charlie Chaplin's mother-in-law!"

She phoned Grandpa. He said he'd drive right over.

When he pulled up and was admitted into the house by a baffled houseboy, we were ready. Mama carried Charlie junior and an overnight bag, and I had Sydney and a valise. At that moment Kono strode into the hall. I ignored him and asked the houseboy to bring down the suitcases he'd just taken up. Kono raised his hand imperiously. "I do not know what is happening," he said coldly, "but there will be nothing removed from this house until—"

My seventy-two-year-old grandfather towered menacingly over Kono and thundered, "Simmer down or I'll tear you limb from limb, you son of a bitch! My daughter and granddaughter can take anything that's rightfully theirs!" To the houseboy he barked, "You! Do as you're told! Get that luggage and snap to it!" The houseboy swiftly obeyed.

Kono turned on his heel and left, muttering that Mr. Chaplin would be informed. The houseboy came down with the suitcases and carried them to the trunk of Grandpa's Lincoln. We followed him and drove home, where Grandma met us at the door and took the babies.

In my grandparents' parlor, Grandpa told Mama to be quiet while I talked. I did. In a rush of emotions spurred on by the fear that Charlie would catch me and punish me, I talked of the cruelty, the adulteries, the demands, the tyrannical threats. Mama tried to interrupt, to announce that nothing could be as black as I was picturing it. Grandpa angrily shushed her, grumbling, "Who's married to the son of a bitch, Lillita or you?"

241

Finished with my recital, I was drained.

Grandpa sat silently for a moment, then said, "The next step is very important, child. As long as there's a breath left in my body you're not going back to that filthy bastard. But you've got to make the decision about divorce by yourself. Are you absolutely sure you want to rush into a divorce?"

I nodded vehemently. "Absolutely sure. I don't want a penny from him. All I want is to stop being his wife as soon as possible. I don't care what he does to me, I won't be his wife. I'll go away and wait tables to support the children if I have to, but I won't stand his torture any longer."

Grandpa went out of the parlor just as I began having private, worried second thoughts about everything I'd said over the past three quarters of an hour. Had I done the wrong thing in leaving Charlie, especially in the way I had? Was he really less a monster than I'd just made him out to be? Should I have listened to Mama first before walking out of the house I'd lived in for two years?

Then Grandpa came back, his jaw set. "I've called your uncle Edwin in San Francisco. He's a blood relative, so they won't be able to buy him off. He'll be down in a couple of days. In the meantime, he said for you to talk to no one outside this house."

Mama sighed. "Oh, Dad, do we have to go into all this right away?"

"Of course. You dasn't make a move without an attorney."

I don't know how I knew, but when the telephone rang I knew the caller was Charlie. I picked up the phone, said, "Hello," and heard Charlie's voice.

"Lita," he said slowly, wearily, like a man just this side of losing patience with a child he's indulged. "Very well, you've played your nice little game, you've proved you're an assertive grown-up lady. Now it's time to come home. I'll send Frank for you and you'll come back where you belong."

"What about the children? Should I bring them, too?"

"Naturally! What a question!"

I was amazed that there was volume in my voice. "If I decide to leave again, which one of the children will you decide to hold for ransom? Sydney again? Or Charlie junior this time? Or maybe both? Yes, that would work out just fine for you. You could tell the newspapers and the judge and everybody that I ran away with a bunch of lovers and I deserted not only you but both my children. Oh, everybody would take terrific pity on you!"

"What is this claptrap your family's been putting in your head about ransom—was that the word you used? I'm sending Frank over to fetch you. If you like, if it will make your family happy, leave the boys there for the time being. You've made a silly mistake, Lita. Come here where you belong and we'll discuss it, calmly, quietly, without everyone on our necks. I'll show you that—"

"That's the second time you've said 'back where you belong,'" I broke in. "When did I start belonging there? I'm scared, Charlie, but you sound even more scared. What are you afraid of? Are you afraid I'm not under your thumb any more?"

He gave a reproachful sigh. "Look, this isn't you talking. It's that meddling family of yours putting these absurd words and accusations in your mouth. Come home where you be— Come home and speak for yourself."

Distance furnished courage. "Don't call me again," I said. "You're a brilliant man and I'm a dumb girl, but I'm not rotten. You are, Charlie. You're not only rotten but you get pleasure out of being rotten. I may be dumb, but I'm through taking rottenness from you."

I hung up.

Grandpa was nearby, sucking on his pipe. "I came in on the tail end just a few seconds ago, Lillita," he said. "Your Uncle Edwin claims you shouldn't have any communications at all with the great Mr. Chaplin, but I must say you treated him like a woman who knows her own mind."

"I'm not a woman, though," I said, and went upstairs to my sons.

By the time Uncle Edwin arrived from San Francisco, ready to go to work, I was at my wit's end. He was a brusque and businesslike Scotsman, bursting with confidence and capability, a boldly aggressive and articulate lawyer prepared to tear Charlie apart.

And only because I'd been stupid and hysterical when I'd come back from Hawaii, I told myself. I'd been all in favor of making trouble that day, spurred on by my grandfather's reassurance that I was right and my husband was wrong. Now, after sleepless nights and uncontrollable sobbing, I would have given anything to avoid trouble. I had pulled a protective black curtain over the part of my mind that remembered indignities and threats. Of course Charlie wasn't blameless for what had gone so sour between us, but neither was I. I should have been a better wife, a better person. Maybe if I had stayed to talk with Charlie, maybe if we could start again . . . maybe . . . maybe, maybe, maybe. . . . I kept seeing him at home, brooding, wandering over the deserted grounds, trying to bring himself to come for the children and me, to take us back and start over. I was bereft, naked without him. . . .

Grandpa had outlined the problem in his long-distance call, but now that Edwin McMurray was here, in person, it was expected that I go into everything, and in full detail. I found myself stammering, unable to make sense; when I tried to repeat the charges I'd made so vehemently before, what came out was rambling, diffuse, formless. Only Mama seemed relieved that I'd lost steam over the past few days of waiting. Grandpa was annoyed that after he'd summoned Edwin to Los Angeles, I was making a clear case of cruelty sound like a vague headache.

Edwin spoke up. "I'd like to make a suggestion, Will. Let Lillita and me have some time by ourselves. You and Lillian go in another room, or take a drive, or do something. The girl's been through a lot, and she's going to go through a lot more, and she's confused. Go ride around in that shiny new car I saw sitting outside."

From that moment on Grandpa backed out of the picture completely and left everything in the hands of my uncle, who, because he gave me the feeling he was very much in my corner, soon got me to tell him all there was to tell. He asked hundreds of follow-up questions, but he didn't pounce on my answers. He scribbled notes on a long yellow pad and behaved as if he had infinite patience. He talked, too, but I appreciated the fact that he wasn't putting words in my mouth.

Then he began discussing the procedure of bringing a divorce action.

"I'm—not sure I want to divorce him," I said.

My uncle frowned at me. He sat back, laced his fingers across his chest and asked quietly, "Well, what do you want, Lillita?"

I was fumbling now. "I'm not sure I know. Not yet, anyway."

" 'Not yet'? When do you suppose you'll decide? And while you're deciding, will your grandfather buy the milk to feed your babies? Is it your grandfather's obligation to take care of you and Charlie Chaplin's babies?"

Money hadn't occurred to me. I admitted it hadn't.

"I strongly suspect that money *has* occurred to your husband—who has a great deal more of it than your grandfather has," he said. After a pause he added, "My understanding is that your husband is worth in the fancy neighborhood of sixteen million dollars."

"I don't want any of it," I said hastily. "I mean, if I *do* divorce him I don't want to skin him alive or anything like that. The children should be provided for, of course, but . . . I feel just terrible. Talking about money this way, it—well, it's just that—" I took a deep breath. "Do we have to go into these things? Charlie's so careful with the money he's made. He'd get awfully angry. He'd never give up money on his own. Can we—I don't know . . . can you work things out so he won't get too angry?"

Edwin sat forward again and sighed. "Have you any real conviction that Chaplin intends to be a loving, responsible husband and father?"

"No . . ."

"Forget his being angry for a minute. Is there anything to justify his having the fortune he has and not decently providing for his wife and children?"

"No . . ."

"Then let's stop this shilly-shallying," he said, and reached for his pad. "The first thing we go after for you is temporary alimony. You're afraid of making that man *angry,* for Heaven's sake? What sort of talk is that? What are you, a baby?"

Although Edwin warned me in person, as he had warned Grandpa on the telephone, that I must have no communication with Charlie, I couldn't live with the burden of not seeing him again, especially now that my uncle had begun to put such hostile measures into motion. I had reversed myself for the thousandth time: I was convinced again that Charlie and I had no future together; Edwin McMurray had spent an entire evening helping me to convince myself. But there was a crowd of us and only one Charlie, and we were preparing to gang up on him. The prospect of setting a lawyer on him without talking with him about it first was too cold, too mercenary, too ruthless.

I can't say I called him against my better judgment for at the beginning of November, 1926, I had no continuing judgment of any kind. I waited till I was certain my family was well out of earshot, and phoned him. He invited me to the house on Cove Way. His voice was pleasant.

I got out of my grandparents' house by saying I was going to see a movie. Ralph opened the door and admitted me, nodding uncertainly as though he wasn't quite sure how he should greet me, and told me that Mr. Chaplin was in the music room.

Charlie, an untutored yet natural musician, stopped playing the organ as I entered. His thick, curly hair was uncombed, and he was dressed in his regular home outfit of sweat shirt, shapeless pants and sneakers, but he was still, as always, the last word in handsome dignity. He half smiled and half rose as I came close—though not too close. "Hello, Lita. You look tired."

"So do you," I said, sitting in the red leather armchair. "That was a pretty tune. Did you make it up?" Charlie didn't take himself seriously as a composer and often said he played the organ or piano for relaxation only. When snatches of music he invented stayed in his mind, though, he invariably had them written down. This was farsighted, for when sound came to pictures, and when he finally gave in and conceded that there would have to be sound in his pictures as well as in those of others, the musical scores were composed by him. He wrote the haunting "Limelight Theme," for instance, and tucked it away a full fifteen years before *Limelight* was released in 1953.

"Yes. It's not bad, but nothing anyone will remember to whistle tomorrow," he said, and lighted one of his very infrequent cigarettes. "Let's see, what can I get you? Shall I ring for a brandy and soda?"

"No. Thank you. You have one, though."

He shook his head. "Lita, I just can't understand why we're sitting here like two strangers when clearly we're not."

"Maybe that's what we are. I wish we weren't, but maybe we are," I said, trying not to sound like a scold. "I don't really know what we are to each other. I guess that's one of the reasons I came here—to maybe find out."

Charlie studied me. "What were some of the other reasons, Lita?"

I paused, then softly plunged ahead. "I came to tell you I'm divorcing you."

"You told me that on the telephone. Did you make a special trip here to repeat it?" When I didn't answer, he asked, "Would you like to let me know what on earth's come over you? Why did you run away like a thief in the night? Why aren't you living here?"

"Because you don't want the children and me to live here."

"There you go, being childishly dramatic again. I admit I said some harsh things, but then I work hard and my temper isn't always all it ought to be. I'm not a malicious man, I'm—well, I'm who I am. If you were looking for a simple bed of roses, life of cotton candy, then you should've married a drugstore clerk. But you married me. It mustn't be easy being married to me, but after all there's—"

A bell rang in my mind, and I was no longer the unsure little waif.

"Somebody said the same thing to me, in almost those same words," I said. "Somebody told me, 'If you want a bed of roses, go marry a drugstore clerk. If you want Charlie, put up with him.' Do you know who told me that? Marion told me that. Marion Davies. That's some coincidence, isn't it?"

"Marion? What does she have to—"

Now I was stronger than ever, more certain of myself than ever. "Charlie, you're a fake and a liar and I'm dropping you before you have the chance to hurt me more. I came here to tell you the babies have to be fed and clothed. I came here to tell you it's not my grandfather's job to feed and clothe them, but yours. I want you to tell me here and now whether you want the children and me back because you love us and want us or because you're afraid you'll have to give us money."

"Who's saying these insane things to me? Not you, you dimwit. It's that mother and that grandfather of yours. They sent you here, they rehearsed you, they drilled these clumsy, insane speeches into you."

"No," I said. "It's my lawyer. He's smart, he's smarter than all of us combined, and he's set to take you to court and make you pay."

"I see now," Charlie said, his voice an ominous whisper. "You got yourself a dime-store lawyer and he sent you here to hand me a progress report, right? If I nicely agree to let you rob me deaf, dumb and blind, I can go into the poorhouse and no one will bother me. If I have a quibbling question or two, you'll all cut my balls off once and for all. That's about the size of your message, right?"

"Nobody knows I'm here. I was warned not to talk to you," I said. "I just want to make things as easy for you as I can. I don't want this to grow into a great big fight and get in all the newspapers any more than you do. If you give me some lump sum to make sure the children will be taken care of and give me a chance to start out again on my own, then I'll dismiss the lawyer and you'll never hear from us again."

His eyes were slits. "And how much would that lump sum be?"

The round figure had come to me on the way over. "Ten thousand dollars," I said.

He blew up. "Ten thou— Are you serious? Why don't you ask for a million?"

"Ten thousand sounds fair, doesn't it? All your other troubles have cost you into the hundreds of thousands."

Incensed, Charlie paced the room, never taking his eyes off me. "Money, eh? You've come here for money, have you, you stinking little Mexican slut? Well, you can go back to those other holdup artists and give them *my* message—you don't get one goddam cent of my money. Who the hell are you, what the hell have you done to merit anything from me? If your family won't feed you don't come sniveling around me. Get off your backside and use it for something besides sitting on. Rent it out, you common whore. You'd be fine at that kind of work, and you'd earn a lot more that way than you'll ever bleed out of me!"

I got up.

He was still roaring his filth as I silently let myself out.

I went back to my grandparents' house. And embarked on nearly a year of my life I would have given my soul to be spared.

Chapter Seventeen

It would be comforting for me to say that everything that happened between November, 1926, and August, 1927, was done without my cooperation, for on looking back I realize the picture one is likely to get of Lita Grey Chaplin is that of a ruthless, mercenary female out to get Charlie Chaplin's money and destroy his name. But I can't say that, because I surely must have known, from the minute I gave Edwin McMurray the green light to proceed, that the roost would thenceforth be ruled by the tactics of expedience. I could defend myself by saying that I was still very young and that I assumed, when people looking out for my interests kept repeating, "We know what's best for you," that they did indeed. But I can't use that as an excuse; I must have had some awareness that they were going to work to hurt my husband, and I didn't stop them.

At the outset, I still hoped that both Charlie and I could come out of what lay ahead with dignity. It was one thing to confide mistreatment to my mother and grandfather and lawyer in private; it would be quite another thing to publicize it to the world. Frankly, too, I was worried that the angry Charlie, who was indeed powerful and capable of pitiless retaliation, might actually carry out his threats to me. Would he say, or have his attorney say, that I was an unfit mother to my children, that I drank, that I had lovers? If I denied these preposterous charges and he repeated them publicly, and if he had the servants and hired perjurers repeat them, which of us would the world be likely to believe?

But most of all I worried about the children. They were babies now, but they would be young men some day, and for the rest of their lives they would be the sons of Charlie Chaplin. Their parents brawling in public could stigmatize them forever.

My uncle Edwin moved from San Francisco, and because it was advantageous for him to work out of a Los Angeles firm, joined the law offices of Young, Young and Young, who entered the case in cooperation with him. Preliminary hearings were held after Charlie's attorneys reported that Mr. Chaplin had no intention of offering a dollar in settlement, because he, not I, was in the right. Suddenly I wanted out, yet I didn't know how to get out. I was to blame for what was happening to Charlie. I had not only let the wheels go into motion, but I was standing by in a sleepwalker's daze as my uncle—and the clever attorneys who had joined the parade of Lita Chaplin protectors— hurled charges of neglect, infidelity, penuriousness and mental cruelty at Charlie. His side shot back that he had bathed me in limitless luxury and denied me nothing, and that I had repaid him with coldness and selfish indifference to his love. I was simultaneously horrified and benumbed.

By the time I was able to shake the cobwebs out of my head and tell Edwin I wanted to be more than merely an outsider when it came to making decisions, that I wouldn't abide having the suit get too rough, it was too late. The lawyers had taken over completely. I was, for the most part, ignored.

On January 10, 1927, the divorce complaint was ready to be submitted to the court, but I didn't get to see it much in advance, chiefly because Edwin—who by now was bothering to talk with me less and less—gave me his assurance that it was written in pure legalese, understood only by other lawyers.

I saw it just before the public did—and I was thunderstruck. It was filed, for purposes dealing with the complexities of Charlie's income, savings and investments, not against him alone but also against his studio and United Artists, Alf Reeves, four California banks, miscellaneous "John Doe" companies, and even Kono. Yet the central villain was Charlie. The complaint consisted of forty-two pages of charges and requests that were in language not nearly so esoteric as my uncle had claimed. I understood most of what I read, and apparently I wasn't the only layman who did; by January 12 someone had got hold of it long enough to have it mimeographed, and thousands of copies were being huckstered on street corners throughout the city. Every newspaper reported the complaint, though they touched delicately, if at all, on those passages that were considered, in 1927, too juicy for public consumption. Only the complaint itself contained the gaminess in its lipsmacking entirety.

What I read was devastating. The most damaging complaints I had confided to my uncle were included, and in several instances cleverly, shockingly enlarged upon or distorted. Charlie's neglect and miserliness and temper, his indifference and his threats, were discussed in such detail that I was embarrassed now that it was all here in cold print.

... defendant at no time during their co-habitation, entered or maintained with plaintiff, the normal and ordinary social relations and matrimonial intercourse, usually existing between man and wife.

In this connection plaintiff alleges with regard to the sexual relations heretofore existing between said parties, that the defendant's attitude, conduct and manifestations of interest therein, have been abnormal, unnatural, perverted, degenerate and indecent, as shown by the following particulars, to-wit:

That throughout the entire married life of said parties and at times too numerous for plaintiff to more particularly specify, defendant has solicited, urged and demanded that plaintiff submit to, perform and commit such acts and things for the gratification of defendant's said abnormal, unnatural, perverted and degenerate sexual desires, as to be too revolting, indecent and immoral to set forth in detail in this complaint. That the aforesaid solicitations and demands were so revolting, degrading and offensive to plaintiff, and were such infamous personal indignities, and showed such a lack of respect, and such a contempt for plaintiff as a wife and a woman, that they were a shock to her refined sensibilities, repulsive to her moral instincts, and abhorrent to her conception of moral and personal decency.

That the aforesaid open solicitations and demands were the culmination of a course of conduct in respect thereto on defendant's part which commenced shortly after said marriage, and which included his reading to plaintiff

253

from books on such subjects, conversing with her thereon, and recounting to her in detail his personal experience with five prominent moving picture women involving such practices.

That the aforesaid course of conduct was of such duration and of such a character, that plaintiff is informed and believes, and upon such information and belief alleges the fact to be, that it was the result of a deliberate and general intention and plan on the part of defendant, to undermine and distort plaintiff's normal sexual impulses and desires, demoralize her standards of decency, and degrade her conception of morals, for the gratification of defendant's aforesaid unnatural desires, and his said solicitations and demands in reference thereto.

That the aforesaid acts, conduct, solicitations and demands of defendant, in addition to their aforesaid effect upon plaintiff, were the cause of continual friction, unhappiness, quarreling and unpleasantness between said parties, and resulted in a further disagreeable and neglectful attitude on defendant's part toward plaintiff on account of her persistent refusal to yield or accede to defendant's said demands and solicitations.

Plaintiff alleges further in this connection, that approximately six months before the separation of said parties, defendant was home in the afternoon shortly before dinner, and continued his solicitations and demands that plaintiff commit the act of sex perversion defined by Section 288a of the Penal Code of California. That defendant became enraged at plaintiff's refusal and said to her: "All married people

do those kind [*sic*] of things. You are my
wife and you *have* to do what I want you to
do. I can get a divorce from you for refusing
to do this." That upon plaintiff's continued
refusal, defendant abruptly left the house
and plaintiff did not see him again until
the next day.

That approximately four months before
said separation, defendant named a girl of
their acquaintance, and told plaintiff that
he had heard things about said girl which
caused him to believe that she might be willing
to commit acts of sexual perversion; and asked
plaintiff to invite her up to the house some
time, telling plaintiff that they could have
some "fun" with her.

By the liberal standards of the 1960's, phrases like these
might seem comparatively tame. But in 1927 such words
as "abnormal," "unnatural," "perverted," "degenerate"
and "indecent"—especially as applied to the world-beloved
Charlie Chaplin—struck several million sensation seekers
with bombshell force.

And though the document was signed, not by me, but
by my attorneys, my name was nonetheless on the first
page as plaintiff. I wasn't just asking for support. I was
smearing Charlie's name, maybe beyond repair.

I found Edwin and told him I was mortified.

"Oh? What did you expect me to do with all that
material you gave me, bury it?" he asked.

"But I never thought it would be made public . . ."

He heaved one of his reproachful sighs. "Well, it was.
Lillita, if this separation had been left in your hands, you
would not only wind up getting nothing from Chaplin,
you'd probably be sending him checks every week for the
privilege of scrubbing his floor. Look, there's just no
compromise between kid gloves and boxing gloves in a
suit like this—especially when it's as clear as daylight that

Chaplin is all set to be twice as rough and dirty as we could ever dream of being. We tried any number of times to reason with his side, to have them agree to a decent settlement, and at every turn the only terms they're willing to talk are chickenfeed. We're going after a four-thousand-dollar monthly temporary alimony award for you. *They* can't understand why we won't jump at their ducky offer of twenty-five dollars a week for you and the kids. They're still ready to settle here and now—oh, you can bet your boots they are!—but they're trying to settle for peanuts—maybe a couple of thousand dollars. That's a laugh. We're going for millions."

"Millions!"

The sigh again. "Lillita, will you grow up? We have your husband over a barrel and those attorneys of his know it, because they're well paid to be as smart as they are. If we decide we really want to push this thing, we can not only get you and the children a better than substantial settlement but we can put the slippery Mr. Chaplin behind bars. There happens to be a section in the California Penal Code that looks very darkly on men, even married men in their own homes, performing the oral copulation that we referred to in the complaint. If we want to press, he can go to prison for fifteen years."

"Wait a min—"

"All right, maybe it's a ridiculous law that never should've been on the books to begin with. But it's there, and Chaplin's counselors know it's there—and they know we can use it."

I felt ill. "What did I get myself into? I don't need or want money that much. Don't ever, ever bring that up again!"

Edwin McMurray shrugged. "This is how the real world revolves, child. A certain amount of hearts and flowers on your part is admirable, but you ought to be braced, prepared for what's to come. Before Chaplin gives in he's going to try his best to cut you to ribbons."

The judge awarded me three thousand dollars in temporary alimony and the use of Charlie's house pending final disposition of the case. It was the judge's decision that the boys and I should, in his words, "live in the style to which they have become accustomed."

Where would Charlie live? I asked. I was told that he had fled to New York, to his East Coast lawyer, Nathan Burkan. The court was about to approve receivership. An attachment would be placed on nearly everything tangible that Charlie owned in the state of California.

The more I was congratulated for having won so many victories so early in the suit, the more helpless I felt. If a good life with Charlie was impossible, then the only thing I wanted was a fair amount of support for the babies and me. I didn't want to go back into Charlie's home—empty without Charlie—as a nose-thumbing conqueror. I recoiled at hearing myself called "Plaintiff" and Charlie called "Defendant." His camp was storming at me in print, and maybe they had a right to; if it hadn't been for me, the law wouldn't have allowed the locusts to take Charlie's property and possessions away from him.

Charlie was served the divorce complaint in Nathan Burkan's New York apartment, and later met reporters to issue a statement that was untruthful but—for him—comparatively tepid: "I married Lita Grey because I loved her, and like many other fool men, I loved her more when she wronged me, and I am afraid I still love her. I was stunned and ready for suicide that day when she told me she didn't love me but that we must marry. Lita's mother often suggested to me that I marry Lita and I said I would love to if only we could have children. I thought I was incapable of fatherhood. Mrs. Grey deliberately and continuously put Lita in my path. She encouraged our relations."

It seemed as if everyone who could read a newspaper or listen to a random rumor quickly became an expert on, and a judge of, our marriage. Sides were vociferously taken. You were either on Charlie Chaplin's side no matter what, or you were on Lita Grey's side no matter

257

what. Charlie was the unhappy little clown crushed by another marital fiasco, the wistful little creative genius once more torn asunder by the unscrupulous, the pathetic mime from the London slums who deserved deification and who, instead, was being crucified. I was the blackmailing, gold-digging, promiscuous, ungrateful Mexican peon whose illiterate and money-grabbing family was intent on bleeding the adored Charlie of his last dollar and his last shred of dignity. I had smelled the erotic scent of gold and glory, and I had cleverly seduced Charlie into seducing me.

But public opinion gave Charlie a rocky time of it, too. He was castigated in some violent quarters as a depraved foreigner who went around deflowering unspoiled maidens. He was pictured as a hedonist convinced that money and power and fame gave him the right to pursue immorality at his whim, and that laws applied to others, not to him. He was criticized as a selfish, self-absorbed satyr who viewed marriage and its obligations without respect, and who was indifferent to the well-being of his babies. Ministers blasted him from their pulpits. Citizens who had no trouble breaking one or more of the Ten Commandments daily banded together to boycott Charlie's "morally offensive" films, and some outraged states banned them from being shown.

Somewhere along the sidelines of these extreme feelings stood the less impassioned observers, who suggested that the failure of a marriage is seldom the doing of one spouse alone and blamed both Charlie and me. Many people, most of them Europeans, rebuked the critics who wouldn't separate Charlie's personal life from his work (an attitude, by the way, that was to burden him every time he got in trouble with women and eventually politics; those who were out to get Chaplin the man invariably went about it by attacking Chaplin the artist). H. L. Mencken, no slavish admirer of Charlie's movies, wrote at one point in the divorce proceedings, "The very morons who worshipped Charlie Chaplin six weeks ago now prepare to dance around the stake while he is burned."

Mama, the children and I moved back to the Cove Way house to find it desolate. Charlie had taken Kono with him to New York; the other servants were missing. I was almost penniless except for a little cash I had accepted from Grandpa, but I contacted Tomi and Todah—whom Charlie had had fired—and persuaded them to come back. I wasn't worried about their salary because, while Charlie had formally announced he was no longer responsible for my debts, thus cutting off all my avenues of credit, the temporary alimony was expected soon.

Or so I'd been told. The money didn't arrive, in spite of the judge's ruling, and it was explained to me that Charlie had no free access to his money; the federal government had just filed a case against him for having neglected to pay $1,133,000 in income taxes. Loyd Wright, Sr., his chief attorney in Los Angeles, renewed his offer to send me twenty-five dollars a week to support the children and myself until the outcome of the hearing. In fact, he actually sent the checks. There was so much stalling, and I was getting so broke, that I was on the verge of cashing them; at least we wouldn't starve, and maybe I could talk Tomi and Todah into taking a smaller salary for the time being. Edwin flatly rejected Wright's offer and was furious with me: "Let them have their way just once and a precedent is set. Don't worry. We'll get that money for you."

While he was getting it, Edwin wasted no time in informing the press that Mr. Chaplin's attorneys were not only flagrantly contravening a court order that I receive three thousand dollars a month, but they were callously resuming their offer that my children and I live on twenty-five dollars a week; neither did he miss a chance to refer to The Penniless Mrs. Chaplin and Her Starving Little Boys and to The Merciless Charlie Chaplin Whose Assets Exceed Sixteen Million Dollars.

It was an effective performance and it made me the object of maudlin pity. Women's clubs across the country started to rise to my unasked-for defense. A Mrs. M. R. Brownfield of The Ebell Club made headlines by publicly stating, "If Chaplin thinks he can starve his child-wife into submission he is reckoning without the women of Hollywood. Thirty women, representing twenty clubs, met Thursday, and we already have begun to raise money to properly feed and care for Mrs. Chaplin's little boys. We are not prejudicing Chaplin nor taking sides in the divorce suit, but we are not willing that this eighteen-year-old wife and mother shall suffer from want while the husband, whose superior age and experience should have made him more tolerant, is employing his expensive lawyers to deprive her of use of money the judge said she should have and which Chaplin can well afford." The New York *Sun* concluded, after reporting Mrs. Brownfield's speech: "It is understood that each of the thirty women pledged to contribute $100 by the end of the week, which would give Lita $3,000 to meet immediate demands. The women plan to canvass the city for funds until Chaplin relents or money is released for Lita's use."

The statement by Mrs. Brownfield caused a national furor, because it came exactly when it did and because, in language that tugged at the heartstrings, it presented Charlie as the worst kind of ogre—one who cared nothing about the plight of his babies. Charlie responded to it quickly because, according to Edwin, such a charge left unanswered could ruin him and his movies in parts of the country where people took family responsibilities seriously; his pictures were being barred in more and more communities as it was. He issued a statement.

> I find that I am accused of letting my
> children go hungry for lack of milk. I had
> heard a rumor of it before but now I learn
> the charge has actually been made and is being
> repeated. It seems silly to deny it but I have

had to deny so many other silly charges that I must now give my word that this charge is not only untrue but was manufactured for the sole purposes of injuring me and holding me up.

I don't believe a man has ever lived who would refuse milk to hungry children. And when you realize that I have no other interest in the present controversy than to regain my children and look after them, you will also realize the absurdity of the charge that I am letting them go hungry. As a matter of fact, Mrs. Chaplin's lawyers have checks of mine in their possession which could buy milk. The reason they have not cashed them is that they want bigger checks. They do not want milk for the children. They want to milk me.

I will make a fight for the sake of my children. They will never want for anything that I can give them. But it will be a tedious fight and you will hear many rumors and charges. You can trust a group of lawyers who are out to hold me up for money and publicity to do everything they can to intimidate the defendant so that he will settle with them for cash.

All I ask is that the public suspend judgment until the case is decided. I can fight an unjust charge even though all the lawyers of California are behind it. But I do not think it fair to ask me to fight all gossip and all charges and all rumors that are spread against me by people whose only interest is to make money out of me.

This public reply, the first in which Charlie himself displayed personal anger at the conspiracy against him, was inaccurate on two counts. One point he neglected to mention was that the uncashed checks amounted to twenty-five dollars each, although he clearly gave the impression that they were for higher, very generous amounts. The other inaccuracy disappointed me infinitely more, for it suggested that he had deep concern for the boys. The fact is that not once, from my last encounter with him in the music room throughout the divorce suit and for months thereafter, did he or anyone representing him make the slightest effort to inquire about the boys' health and well-being.

I made my own public statement, thanking my well-wishers and announcing that I would accept no charity, that any money received would be returned immediately, no matter how spontaneously offered. Fortunately, the first temporary alimony payment came through just as I was about ready to overrule my Uncle Edwin and cash the twenty-five-dollar checks, for I was indeed almost penniless. The check for three thousand dollars had all those beautiful zeros and looked sumptuous, but it was scarcely free and clear, for the judge had directed that all obligations in caring for the house would be mine. The Chaplin mansion was in fact an estate, requiring three in help for the grounds, a man to keep the pool, organ and motion-picture equipment in condition even if they were not used, domestic help to keep the home running smoothly on an overall basis, plus people here and there who had to be paid to come and perform myriad small jobs. This meant that three-quarters of the monthly three thousand dollars went out in expenses. But I didn't mind that as much as I minded our living here, in a home and in a life that wasn't ours. I hated this grossly unnatural limbo, and on top of everything I was getting scores of letters and telephone calls, most of them anonymous, none of them welcome. The patronizing ones offered condolences for my having been in bondage to a fiend. The pathetic ones proposed marriage. The sad and sometimes abusive ones asked me, even ordered me, to lend them money. The frightening ones—and there was such a flurry of them, all within a short span of time, that I had to call the police—threatened to kidnap my sons or kill me unless I instantly called off the divorce action against the greatest man who ever lived.

I didn't belong here. But did I belong anywhere?

I was becoming, for want of a more respectable word, a celebrity.

As the suit fulfilled its promise to be a long one, as both sides wrangled endlessly over one legal technicality after another, as their side came up with new offers for settlement and our side turned them down, I began to see my name in newspaper headlines every day—in *The New York Times* as well as in the scandal sheets.

And seeing my name was getting to me. I was no longer the gawky, unsure kid my mother shunted aside every time she met a potential new husband. I wasn't the barely acknowledged shadow of the world's most famous man. I was Lita Grey Chaplin, an identity, someone, a person. The devil with people who made me the butt of dirty jokes at smokers. The devil with people who pitied me. There were people who cared about me, who believed every word of the positive image my lawyers painted of me, who were concerned.

I began to change. I stopped viewing Charlie as the sinned-against innocent and myself as the heartless vixen. I began to listen more receptively to those thunderings of my Uncle Edwin that went: "He's the *father* of your *sons!* Does it make any sense for you and those sons to wind up with nothing?" Now I paid attention to them as they repeatedly characterized Charlie as a swine and reminded me vigorously that the children and I deserved every penny we could possibly get.

This change in me hadn't come about overnight. From the day my Uncle Edwin had announced he would petition the court for temporary support and I hadn't jumped up and ordered him to go home, I'd suspected that it wasn't all wishy-washiness on my part, that I wanted to pay Charlie back for his cruelties. I had allowed Edwin to go farther, to have a divorce complaint drawn that appalled me—yet not enough to disavow it. The press was quoting remarks I had never made. I would complain, but I wouldn't deny the inventions publicly. By not speaking up to Edwin and the others, which would have been my right, I had been going along with them.

But now it was more than just going along. While before I had vacillated between anger and self-pity and hurt, lonely bewilderment—I'd had periods of feeling so hurt and lost that I'd wanted Charlie to take me back under any conditions—now, as I heard the ugly facts and ugly memories rehashed, I wanted with as much intensity as I'd lacked before to inflict pain back on him.

Charlie and his camp helped crystallize my new decisiveness. When he finally made it, his formal answer and cross-complaint to the court denied that he had been anything but a constantly devoted, doting husband and father. It denied that he had sought to avoid marrying me once my pregnancy was established. It denied that he'd demanded I have an abortion; denied that he'd ever been cross or unavailable for long; denied that he'd ever harbored any feeling other than love for me, even though I gave him neither love nor loyalty; denied adulteries. It did assert, as he had warned it would, that I was an unfit mother who preferred wild parties to caring for the children, that I was a confirmed drinker and that I'd had infatuations with other men after I'd become his wife. No proof was offered to support any of these remarkable charges, but they were phrased as incontestable indictments. He didn't ask for a divorce, but he did ask for custody of the children.

At this point the change from passive waif to determined plaintiff was complete. I realized at last that the distance between Charlie and me was real and unbridgeable, that nothing in either his or my behavior showed the slightest trace of warmth or compassion. Supported by those who were looking out for my interest, I began to feel more anger than pain for the first time in a very long while.

One day, Uncle Edwin and Lyndol Young called me to come downtown. "We've gone over this a dozen times, Lita, but let's talk turkey now about your character," said Mr. Young. "Is there anything you'd like to tell us that you may have—ah—forgotten to tell us up till today?"

"I don't understand."

"Those charges of Chaplin's," Edwin said. "If their side can prove, or even plant a seed of suspicion in the judge's mind, that you enjoy your liquor a little too much, or if you've even said hello to a good-looking postman, or if you haven't been a capable and devoted mother twenty-four hours a day, it's quite possible you're in for some unpleasantness. Chaplin won't give up till he's on his knees. It would be very much to his interests to discover that you haven't been the paragon of virtue you've been made out to be."

"Mr. Young is right," I said, less than serenely. "We *have* gone over this a dozen times. If I'd been that sort of person, wouldn't I have admitted it to you before this? I don't drink because I don't like the way alcohol tastes—everyone who knows me knows that. I'll swear on anything that's holy that Charlie has been the only man I've ever even dated, much less been intimate with. And what were the others? Oh, yes, wild parties and not being a proper mother. I wouldn't know what to do at a wild party, unless he's talking about the night I brought those kids to the house and we played the Charleston on the record player. And whether or not I'm a good mother . . . well, what can I say? I adore the children. They're everything to me. I'd never let anyone take them away from me."

They reminded me of what I'd originally related to Uncle Edwin: that Charlie had threatened, if his hand was forced, to summon the servants and even hire outsiders to lie about me. "That isn't likely," Mr. Young commented, "because perjured testimony calls for a most severe penalty, and if your husband somehow didn't know it at the time you can be sure his lawyers have apprised him of the fact. But we mustn't be lax about anything or assume for a moment that the other side isn't thrashing about for anything they can lay their fingers on. I'm sorry to hammer at this, Lita, but I must ask you one more time—is there *anything* they can begin to use against you?"

"No! If they have any proof of anything, isn't it their job to bring it up?"

They tried, over the months that followed, and could make nothing stick. I waited for the promised bombs to burst, and Edwin kept me posted. Of Charlie's corps of Japanese servants, one—Imu, one of the houseboys—appeared nervously to testify that I had sneaked men onto the estate for illicit purposes when I knew Mr. Chaplin would be away at work. Under Lyndol Young's grilling, however, Imu fell apart. He hadn't seen or even heard of any such thing, he finally admitted. He had been coached to come forth and say so. He had been warned that he would lose his job and that his parents in Japan would be in danger if Imu didn't do and say as he was told.

For a time there were rumors that Minnie Chaplin, the wife of Charlie's half brother Sydney, was going to materialize to testify that my adulteries and alcoholism had made my suffering husband's life miserable. This seemed possible, for Minnie worshipped Charlie, but she backed down to the point of silence well before she could be of any use to the defense's side, claiming that she would have had nothing substantial to present anyway.

We gained a point for our side the morning one of Charlie's ex-chefs entered the offices of Young, Young and Young and revealed, through an interpreter who spoke enough English to be understood, that Mr. Chaplin had paid him five dollars to get out of his basement room for half an hour, and that Mr. Chaplin had taken a woman in there. The chef recalled the date: March 30, 1926, while Mrs. Chaplin was upstairs, in labor with Sydney. He also recalled the woman: Marion Davies! At this point I was beyond surprise.

Mr. Young's telephoned report to me that we were

getting closer and closer to an airtight case against Charlie delighted me. I was by now as worked up for vengeance and profit as my attorneys were for settlement and profit. I was dimly aware that my aspirations for victory were no less sleazy than theirs or Charlie's, but I refused to think in those terms for long. My uncle had worded the complaint without my help, but now I was ready to support it for all it, and I, were worth. I would be mercenary, and gladly.

Attorneys argued among themselves, quit and were immediately replaced by other attorneys, after new briefs, new documents and new petitions were drawn up and likewise replaced. Attorneys got into heated hassles with the dogged Edwin, claiming he was pushing too hard and demanding too much, that he should calm down, listen more courteously to Charlie's men and agree to compromise. What did he want to do, make a life's career of the Chaplin case?

"You're damned right I do if I have to!" he answered.

The suit dragged on month after month, mired in technicalities and impasses, with neither side willing to budge an inch. Charlie applied for, and was granted, the right to have some of his impounded funds released so that he could resume filming *The Circus,* which had been pretty well on its way toward completion at the time the divorce action had been instituted. He behaved erratically, one day zealously avoiding reporters and the next day meeting them to repeat his cry that he was grievously misunderstood and wished only peace and harmony, but that my gang of lawyers and I were determined to destroy him.

He was quite right about my intentions. I was no longer guilty Lillita McMurray; I had become hard, out now only for the children and myself, and being aware of this didn't disturb me in the slightest. I wanted very much to hurt him.

Charlie's camp exhausted every last effort to come up with some flaw in my reputation they could exploit. They couldn't, and they had no case, but they refused to give in to anything close to the whopping settlement we were demanding. Then Edwin reviewed the tactic he had wanted to pursue from the outset. "Those women Chaplin told you he was intimate with," he said. "We mentioned we'd name them, but you said no. Well, we've been with this suit for a long while, Lillita. If you're ready to change your mind about those names, we can close this up fast. Even Chaplin couldn't take the prospect of having his famous lady friends in all the headlines."

"That would be playing pretty rough, wouldn't it?"

"Yes," said Edwin placidly. "But he did commit adultery with them, didn't he?"

I phoned Marion Davies and asked to see her. She invited me to her house.

When I arrived, she appeared bothered that I didn't return her kiss on the cheek, but her smile was as unperturbed as ever. "We sure got out of touch, didn't we, sugar?" she said. "All I know about you these days is what I read in the papers."

"Oh, I'm sure Charlie's been keeping you informed about me all along," I said sweetly.

"Charlie?"

"Or haven't you been to bed with him since I left him? Maybe my leaving took all the fun out of it for you."

"What're you talking about, Lita?"

I didn't try to control my anger. "How many laughs did you and Charlie have, Marion, while I was coming here as a friend and you were saying you and he weren't having an affair? Who laughed louder that I believed everything, you or Charlie?"

Marion blinked, but made no attempt to squirm out of my accusation. "Charlie told me he told you about us. I was sore. He shouldn't have done that."

"And you shouldn't have made a fool of me."

She nodded solemnly. "No, I can't argue there. It was cheesy of me. I just—well, I didn't *love* Charlie or anything like that, so I didn't think we were hurting you, or anybody." Then, visibly worried, she asked, "Why are you bringing this up now, all of a sudden? It happened 'way back last year and you've known about it all this time."

"Your friend Mr. Hearst would feel awful if he heard about it, wouldn't he, even though it happened 'way back last year?"

Her panic was very real. "You'd go to him? You hate me so much, or Charlie so much, that you'd go to W. R.?"

"No, but he'll find out," I answered. "Unless you co-operate, that is."

"God," she moaned. "God, W. R.'d go through the ceiling . . ."

"My lawyers and I want to end the suit and get me a sizeable settlement, but Charlie's stubborn. Now listen to me carefully, Marion, and don't think for a second that I'm not being one hundred per cent serious. Charlie bragged to me that he'd had affairs with six women over the past two and a half years. Five of them are well known, and you're one of those five. We won't have to prove a thing. All we'll have to do is name those six names, with Marion Davies topping the list, and then just sit back and see what happens. You can swear to W. R. that it's not true, of course, and he'll probably believe you. The point is, will you enjoy the mess?"

After a troubled pause she said in a hollow voice, "I knew you when you were different. How'd you get so hard?"

"Easy," I said. "I married Charlie Chaplin."

It worked. The story goes that Charlie summoned Nathan Burkan to Los Angeles, a distance of 3,000 miles from New York, and met him at the train station. They went into a coffee shop and Charlie asked, "Nate, what shall I do?" Burkan answered in a single word—"Settle"— and took the very next train back East.

On August 22, 1927, I made my one and only appearance on the witness stand. I was questioned for ten minutes about the validity of the complaint and I replied that point after point was accurately stated. Judge Walter Guerin granted me custody of the children, and I was made guardian of their persons and estates. Each of the children was awarded a trust fund of $100,000. I was awarded a settlement of $625,000. Charlie was not in court.

How ironic, I thought. If Charlie had accepted my offer that day in the house, it would have cost him ten thousand dollars. Now, complete with attorney's fees, it was costing him much more than a million.

Chapter Eighteen

Four days after the judge's ruling, Mama was rushed to the hospital for an emergency appendectomy. Five hours after she was wheeled into the operating room, the surgeon came to me and said, "First of all, she's alive."

"Thank God," I whispered.

"Now I'll tell you the rest of it. Your mother had considerably more than appendicitis. I found tumors in both her tubes and a tumor in the uterus. They're out, but it's too early to judge yet whether she's going to make it."

I gasped and grabbed his wrist.

"Be as strong as you can, Mrs. Chaplin, because you'll need a lot of strength over the next few days and maybe longer, until she either passes the crisis—or doesn't. This condition was building for at least a couple of years—I don't know how she lived this long without treatment. Is it possible she didn't even suspect something was wrong with her?

I shook my head and struggled to form words. "There were warnings. She was advised over two years ago to have an operation. She kept putting it off. I tried to make her go into the hospital and then—I didn't follow it through because the only person I was thinking about was myself. . . ." In terror I asked, "Is that all you can do—just wait? Can't you give her anything, do something more for her?"

"Not yet. We can only wait."

I didn't leave the hospital for three days. Grandpa and Grandma paced the corridors, mutely though gravely worried, but they had the sense to conserve their strength by going home from time to time to rest. The floor nurses got to know me, and when they couldn't persuade me to go home, treated me warmly, and when it was possible, sat with me.

On the third post-operative day I went into my mother's room. The surgeon, Dr. Friedman, and a nurse flanked the bed. The first things I saw as I went nearer were two needles, the size of ice picks, in her breasts.

The sight made me reel, and I grasped the metal rail at the end of the bed for support. Her eyes were wide open, but she was in a coma.

Dr. Friedman guided me out into the hall. "I won't try to fool you," he said. "The third day after an operation like this is the really rough one. Your mother is in surgical shock, and she may come out of it or she may not. We're doing everything we can. We'll know some time today."

I hadn't left the floor in three nights and days. But now, perversely, when everything pointed to my staying, I found I couldn't wait to escape from the hospital. I hurried to one of the nurses who had been so comforting and asked, "Will you do something for me and not think I'm insane? I'm going to Griffith Park and ride a horse. When you hear anything about my mother—anything—would you call me there and tell whoever answers what . . . happened?"

"Of course. You're being very smart."

All during the taxi ride to the stable I was sure I was losing my mind; what was this compulsion to ride a horse, now of all menacing times? What possible justification could there be for my cowardice? My mother was dying and I hadn't the guts to do anything but run away from her!

I told the man who rented me a horse that I was expecting a telephone call, and I asked him to send someone out to find me and give me the message the minute the call came in. The man lifted a quizzical eyebrow at my strange request, but he agreed.

I was far from an expert horsewoman, and my nerves were screeching with anxiety and lack of sleep, but I rode for hours, mostly running the horse, seldom actually stopping. As much as I had always scoffed at black magic and superstition, I couldn't wholly dismiss the paralyzing suspicion that God was punishing my mother for my sins. Over the long months between January and August I had finally become a woman, all right—a callous, hungry, greedy woman so intent on sucking great amounts of money out of her husband that she was ready to drag the names of other women—even one who'd been her friend— through the mud. And God was taking it out on Mama and making her die.

The August wind whipped through my hair as I rode. My eyes smarted, and I prayed. I promised God that if Mama were saved I would never take anyone for granted again. She had done so much for me and I had given her so little in return. A doctor had advised her well over two years before that she had tumors and she should have them removed. I had been in that office and I had heard him, and I had let it slide. I could have talked her into entering a hospital. It would have been a simple operation then and she would have come out in no time, better than new. And I hadn't done a thing because I'd been selfishly wrapped up in myself. Always the child, always the resolutely dependent little girl waiting for others to hold my hand and take me across the street . . . And had my marriage really been all that hopeless from the start? If I'd been less the perpetually helpless child, if I'd worked a little harder to do some growing up on my own, then maybe . . .

God, don't let her die. I'll be good.

Almost as if I'd planned it, I realized within the next quarter of an hour that I was lost. I was in a part of Griffith Park completely unfamiliar to me; instead of one path there were many surrounding me, but I hadn't a notion of which one to take.

I didn't feel panic or even conscious worry. I dismounted and simply sat on a boulder, a weary child who knew some grownup would come and rescue her.

And that's the way it happened. Some time later I heard the sound of horse's hoofs, and a groom from the stable rode up alongside me. A nurse had called, he said, to tell me my mother was going to be all right.

I seldom left Mama's side during her recovery, which was slow but complete. When there was absolutely no doubt that she would soon be restored to health, I said, "We've never been to New York. You and I are going to take the boys there. We'll stay at the best hotel and see the shows and eat at the fanciest restaurants so we can fatten you up and put back those twenty pounds you lost. And we'll buy everything in sight."

"You're talking foolishness," she objected. "Just because you have a lot of money now is no reason to squander it."

I laughed. "You're the one who's talking foolishness. We're *rich*, Mama! What's money for, anyway? I'm going to show you the time of your life. You took care of me all these years, now I'll take care of you."

We went, and took Tomi with us. We spent three marvelous months in Manhattan in high, giddily carefree style, and I spent money like water because it *was* water, so plentiful it seemed impossible that the supply could ever end. In the beginning Mama cautioned me against extravagance at every turn, but I was truly free, truly independent, and having so much unsuppressed fun that she gave up and indulged me by letting me shower her with luxuries.

Not that she didn't soon discover that luxury-showering was an immensely easy and pleasurable habit to fall into. We visited all the night clubs and theaters and went deliciously berserk in the stores. Nothing was too good for Mama—or me, for that matter—in those early months of 1928. I spent $20,000 on coats, dresses, suits, furs and jewelry for us both. Mama kept protesting, but she sent nothing back and did indeed have the time of her life. Late at night, after the wild shopping sprees and shows and cabarets, she would begin to sigh about Charlie and dabble in regrets about the origins of our wealth and finery. I would forbid her to mention his name.

It was mentioned, of course, by nearly everyone we met in New York. I had called Buster Collier, the handsome young actor and swain of Constance Talmadge, to say hello; Buster was a passing friend from the Santa Monica Swimming Club days, now appearing on Broadway. He invited Mama and me to a party, which brought invitations to other parties and still other parties. We attended them all, because Mama enjoyed goggling at the nonstop glamour and because I was thrilled at so often being the center of attention. At one party I met Lou Irwin, the peppery theatrical agent, who not only suggested I go into show business but offered to represent me. "Now's the time for you to try vaudeville," he said. "You can pick up a fortune and salt it away for your old age. An hour from now I can guarantee you fifty-two weeks' bookings."

"Vaudeville? What would I do there?"

"Can you spell your name out loud? All right, do that and I can get you fifty-two weeks' booking at the top price."

I thanked him and said no. "Not now, Mr. Irwin. I'm having too much fun. And I've got too much money. Why should I go to work, and at something I don't know anything about?"

By the time we got back to Los Angeles, I was fired with a new idea: I wanted a new house, one for Mama and me and the children. And I had one built, next to my grandparents' home on Beverly Drive. The plans called for eighteen rooms, the best and most opulent taste possible, and a final bill of $90,000. Grandpa watched the construction in eye-bulging disapproval and criticized what he called my senseless extravagance. He warned repeatedly that I was riding for a giant fall, that before I knew it I wouldn't have enough money left for investment. I lovingly told him to stick to his knitting; the world was my oyster now that I was independent. I was free of domination, and I was going to live as *I* pleased for a change.

Building the house worked instant miracles for me, for now I had friends in droves. Scores of people would come on weekends and I would greet them, and the friends they brought along, with plenty of food and liquor. I was Lita the party-giver now, Lita the sport, Lita the generous wowser who encouraged the booze to flow. It didn't matter that most of them would come and go and be replaced by others who would come and go. As long as I had company I hadn't an enemy in the world; everyone was my friend.

To get as gay and lively as my guests, I began to join them in a drink. The taste of liquor was still unpleasant, but I found that rye went down well if it was camouflaged by ginger ale. Before long, two or three or four glasses of rye and ginger ale relaxed me and didn't make me sick or silly. And since Mama had no use for alcohol or people who drank it, it became a game to spike my ginger ale secretly with whiskey. I came to enjoy fooling her; standing beside her slugging down drink after drink while she thought, if she gave it any thought at all, that I needed no more than soda pop to make me the bubbling life of my parties.

The Circus was another Chaplin picture that opened and played to packed houses, in spite of the fact that there were communities across the United States that were still adamantly banning any project that had the name Charlie Chaplin associated with it. Charlie next went on to one of his most ambitious films, *City Lights*. I didn't hear from him, but one day Kono called, reporting that Mr. Chaplin would very much appreciate having the children brought to visit him. After studying the implications of such a visit from every angle, I agreed, and Grandma took them to the house in Beverly Hills. They were brought back a little bewildered but cheerful, and when the request was repeated I let them be taken again.

Over the next weeks and months the boys fell into the routine of spending weekends with Charlie, while my weekends continued to be spent in throwing big, expensive parties for guests who came and went, came and went. I told myself I enjoyed my parties, and the rye, hidden safely in the ginger ale, helped me believe it.

I began to have dates, sometimes four and five a week. With luck, and by some inexplicable sixth sense, I had no real trouble in sorting out the genuine young men from the ones who were more interested in my money than in me, and in cutting off the latter in short order. I could have gone into an eclipse of fleeting affairs, but promiscuity was the last thing I wanted; the very prospect of "liberating" myself by hopping in and out of bed left me depressed.

Instead, there was a series of serious affairs, each one long, each one clinging, each one meaningful at the time. And each one ultimately an empty failure because I was rootless, with no substantial sense of who I was or what I had to give to a relationship. I retreated from men, and I gave up the parties, too. Intense restlessness set in—and then, ominously, insomnia, an insomnia that could be overcome quite magically by a glass of ginger ale and rye and then rye and ginger ale, and then rye. . . .

There was still a ton of money left in 1929, but nothing could remove the fact that Hollywood was Charlie Chaplin's town, not Lita Grey's. And certainly not Lita Grey Chaplin's. When another offer came in for me to sign up for vaudeville—at a guarantee of $2,500 a week for fifty-two weeks, and better yet, the opportunity to keep on the move—I grabbed it. Mama put her foot down, or tried to, with the argument that my first obligation was to my sons. "You'll be sorry if you go through with this," she warned. "Your children won't love you when they grow up, and I won't always be around to help take care of them."

She was talking nonsense. I chose my own survival and signed the contract.

Billed as Lita Grey Chaplin, I went East with the Keith Circuit and toured in vaudeville as a singer without much of a voice but a sensational draw at the box office. I bought crutches for myself—the best orchestrations, an expensive wardrobe, two pianists and eye-catching sets and backdrops. I would work for endless hours at a stretch, exercising a voice that would drive no other professional vocalist out of business, slaving to acquire a brand of personality projection that could carry throughout a crowded theater, striving to become a "performer"—which is translated, in my case, to mean a singer who couldn't sing very well—and trying desperately to perfect every trick to make audiences see me, not as a freak, but as someone giving them their money's worth. I was determined to develop an identity of my own, to find approval, respect and vindication for all the ugly publicity—but apparently I wasn't so determined that I insisted on having the Chaplin part of my name dropped from the marquee. My rationalization was that I *could* make a career, and in a place where Charlie Chaplin wasn't king; I *could* shine, and in my own right, in a branch of show business that wasn't his medium

—but where his name would add luster to my efforts. And he owed me a start, I told myself.

With unceasing work I finally reached a point where I could step on a stage and feel I wasn't cheating the customers. I had sunk a lot of money into special material, medleys of popular songs strung together with lyrics changed and rewritten. I performed with growing self-confidence, and the audiences liked me. Once I was reasonably sure of myself, I sent for Mama and the boys to join me. Money was still no problem; Mama had rented the house for $2500 a month, and of course I was guaranteed $2500 a week. Pat Casey, one of my pianists and a dear friend, talked me into putting $75,000 into an irrevocable trust. The act became a bigger and bigger success, and soon I was working with pros such as Jack Pearl, Phil Baker and Jack Benny, who talked me up into believing I merited the marvelous notices I was getting.

My style did come to full bloom, and though I was still afraid to go it alone as Lita Grey, I was being starred to increasing applause at the top theaters on the circuit. I was sneaking drinks as a matter of course to ensure sleep, but that was all right because it was only therapeutic. I was able to handle whiskey as I handled audiences—with the carefree ease of the young and unthinking.

Mama took the children back to California when living out of suitcases proved too much for her. I was sorry to see them go, but I was lucky in finding Gladys Thompson, an immensely warm and understanding young Jamaican whom I hired as a dresser and who became a surrogate mother and life-long close friend. Gladys called me "Skipper" and toured everywhere on the circuit with me, chiding me when I took one tiny drink too many but never failing to be right beside me when anything, of large consequence or small, made me falter.

In the fall of 1929, Grandpa's ramrod body finally succumbed, and he died. I was terribly shaken by a loss that was uniquely personal, far more than I would have expected. The loss of Grandpa meant, too, a loss of some of the confidence and a touch of self-esteem that he had given me while he was alive, even though I gave him little conscious thought. He had worked to teach me to respect myself, and in his way, he had worked at it more meaningfully than had anyone else in my life.

By some eerie coincidence, my paternal grandfather died the very same night Grandpa passed away. And the same week, the sixteen-year-old daughter of Mama's brother Frank was killed in a car accident.

Hard on the heels of these tragedies came the Wall Street crash. The rent on my house dropped to $1,000 a month. My $2,500 salary was cut to $1,750 a week.

I couldn't cope with it all. Instead of signing up with Keith for a new season, I booked passage on the *Ile de France,* arranged for Tomi and Todah to care for the children and sailed with Mama for Cherbourg.

We checked into a luxurious suite at the George V in Paris and fell in love with the city and its people. I was twenty-one, pretty, rich and convinced that Charlie was out of my system. I was ardently ripe for a love affair.

I was introduced to Georges Carpentier, former pilot and World War hero, former light heavyweight champion of Europe and knockout victim of Jack Dempsey, and former friend of Charlie Chaplin. He was a man of enormous charm and physical magnetism, and I was flattered when he asked, in surprisingly good English, to take me to dinner. I politely refused, telling myself there was no future in getting mixed up with someone who had a wife and child—but knowing deep down that I was eager to be pursued.

The more I turned him down over the next three weeks the more he pursued, and the more I worked to persuade Mama that she ought to go to London for a while to visit distant relatives. She went, finally, leaving me alone—for a time—in the plush suite.

Georges took me to the Scheherazade, a smart night club with soft lights and a splendidly romantic atmosphere.

In such an atmosphere it wasn't long before Georges and the champagne mingled to put me in a mood of mellowness and active receptivity, and when we got to my suite we were in each other's arms almost before the door could be bolted. For the first time I felt the exquisite sensation of wanting a man totally, of truly being immersed in every part of him, emotionally and physically.

From that night on I was so in love with Georges that I was sure I would go crazy when he took five minutes longer than promised to arrive or telephone. He had explained that there was nothing furtive in our meetings, that his wife had a lover and that, in peculiar fact, he and they frequently played bridge together. I winced when he called me his mistress because the term seemed to signify something passing and eventually forgotten. I was jealous of the respect he had for his wife and even of the love he had for his daughter, and I withered every time he said he had to go home.

Mama learned how serious I was about Georges and blew up. "Charlie will find out and he'll have the children taken away from you!" she scolded. "Is that what you want, to have an affair with a married man and risk losing your children?"

I told Georges we couldn't see each other again, not really because I feared that Charlie would try to claim the children but because I couldn't go on being Georges' "wife" at his convenience. He insisted he loved me and would do anything for me—anything short of divorcing his wife.

I insisted that the situation was hopeless and said it was for the best that the break be quick and clean. Mama and I left Paris for London.

Georges followed me.

Mama and I sailed back to the United States.

Within two weeks, he followed.

He stayed in America for five years, and for five years we were rarely apart. I had returned to show business, traveling extensively now, breaking in new material in

Newark, playing such theaters as the State-Lake in Chicago and ultimately the Palace in New York, picking up professional and personal polish along the way. If I wasn't content, I was at least resigned to the fact that Georges and I were lovers, that marriage just wasn't going to happen. His wife knew about us, of course—as did every gossip columnist—but every other letter she wrote reminded him that she was a Catholic and divorce was out of the question. I lived without a future because I had Georges.

And I had liquor. I wasn't addicted to it—I could go to parties after the last show and nurse a single drink, and there were still nights when I could get to sleep alone without anesthetizing my brain with a few shots—but I did turn around one day to realize that liquor was nonetheless a part of my life and that I'd be pretty uncomfortable if I were some place where a drink wasn't handy. Mama had discovered with loud, sighing sorrow that I enjoyed a drink now and then, but she still didn't know how much or how often. Georges lectured me on the evils of alcohol, though never for long; he believed, as I did, that drinking was nowhere near being a problem with me.

At long last Georgette came through: if Georges really wanted me, she would give him his divorce. The thoroughly unexpected offer caught us both by surprise. I didn't say so, but after five years of being the second woman, yet deluding myself that I was the first, I wasn't so sure now that I wanted to be his wife after all!

Georges, I could tell, was having second thoughts, too, although he didn't voice his, either. Before he sailed for France he kissed me—rather perfunctorily—and promised to cable me the minute all the divorce arrangements had been made.

Why couldn't I stop crying for days after he left? The gin bottles were beside my bed and I drank myself into one stupor after another, despite Gladys' worried scoldings that I was trying to kill myself. Finally she was able to get me into a tub, and the bath revived me. I had a

Martini and phoned a man who'd been after me for a date for months. Word of this other man crossed the Atlantic, as I'd known it would, and Georges immediately stopped the divorce proceedings.

A few years later he did divorce Georgette, and shortly after he married a girl young enough to be his daughter. Today he is the owner of a bar in Paris, and I'm told that his young wife sits there every evening, watching him greet old friends.

Chapter Nineteen

By the mid-thirties there were rumors that Charlie had taken a Ziegfeld dancer named Paulette Goddard as his third wife. And there were equally intriguing rumors that he hadn't. One rumor had it that they'd married in 1932 on a yacht cruise, which neither of them bothered either to confirm or deny. Another rumor went that they were merely living together in the Beverly Hills house, which they also neither confirmed or denied. Women's clubs and church groups got after Paulette for what they termed her flaunting of immorality, a campaign that was later to cost her the role of Scarlett O'Hara in *Gone with the Wind*.

Charlie and I hadn't seen each other since our divorce, although we did have another legal tug-of-war when Warner Brothers offered me a sizeable sum to star my children and me in a movie. I agreed. Charlie was livid, claiming that I had no right to turn our boys into actors before they were old enough to decide if that was what they wanted. He was right, of course, and I was wrong. I'll always be grateful to him for refusing to let me do it.

But even though we didn't see each other, we did talk together by phone several times, mostly about the children, who were seeing him at every available opportunity and who clearly adored him. Our conversations were usually rather awkward—he would ask me questions about myself without really hearing my answers, and when he talked about himself it was in generalities—but there seemed to be surprisingly little rancor in his voice. I never asked if he and Paulette Goddard were married or not, but I had seen pictures of her and heard that she was a bright, clever girl, and I complimented his taste. He seemed pleased.

At Christmas I rented a suite at the Ambassador Hotel in Los Angeles and gave a party for the children. I phoned Charlie and invited him to come. To my amazement he accepted. He arrived about half an hour after the party had started, carrying an armful of presents and looking little older than when I'd last seen him, eight years before. The boys rushed to him, then quite formally introduced him to their young guests. Charlie was charming with them, as he could always be with youngsters if the time and situation lent themselves to spontaneity. Then he came to me, and his smile was open, even approving.

"You're looking fit, Lita," he said. "Have you been well?"

I looked for a hint of sarcasm, but I found none. I was positive that I didn't look fit at all. I was drinking more heavily these days than ever before, sleeping and eating little because that required quiet and effort, and I was sure every day of dissipation showed on my face. Charlie, on the other hand, looked as though he'd just returned from a year of solid rest; bronzed and bursting with health, he'd never been so attractive. "I couldn't be better," I said.

"What've you been doing with yourself, Charlie? You get younger all the time."

He laughed. "Blame it on Paulette. She's a fresh-air fiend—has me out sailing and playing tennis from dawn to dusk. Which reminds me—I can stay only a minute. Paulette's waiting in the car downstairs. We're going on to an engagement."

"In the car? Why didn't you bring her up? I'd love to meet her."

Charlie, who could be boyishly shy when you least expected him to be, asked, "You would, really?"

"Of course! What a thing, making her sit down there by herself. Please get her. I can send for some champagne."

He telephoned down and had the doorman deliver the message. Five minutes later Paulette entered the suite, a dark-haired, buoyantly alive vision in black velvet. I liked her instantly, liked the aura of vitality and genuineness about her, and we hit it off together right away. After a couple of minutes Charlie joined the kids for ice cream and cake, and Paulette and I went to the sitting room, made ourselves comfortable and began to talk easily, as if we'd known each other all our lives.

As a moviemaker Charlie had done the impossible; at a time when everyone insisted there was no market for silent pictures he had made *City Lights,* a picture that was silent except for background music and occasional sound effects, and it had been an artistic and commercial triumph. Now he was preparing *Modern Times,* another silent, and his leading lady was Paulette Goddard. She was on Charlie's pedestal now, and surely knowing all about the vicious, treacherous Lita Grey, she could have blithely chopped me to mincemeat and gotten away with it. She had class; it was obvious in every word and gesture.

Yet Paulette was utterly without affectation or guile. She put me at my ease by ignoring herself, bypassing mention of Charlie and telling me what a colossal performer I was. "I saw you when you played the Palace," she said. "I stayed for two shows, in fact. You really know how to put an audience smack in your palm." She informed me she was plain Pauline Levy from Long Island. I informed her I was plain Lillita McMurray from Los Angeles. We chatted about the people and places we both knew in New York until Charlie tapped at the door to say it was time to go. Paulette rose and smiled warmly. "I like you, plain Lillita McMurray from Los Angeles," she said. "I'd love to see you again."

I saw them out, admiring and envying that bubbling, beaming girl. In the years that followed I was to admire her even more and be in her debt for the endless kindnesses she showed my boys when I became helpless as a mother and as a human being. She lavished affection on them, taking them along with Charlie on fishing trips, guiding them up ski slopes, lovingly forcing them to re-learn the French they had learned and forgotten. When I entered a hospital for an operation more than a year after our short, single meeting, my room was flooded with baskets of flowers and other gifts. The card read, "Get up and out of there fast. Love, Plain Pauline Levy from Long Island."

Now, in the Ambassador suite, I realized without pride how envious and empty I felt. I still loved Charlie, still wanted to be his wife. Paulette was everything I hadn't been when I'd had the chance: alert, knowledgeable, out-going, confident—and yet every inch a man's woman. I had money and a career. And nowhere to go.

From $2,500 a week my salary in vaudeville went down to $550; I was still box office but no longer a sensational novelty. Ironically, I could feel myself getting better all the time as an entertainer—but show business was becoming less glamour and excitement and more treadmill and unrewarding repetition. Now, with my popularity waning, it seemed a good time to quit.

Then came the shock of being told that my money was seeping away, that I would have to stay in show business to pay the bills.

That seemed impossible. How could anybody even begin to go through $625,000 in less than a hundred years? I took out a pencil and pad and found it wasn't impossible, that I'd been nearly successful at it. My attorneys' fees had taken $200,000. An additional attorney's fee of $16,000 had been charged me by my Uncle Edwin McMurray, who'd come to my grandparents' house for dinner one night after the divorce, answered a few legal questions of mine and later billed me. (Grandpa and I, both irate, had protested, and the case had come before a judge, who'd ruled that I would have to pay.) My house had cost $90,000. I'd set up an $80,000 security for Mama. I'd set up a $75,000 trust for myself—irrevocable except in case of serious illness—with The National City Bank of New York.

I had been advised, and had been only too ready to believe, that a great deal of front was necessary for the ex-wife of Charlie Chaplin. I stayed at the most expensive hotels and dined at the most expensive restaurants. Hairdressers and manicurists had, I thought, to be constantly available. Friends, and friends of friends, viewed me as Mrs. Moneybags and came to me, especially in the early days of the Depression, to confide to me with tears in their eyes that they were broke, that they needed an operation, that they would pay me back next month. I gave thousands away in loans that were never repaid and that I never expected to see repaid.

The rest went, or was rapidly going, up in smoke. I wanted to buy a gift for everyone on earth and I almost succeeded. I fought to pay every check and I almost always won. I paid for everybody. Everybody loved me.

Aside from the vanishing $625,000, I discovered by simple arithmetic that I was occasionally paying out more than I was earning in vaudeville. I paid an average of $28 a day for hotel rooms, food and incidental expenses for Gladys and me; Gladys received $60 a week; my road manager got $250 a week; my agent got a straight ten per cent of my salary; my two pianists were paid $250 each a week. I paid the railway fares not only for Gladys and the pianists and myself, but for the pianists' wives as well. I paid for insurance, publicity, new stage gowns, new special material, train freight for the scenery for my act; tips, medicine, taxes, everything, everything, everything.

And nothing inside me was getting anything in return.

The hard drinking began in dead earnest. I was missing or hurting none of my performances because of liquor, but I had become so dependent on it that I needed an eye-opener when I woke up and a stiff jolt or two every hour or so to see me through the day. I wasn't the kind of drinker who experiments with different kinds of alcohol and then selects and sticks with one; I would take any-thing—Scotch, rye, bourbon, rum, gin—because one tasted no less awful than another and because I was interested only in the effects. Any alcohol could stimulate me when I needed to feel I was the friendliest and most popular girl at a party, could subdue me when I was ready to jump out of my skin with nervousness, could knock me into unconsciousness when I needed sleep.

Liquor depressed my appetite, both for food and for men. I would gobble pretzels and peanuts as though famished at impromptu get-togethers after the curtain came down, but in my hotel room or a café I would hope-fully order a meal and then, when it was delivered, get bored with the business of chewing. Gladys would shake her head and complain that a bird couldn't live on what I ate. I would pour another drink, laugh and tease her. "What're you afraid of, Gladys, that I'll wind up on Skid Row? I've got the constitution of an ox. Anyway, if I don't eat I don't get fat, right?"

As for men, I was lucky that I made so few mistakes. I would see girls strolling off with men, obviously in the direction of the nearest bedroom, their senses immersed in the courage that booze provides, and I was afraid it was merely a matter of time before I'd become a veteran traveler on those empty journeys. I had been drifting through a series of empty affairs, to be sure, but some still remaining sense of self-esteem made me set up an unwavering rule: I would never, no matter how sozzled I'd been the night before, wake up in the morning to find a stranger sleeping next to me. And I never did, because I scrupulously forbade any man to get within touching distance of me when I was drinking heavily.

How much did I drink? I didn't count them in 1935, partly because I couldn't be bothered but chiefly because it didn't really occur to me that my drinking was getting out of hand. I could point to others and say, "There's a rummy just begging to be committed to the alcoholic ward." But I was no rummy. I could laugh and sing louder than anyone else at parties, but I never made a pest of myself, never had crying jags in public like other girls, never dropped glasses or threw them against the walls, never threw up on the host's rug. I always made my show in plenty of time and I always gave my best. I had to know there was always a bottle handy, sure—but that was just a temporary condition; giving it up would present no problem when I was ready.

A big break came when I needed one badly. I was offered the co-starring role with Milton Berle in the national company of *Life Begins at 8:40,* a Shubert musical that could do great things for me. I said yes, relieved to be free of vaudeville and all its responsibilities, glad to play opposite Milton—brash and professional and soon to become one of my most valued friends—certain without knowing why that this trip would be the personal making of me, that I would finally somehow find myself.

We rehearsed for four weeks, weeks so invigorating and happily challenging that I seldom even thought of taking a drink. We all set out with high optimistic hopes. The national company, unfortunately, didn't go very national. The show closed in eight weeks.

I saw the show's failure as my own, which made going back to the bottle an obligation. I would sit for hours in a chair, not moving except to pour a drink or light a cigarette, and play a subtraction game called What Happened to the $625,000? I would get the irresistible urge to make a long distance call to my babies and my mother, and on reporting this urge to Gladys, would be advised against it because my words were slurring. I would say, "Okay, I'll wait," and then place the call immediately. Sometimes I would call and Mama would say the children were spending the weekend with their father and then ask, "Why are you drinking?" Other times I would call and talk with each of the boys for an hour or more, delighting in what fine young men they were, biting my lip to keep from crying, "Come to me, children! Come and let your mother love you!" Mama would get on the line and ask me what I was doing in the East, what I was trying to prove, why I drank, why I wouldn't come home where I belonged.

"I don't know, Mama . . ." I would say.

But I did know. I was staying away from the three people I loved most because I was ashamed to have them see me before I could straighten myself out. I was a drunk. The mother of those darling, perfect boys was a drunk. And a coward. And a failure, a failure in life. And a fake, a dame who made imposing noises about her desperate need to grow up but who wouldn't recognize maturity if it fell on her.

My agent, Lou Irwin, called me into his office some weeks after the Shubert fiasco with the suggestion that I tour Europe. "Your career's limping, honey," he said from behind his cigar, "but I've worked out a sort of bargain with the European bookers. You play the British Gaumont Theatre Chain throughout the British Isles and a couple of second-rate theaters. If you agree to go the whole route, and that's frankly the only way they'll book you, they guarantee to give you star billing at the Café DeParee in London." He squinted at me, waiting for the enthusiasm. "It'll tire you out, jumping all over the place, and I might as well tell you right now that the best salary I could get for you is pretty crummy, but a credit like the Café

DeParee'll be nothing for anybody to sneeze at when you get back home. It'll sure build your career."

I sighed. "God, I wish I could throw my arms around you, Lou, but I'd feel washed up before I begin. That's no way to begin a tour."

"What's wrong?"

"Me," I said. "I got lost somewhere. I hate the kind of person I've turned into. I spend every minute of my life pitying myself. I'm drinking as if there's some little man crouching on my shoulder with a whip and yelling 'Drink! Drink!' I'm scared to go back to California and see my children because they're so clean and I feel so dirty. I'd bill myself as kind of an unholy mess, wouldn't you?"

Lou, leaning forward to light my cigarette, saw my hand shake. "A head doctor I'm not, honey," he said. "Even a gambler I'm not. A sure-thing businessman I am. I've known you long enough to know you got your troubles. I also know you've never loused up a show and you never will. On the one hand, if you pass this up and I get you little jobs here and there, there's no guarantee you'll straighten out—on the other, if you go to Europe and knock 'em dead and everybody applauds you and loves you, maybe the little man with a whip'll go somewhere and fly a kite. You got anything to lose? You got a whole lot to gain."

Lou Irwin, bless his Jewish mother of a heart, couldn't have been more wrong. I had everything to lose in Europe. And I did.

Chapter Twenty

Gladys and I sailed for England early in 1936. What had finally persuaded me to make the trip was that New York had begun to oppress me. Steady drinking had led to trembling, stomach quivers and hangovers so unendurable they could be conquered only by a quick brace of bracers. Somehow I managed to place the blame for the horrid things happening to me on the city noises, the always unexpected explosions of sound. I couldn't bear the steady ratatatatat of street drilling outside my window, and this seemed reason enough not to move from my room, where I could drink all the more, in hope that liquor would soon deaden the sound.

From the beginning the voyage was miraculously therapeutic. The relaxed atmosphere, the relative quiet and the salt air helped me to calm down, being in the confines of a ship made me feel as though I were in a safe, warm cocoon. I drank, but only with my meals, and only champagne. I spent hours blanketed cozily in my deck chair, reading or chatting with Gladys. I ate everything put before me. To my relief, I was able to sleep without any struggle or disturbing dreams.

Every evening throughout the voyage, the ship's theater showed a new movie. The night before we were to land in England, the movie was *Modern Times,* starring Charlie Chaplin.

When the ship's captain, a suave William Powell type, sought me out and invited me to be his guest at the screening, I became suddenly panicky at the prospect of sitting in a large room, filled with strangers who knew who I was, and watching Charlie. I couldn't even give the captain an answer. I ran to my cabin and ordered Gladys to tell him I was ill and to offer my apologies. The second she was gone I dug out the bottle of Scotch I'd sneaked under a row of underwear while packing and more or less forgotten till now. I tore off the seal and finished the last drop before I sank into sleep. When we reached Liverpool, Gladys had to shake me and shout at me before I could come fully awake.

Waiting for me in my Dorchester Hotel suite in London were flowers, fruit, candies—and champagne. I downed half a dozen glasses of champagne, despite Gladys's protests, dressed and met the Café DeParee's Jack Harris for cocktails, which I promised myself I would pace. Jack was a cordial and patient man, flattering me shamelessly about how lucky the DeParee was to have been able to book me. There would be a week to prepare the act with not only my fresh special material and what were by now my standards, "I'm the Wife of the Life of the Party" and "I Was Only Looking for a Flat," but to add songs that were popular with the English as well. I was cooperative in the main, although I stood resolutely firm on two issues. I made Harris destroy a set of placards made up to advertise my appearance and featuring sketches of a black brush moustache, derby, bamboo cane and outsize shoes beside my photograph and name. I also gave a flat No to the suggestion that I pose for publicity pictures with Mildred Harris, Charlie's first wife, who was then appearing as a singer in a side-street bottle club.

The rehearsals went well enough, but away from the club I was going to pieces. My nerves were shot and there were times when my mind would drift off into a prickly state of semiconsciousness. I knew I was drinking far too much and not eating nearly enough, but that was essentially all I knew, because except for my obligations to show up at the club and do my best, I had mislaid the ability to control my time.

What I couldn't admit to anyone, even Gladys, was that the peculiar symptoms that had begun in the States were intruding now in full flower. My sense of taste was so off that I had to keep looking to see what I was eating— what I ate. My sense of color was so distorted that blue was pink, black was green. My sense of hearing, hypersensitive in New York, was even more disturbing here in London: the unexpected sound of a common pin dropping on a glass dresser top could literally make me flinch.

But the most frightening thing was what had happened to my sense of smell. Every natural odor had become strange and ominous. When I hadn't enough to drink— or too much, which was now, oddly, the same thing—there were moments when I associated all smells with poison. They—whoever They were—were after me. They were putting something in the very air I breathed to poison me. I carefully avoided confessing any of this to Gladys, for some still safe corner of sanity reminded me that the fears were unfounded, that I was anxious, that I was having brief hallucinations that could be chased away, that if I had just one more drink—well, two—all this strangeness would disappear and the world and I could get up on our toes again. I still wasn't bothering to count the number of drinks I poured into myself, secretly fearing that if I did I would be scared silly by the amount. Not that amounts were mattering much any more. My daily drinking habits were erratic, even though the results were almost always the same; on one day I could polish off two bottles of whiskey or gin over a six- to eight-hour period and be flung into either insensibility or uncontrollable panic, while on another day I could achieve the same effect by consuming no more than a couple of drinks.

To my everlasting surprise I was a smash hit on opening night, although I was as taut as a guy wire and positive I wouldn't get a sound up out of my constricted throat. The café, designed after one of the dining salons on a luxury passenger liner, was packed with beautifully gowned women and escorts in dinner jackets, posh people willing to pay extravagantly to be regulars of DeParee, to see and hear over a single season Beatrice Lillie, Gertrude Lawrence, Helen Morgan—and, incredibly, Lita Grey Chaplin. The applause kept bringing me back. The reviews were kind, and two of them wrote the following day what several other reviewers had written in the United States: that I would have been a star even without the Chaplin name.

After each midnight show Gladys would renew her nightly campaign to steer me back to the Dorchester for a warm bath and a good sleep, but Gladys didn't understand that I needed the chance to unwind. There were always invitations to go to bottle clubs—liquor was served nowhere else in London after midnight—and I would accept them. As long as I was in the crowded, smoky company of new-found friends and admirers who liked me for myself, or at least treated me as if they did, I could handle my nerves and the intermittent hallucinations. Grueling anxieties inevitably started clutching at me the moment I returned to the suite, but heady from compliments and tired from work, I would toss off a couple of quick nightcaps and go under until three or four o'clock the next afternoon.

One early morning I went—alone—to the bottle club where Mildred Harris was appearing. I hadn't meant to, but curiosity got the best of me. Pictures of me seemed to be plastered over much of London, but when I entered the club and made my way to the dark bar no one noticed who I was, which was exactly what I wanted.

The club was seedy, and the handful of customers at tables and bar struck me as no less so. Mildred Harris was over by the piano, balefully singing one moody standard after another in a throaty, weary voice that was neither good nor bad, but rather the voice of a tired professional who has been assured she'll be paid no matter what. The customers were talking, ignoring her, and she didn't appear to care. She was a once-fresh, once-pretty blue-eyed blonde with once-unblemished skin who was going from one tune to the next, taking a sip from her glass or a drag from her cigarette during three-second breathers, drained, bored, interested only in finishing the set. When at last she was done, she plodded to the end of the bar opposite me, oblivious to the fact that the applause was scant and perfunctory.

I watched while the bartender freshened her glass, and then I went over to her. She was hunching forward, bleached and used though still in her thirties, a coldly pathetic, aging woman who glanced at me but barely raised her eyebrows when I introduced myself and asked if I might sit with her.

She shrugged. "It's a free country, like they say. I was sort of wondering when you'd decide to come slumming, Mrs. Charlie the Second. What're you drinking?"

In her sluggish way she said everything she could think of to needle me over the next half hour, sarcastically congratulating me for having nicked Charlie in what some papers had called "The Second Gold Rush," and informing me that if I'd dropped by to take a look at the has-been and offer my shoulder, I was hereby invited to get the hell back to my plush part of town because she didn't need or want a thing.

I was patient. I took offense at nothing. I struggled not to be condescending, mainly because that was the very last thing I felt like being. Only when I could come up with no logical excuse to stay any longer with this sadly, solemnly embittered woman did I realize why I'd really come. In my desperation to be free of the mysterious but terrifying things that were taking place inside me, I had thought of her as the only other woman who understood Charlie as I did. I had come to this wasted, tragic, lost, maybe irreclaimable woman in the hope that she had the key that would save me!

I wanted to give her money, all I had, but I didn't dare. As I got up to leave, she looked at me. "You have two sons by Charlie, don't you? I've seen their pictures in the magazines. They're handsome. Are they good kids?"

"Yes."

She nodded gravely. "Count your blessings, okay? Charlie gave me a baby once—you ever know that? It lived for three days and then it died. Charlie took it hard. Funny thing, isn't it—that's the only thing I can remember about Charlie . . . that he cried when the baby died."

I started to say something, but she picked up her glass. "Go home, lady," she commanded softly. "Go do your slumming someplace else."

The Café DeParee engagement closed with my rallying to some form of workable sobriety only at show time. Gladys had taken to hiding every bottle she could find from me, but I was always too clever for her; I always knew more caches than she did. We toured the provinces to good, friendly English audiences, but by now I was a trained animal act, simply going through the paces, hearing the applause but, like Mildred, not much caring whether or not it came.

We returned to London before embarking on the tour through Scotland. Gladys was hotly insisting that the tour be cancelled: "What do you need it for, Skipper? You're dead tired. You're close to a walking skeleton as it is. You'll collapse for sure if you don't give yourself a long rest."

"I'm going to be fine. I have to play those dates. I gave my word. I'll be all right."

The night before Easter Sunday I went into my usual deep alcoholic stupor, but I shot up in bed a few hours later with my heart pounding so hard I was sure it was about to leap out of my chest. I ran to Gladys, crying, "Quick—the hospital! I'm dying! I'm choking to death!"

She hurried out of bed to find her clothes while I paced wildly like a caged animal, the palpitations building, every nerve end screaming. I couldn't wait. I raced out of her room, out of the suite, and punched the elevator button in the corridor. I couldn't wait for the elevator, either. I found the stairs and ran down one flight after the next, three and four steps at a time, tripping and picking myself up to keep running. I raced through the hotel lobby and plunged through the revolving door until I was out on the damp, cool street, noticing no one and to hell with the fact that I was wearing only a nightgown. Although it was the middle of the night a small crowd gathered, wanting to help, but I could do nothing except pace frantically and scream, "Gladys! Gladys! Oh, God, Gladys!" at the top of my lungs.

She came out, throwing a coat over me and scolding that I'd catch my death of cold. Someone summoned a taxi for us. We got in, and after Gladys ordered the driver to take us to the nearest hospital, she put her arm around me, saying soothingly, "It'll be okay, Skipper, it'll be okay." The palpitations were like drum beats, and I was shaking violently.

Because of Easter there were only interns on duty at the hospital. One intern grabbed my arm as I tried to hurry past him, and he and another one led me to a private room as Gladys followed, telling them everything she knew that could have brought this inexplicable attack on. I fought them as they pinned me to a white table, crying that I was choking to death, begging them to protect me because everybody was trying to poison me.

The gave me some sedation, which began to take effect almost immediately. I don't know how long I was on the table, but I was relatively calm when one of them told Gladys, "It's emotional exhaustion. She's been overstimulated—too much alcohol, obviously. She should stay here the night and then one of the resident doctors can take more comprehensive tests."

Gladys was all for that, but I wasn't. Feeling much better, secretly afraid of what a doctor might tell me, I got up, smiled my most winning smile and said, "Would you nice young gentlemen kindly leave while a lady gets dressed? I'm well now. I could lick my weight in wild-cats—honestly."

They argued, Gladys the loudest. I was persistent and I won. Gladys, clucking her protest, took me back to the hotel, where I found I was indeed ready for restful sleep. What did strange doctors know of the physical and emotional history of Lita Grey Chaplin? Sure, those palpitations had been a warning from my worn-out system; I didn't need strange doctors to tell me that. And I would heed the warning, I promised. I would go to sleep—but in a hotel bed I was comparatively used to, not a hospital bed in which someone once might have died.

The warning impressed me for the several days it took to make the final arrangements for the Scotland tour. I drank nothing except the red medicinal liquid one of the interns had prescribed as a sedative, and my nerves behaved better than at any time since I'd left the States. Gladys was still against the trip. I kept pointing out that I had licked the hooch, that work would be the ideal tonic. She had to admit, at my prodding, that I did have some healthy color back in my cheeks.

The Aberdeen and Edinburgh theaters were a cramped comedown from the lush DeParee, but the audiences were endearingly receptive and I gave them all I had in me.

And I felt so healthy that I started to drink again.

Not very much. Wine and beer could hardly be called alcohol, so I took care of my thirst—or hunger, when I was brave enough to be explicit with myself—with wine and beer. Gladys wasn't terribly happy, but even she had to agree that this was still teetotaling compared to the way I'd been assaulting myself before.

There was only one problem: the wine and beer, even in steadily increasing quantities, seldom provided me with much more than a slight buzz, if that. I was feeling stronger now, and even eating well, so what would be the harm in a few judiciously paced Scotch whiskies?

The harm was that I'd no sooner finished that second wondrous Scotch than it became perfectly clear that a few more would be even more wondrous. By the time we were ready to leave for Glasgow I was back at the bottle once more—with a difference: now I got high and drunk and sick within minutes, after only a couple of shots.

Gladys threatened to hit me, to quit, to find a doctor and bring him. Then, the night before the Glasgow trip, I couldn't stop vomiting. As I knelt at the toilet bowl, light-headed, dizzy, my stomach aflame, I nodded and raised my right hand. "My word," I vowed. "Next time you catch me with a drink, Mother Gladys, you have my permission to shoot me straight between the eyes."

On the Glasgow train, in spite of the fact that the sedative prescription had been renewed, I began to lapse into temporary fogs. Gazing through the window at the glorious green of Scotland, I had a weird hallucination: I thought I saw the menacing figure of William Randolph Hearst standing in a field, watching me go by in the train. "Hearst is a powerful man. He'd do anything for me—he'd have you killed," Charlie had said. Rubbish. Scaredy-cat fantasy. Yet there it was, Hearst's large, bulky form, waving its massive arms and giving orders to have me murdered. I shut my eyes and opened them and—blessed relief—saw that it was only a scarecrow, disappearing into the distance.

This crazy fantasy repeated itself over and over during the ride. "What's going on, Skipper?" Gladys asked. "You're sure acting funny."

I laughed, trying desperately to control my palsied trembling. "It's your fault. You're taking too long opening that deck of cards. Are we playing or aren't we?"

Something told me that when we reached Glasgow I should sneak off at the very first chance and see a doctor for an examination. Something was wrong, awfully wrong. I felt as though I were in my worst, woolliest kind of drunkenness, although I didn't have a drop in me; I was, in fact, full of sedative. I couldn't account for whole minutes of time, and there was an obstinate lump in my throat ordering *Cry*—but I couldn't.

The weather was oppressively gloomy when we reached Glasgow. The inn that was to lodge us was a sorry comedown from the Dorchester and even the less luxurious hotels we'd been in since arriving from America, but I was too exhausted and too tense to throw my weight around and demand better quarters. The old woman who confirmed the reservation enthused over how Charlie Chaplin was her mister's favorite film actor of all time, and whipping away for a moment, came back with a collection of Scotch and English magazines, which she offered to lend me; the magazines, she assured me, had lots and lots and lots of darling stories about Charlie. I didn't tell her that this generosity of hers was in rather odd taste, for I'd got used to strangers who, knowing who I was and all about me, were openly eager to share their love of Charlie with me. I took the magazines, thanked her and promised to return them.

Gladys and I were shown to a dim, damp room with one closet, two bureaus and a single bed. She unpacked while I changed to a robe, hopeful that a bath would settle me enough to allow me to open that night in some recognizably civilized condition. I carried a few of the nine or ten magazines with me to the bathroom at the end of the hall.

The tap water was warm, at least—something that couldn't always be said for the water in some of the better European lodgings I'd been in. Lying back, I could have spent my time in the tub reading stories about Myrna Loy or Clark Gable or Cary Grant or any of the other current Hollywood favorites. Instead, of course, I turned right to the Charlie Chaplin stories.

Charlie Chaplin and Paulette Goddard.

There they were, on the tennis courts, on a yacht, at a premiere. They looked so happy, so damned comfortable with each other. Fine, good. What was it to me? Charlie and I were ancient history, old hat, the guard had been changed and best wishes to you, Plain Pauline Levy from Long Island. I wasn't doing so badly. I had two flawless sons and a career, and I had been pretty enough once to bat my lashes and have all the men toppling over one another to take me out—or keep me in. I had money, or I'd once had money, which is almost as good. So what was I to him, or he to me?

I clapped the magazine shut, got out of the tub and into my robe and hastened back to the room. "Well, that was fas—" Gladys began cheerfully, and then stopped as I stalked toward the underwear she'd laid out on the bed. "Something wrong, Skipper?"

"No," I answered, toweling myself dry. "I just need to take a walk."

Carefully she said, "I'll take one with you."

"By myself," I said, and began to dress quickly. "I want to be by myself for a few minutes. Don't you ever want to be alone?"

"Skipper, when you start acting strange like this, I know someth—"

"Oh, shut up, you ignorant psalm singer! I'm not going out to get plastered. Didn't you hear me? I just want to take a walk for a little while! If you can't get a simple statement like that through your cement skull, why don't you grab your bags and head the hell home? Nobody around here's going to miss you!"

I dressed as fast as I could, in the first clothes I could find, and stormed out of that cell of a room. The damp air outside hit me hard on the face, but I walked on as though I had some vital destination. Ah, I've done it, I thought. Why didn't I go all out and call her a nigger? Who's Gladys Thompson, anyway? The one human being who's stuck by me and with me, who's listened and comforted and mothered and never once said "I told you so,"

303

who's cleaned up my slop and been patient from the beginning, that's all. The one human being who's kept me alive this long, that's all. . . .

I entered the first pub I came to. It appeared to be a man's pub, not the type that catered to a family trade, but when I ordered a double Scotch I wasn't turned away. The drink helped, and the second double helped to narcotize me even more, but my inner bell was still working, and it refused to let me order a third. I paid up and went back to the hotel room, which was empty. So, Gladys was gone. I didn't bother to check whether her possessions were there or not. I simply sat on the bed, and lacing the fingers of both my hands over my knees, I mourned for the good things I could have done, the good person I could have been.

Gladys came in. I was ashamed to look at her, ashamed even to speak. "You all right, Skipper?" she asked. "I ran down hunting for you. Give me the devil if you want, but you shouldn't go traipsing around in this weather without a coat."

I wanted so terribly much to cry when she touched me, and I held up my arms to her. She sat beside me and we huddled close, the friend who gave unsparingly and the perpetually needful, dependent, helpless child. "Forgive me, please forgive me," I whispered.

"For what?" she scoffed. "Now quit this stuff and let's get ready for the theater."

In the wings I shook my head, trying to clear it. The music played my introduction and I walked on stage, beaming, savoring the lovely waves of applause.

I felt fine now, in command, in control. I zoomed into "I'm the Wife of the Life of the Party" as though I'd never sung it in public before, and I sang it with more life, zip, bounce, humor and zestful love than I'd ever given it. My first Glasgow audience went wild, and I ripped into the next number, and the next and the next, using all the skill, and more, that I'd learned in this incredible and sometimes joyous show business career of mine. I was better than fine now. I was the Lillita McMurray—Lita Grey—Lita Grey Chaplin—who had been deprecating herself for a lifetime, but who felt, who *knew,* that this would be marked and remembered as the show of shows, the best show ever, the perfect show for all time to be, the happy summit of Lita Grey, the fulfillment of the till-now unfulfilled crybaby. I knew I was alive and worthwhile, worth something and worthy, that these people wouldn't applaud me and love me just because of Charlie, and here I was, ninety feet tall and all woman, on top of everything and outrageously happy, and starting the change of pace number, "It's My Mother's Birthday Today," so overwhelmingly pleased.

" 'It's my mother's bir—' "

I stopped.

The leader sensed something, let the song continue for another bar, tapped his baton to quiet the orchestra, then started the lead-in for the second time.

" 'It's my—' "

I went limp. There were hundreds and hundreds of people there and my shoulders sank and I slowly began to cry.

I didn't try to straighten myself, to fight, to grin and apologize and start over. I stood there on that long stage in front of hundreds and hundreds of people and wept. The tears were free and they streamed down my cheeks. There was no more music. The lively Glasgow audience gradually hushed. I didn't run off. I stayed. And sobbed. I sank forward to my knees, leaned toward the klieg lights and just sobbed.

The curtains were rung down, and the music began for the jugglers who followed Lita Grey Chaplin.

Chapter Twenty-one

A blackout of days.

I was in a London sanitarium, and nobody was being honest with me.

I was being fussed over by people with white uniforms and grave faces, but nobody would honestly tell me how I'd got here from Scotland, how long they would keep me locked up here, whether they'd brought me here to murder me. Everybody answered my every question—oh, yes, everybody was jolly despite those grave faces. Everybody said I was perfectly safe, that I needed lots of rest and lots of nutrition and soon I would be able to go home. I knew they were lying, they'd all conspired and ganged up on me, that what they called medicine and forced me to drink was poison. It was a terrible thing, killing me slowly. Do it fast, get it over with, I pleaded. Please don't kill me, I pleaded, please make me well and let me go home and I'll never hurt anyone again.

Blackout.

I was on a ship sailing from Southampton to New York, lying in bed for six days, looking at the stateroom ceiling and watching figures playing on it. There was Charlie, The Tramp, The Little Fellow, doing his carefree jig, then glaring down at me and saying coldly, "Get out, you little whore." I shut my eyes. But I kept hearing him.

When we arrived in New York Gladys helped me down the gangplank. Lou Irwin and a friend, Adrian Droeshout, were there to meet us. I kissed them both, apologized for my surely shocking appearance—I weighed less than a hundred pounds now—and told them how grateful I was for their concern. Lou explained that all the arrangements had been made for me to go right to the Neurological Institute, where I would get sympathetic and expert treatment.

"I'm in your hands," I said gaily, but even as I was congratulating myself because I'd become so lucid after such a long interval of behaving like a madwoman, I suddenly felt a wave of resentment against his announcement, and I was sure I caught him and Adrian exchanging a hasty, conspiratorial look. "I feel better already," I lied.

They hailed a cab, and Gladys got in front with the driver. The back seat was roomy, but I felt hemmed in between Adrian and Lou, as though they had seated us this way so I couldn't escape. As soon as we were arranged in the cab, after much slamming of doors—harsh sounds that keyed me up even more—Adrian offered me a cigarette. I stiffened in fright and suspicion. "What did you put in it?" I demanded.

"How's that, Lita?"

I could feel myself going wrong again, all wrong, but I couldn't stop. "You have poison in there. You just can't wait to see me take that first puff."

They did what they could to reassure me that I was safe. They got me to the hospital, where everybody wore white uniforms and grave faces. I wanted to fight them, but instead of fighting, I cried. Doctors and nurses worked for days to keep me sedated, but I spent every waking minute crying, weeping constant, ungovernable tears of grief and fear. I knew that Mr. Hearst had sent someone all the way from California to kill me, and I begged the doctors to protect me. I was fifteen years old and pregnant with Charlie's baby and Charlie wouldn't marry me.

A doctor came to the side of my bed. I grabbed his arm and implored, "Please marry me . . . don't say no . . . please say you'll marry me . . ."

His voice was gentle, his smile kind. "That's a wonderful offer, but I'm afraid I'm already married."

I clung to him and screamed, "I don't care! You've got to marry me! Somebody's got to marry me! Please, please . . . oh, please!"

The bed sheets were cold. Then they were leading me to a bathtub and putting a rubber ring around my neck. To drown me? Yes, to tie me up and drown me. I was begging them to help me, to understand, to take all the money and give it back to Charlie. I didn't want it. I didn't deserve it. I didn't deserve *anything*. They were leading me to a room and explaining that this thing they called electric shock treatments would be good for me, that they wouldn't hurt too much, that I should try to be calm.

There were the long, dark nights with the giant shadows of nurses on the walls. There were the days with those things at my temples, those things around my ankles, those assurances I wouldn't believe that my children weren't dead, that they were all right, that everything was going to be all right.

There were weeks. And gradually there was less panic and no tears at all. Mama came for me from Los Angeles and took me home. I was in a wheelchair, and two porters helped get me off the train.

Miraculously, Lou Irwin had kept all mention of my illness out of the papers, for which I am eternally grateful.

When the weather was warm, I would sit in the back yard of my grandmother's house, staring into space yet knowing vaguely that someday, somehow, I would have to lift myself out of my fog. Mama took care of me, and my boys must have been carefully trained, for they were loving and pretended manfully that their mother wasn't a wreck—and a frightening one to look at, too.

At just the right time, Henry Aguirre came into my fouled-up life. He had a house not far away, and one day an aunt of mine brought him by to call. I was polite but not overly friendly, not because he wasn't a pleasant young man, but because it took nearly all my energy to talk or even to listen.

At first he was simply a nice boy who dropped by afternoons to sit with me. Then, as I came back to life, a bit more, I began to see him for what he was: a genuinely decent young man who genuinely cared that I had been to hell and that I was gradually returning to some semblance of life. He knew something about sickness; he was a dancer who'd contracted malaria while on a tour of the Orient, and he'd had a long, tortured time grappling with it. In an extremely low-pressured way he invited me to talk about myself.

Henry took me for drives in his car, still treating me as a convalescent—though, fortunately, not like glass—and his affection made me feel approved of, wanted. I told him about my breakdown, in considerably more detail than I would have felt free to detail it for Mama. Talking helped me, and his refusal to correct or censure helped me even more. He remarked that he was sure he wouldn't be alive if luck hadn't directed him to a Dr. Edward Franklin, who had worked wonders for him and who might be the one to get me back on the track. In a week, when my head began to clear even more, I agreed and let him make an appointment for me.

I established an almost instantaneous rapport with Dr. Franklin, a bald, chubby man who heard me out for two solid hours and then guaranteed that he would have me completely well in three months. He sent to New York for my medical and psychiatric reports, and while they were on their way, put me on a rigid schedule of daily hot baths and massages and three intravenous injections of calcium gluconate a week. But more, he made himself as available as humanly possible to listen, to answer, and to help mend my mind and frail ego as he was mending my body.

His prediction proved right. Within three months I was strong again, bolstered, healthy. I was hardly in line to win the year's Mental Health Award, but I was eating, sleeping without pills and more serene than I'd ever been in my life.

Henry Aguirre and I drove to Santa Ana and were married. At the time it seemed a sensible thing to do, but the reasons were all wrong: I thought that marriage, even to a boy I didn't love but did trust, would help to give me a stronger sense of continuity; Henry, malleable and easygoing, was willing to marry me because he felt sorry for me.

We were divorced some months later. The marriage should never have taken place, obviously, but it ended without rancor. When we realized that neither of us really had anything emotionally substantial to offer the other, we mutually agreed to part.

In 1938 I married Arthur Day, a reasonably successful theatrical agent. Charlie junior and Sydney were attending the Black Fox Military Institute, and I was working from time to time, earning a living, but performing had long since lost whatever erratic appeal it once may have held for me. Arthur came along at just the right time. He was a happy-go-lucky, affectionate Irishman who persuaded me with extravagant charm that we would make the greatest husband-and-wife team in history.

There is no question that I loved him. I married him in spite of the acknowledged fact that he loved to drink and was convinced that the world would be a better place if everyone loved to drink. I had been warned that I was courting suicide if I ever touched another drop, and I told him this. He shook his head and laughed. "Listen, baby, I'm not going to sneak a snort in your Ovaltine. If you go for this sobersides stuff that's your lookout. I won't gum up your Girl Scouts' code."

Several years after we were married our fights became whoppers. Arthur wasn't an alcoholic in the technical sense—he could function quite well when necessary and when he wanted to—but liquor was such an integral part of his life that he surrounded us only with friends who drank to excess. I would be the sore thumb at parties, the one who cradled a Coke and watched from the sidelines as the revelers carried on. Arthur began to call me Carrie Nation in public, first as a gag and later with a sarcastic bite to his tone. The others would stagger over, tease me for being a wet blanket and try to talk me into taking just one shot. Arthur would join in. I would leave, go home by myself and battle it out the next day with him.

It was vital that I stay married, that I not go back to Mama, who had been against my marrying Arthur Day even more than she'd been against my marrying Henry Aguirre and who would again hoot, "I told you so!"

I gave in and drank with him.

I started by experimenting with beer and then wine, and found the effects from them pleasant. After all, my troubles with drinking in the past had stemmed simply from drinking too much and allowing my chemistry to get out of balance. My chemistry was in perfect working order now. Thoughts of Charlie didn't plague me any more. And as long as I had a glass in my hand, Arthur and I got on swimmingly.

At his urging, I experimented with Scotch and found that the roof didn't collapse on me. At a party in Manhattan, where we were living, I had half a dozen Scotch-and-sodas, got relaxed, got happy, got high—and felt fine the next morning.

Within a year I was back where I'd started. The thought of food was revolting, and I was having momentary hallucinations again, seeing and hearing people and objects that weren't there. My blood sugar and blood pressure plummeted, and I was punishing my nervous system to the brink of disintegration. More and more I discovered myself physically unable to get out of bed in the morning. And when I needed Arthur, he was at the corner bar, laughing it up with his cronies.

I left Arthur in 1943 to flee home to California and Dr. Franklin—and learned that Dr. Franklin had died. My $90,000 dream house had turned into a white elephant, and I was forced to sell it. There was no other home now, for Grandma had suffered a fatal stroke during my years of wandering. Charlie junior and Sydney were both in the service, So Mama and I, alone, moved into a small rented house in the Valley.

I got in touch with Dr. Albert Best, Dr. Franklin's successor, who dug out my old files. He examined me and bluntly told me that the next drink probably wouldn't kill me, but that I wasn't very far from death if I had many more. The severity of his tone and the seriousness of his warning numbed me into a promise that I'd had my last drink—a promise I kept. He went further: I was still in danger and would likely remain in danger unless and until I agreed to enter a sanitarium for complete rehabilitation.

Once home, I telephoned Charlie's house.

There was no reason on earth why he should talk to me. He had just married Oona O'Neill, Eugene O'Neill's daughter, after having divorced Paulette Goddard. He was in the throes of a scandalous lawsuit; Joan Barry had charged him with having fathered her baby. But I had to call. There was no one else I could talk to.

He was summoned and he came to the phone. He was surprised to hear from me, but his manner was anything but brisk. I wasted no time. I told him how ill I was. I told him how desperately I needed to see him.

"Give me your address," he said.

He drove right over, greeted me with unaffected warmth when I opened the door and pretended he wasn't face to face with a haggard ruin of thirty-five. We got into the car and drove past Las Flores Beach, up along the coastline to Malibu. The day was cool. A mist had begun to come in from the sea.

We started talking about the boys and comparing notes, each of us having received wonderfully chatty letters and wonderful photographs from them. We agreed we couldn't have asked for two finer sons. Charlie said, "Something must have gone right, Lita. Those boys couldn't have turned out so well if something hadn't gone right."

He looked older, of course, but the lines in Charlie's face and the gray hair only served to make him more striking. We rode for a while in silence and then he said, with incredible sensitivity, "Tell me everything about yourself, Lita. But before you do, let me tell you something. You're going to get well. Whatever it is, you're going to get well."

I told him everything that had happened to me, the collapse, the constant melancholia and depressions. I told him how hard I had tried to find myself all these years, in and out of show business, searching for approval, for identity. I spoke as simply as possible, trying not to whine, trying not to sound absurd.

Charlie, the man whose uncanny insight into human nature as an artist never functioned in his personal life, listened intently, as though weighing every word. And then, never taking his eyes off the road, he spoke as I'd never heard him speak before.

"Does it help to know we all look for these things, for love, for identity, for true evaluation? It doesn't come easily. Some of us never find it."

"Identity? You've always had that."

He shook his head. "I've been looking for it all my life. If I ever do find it, it will be because of Oona."

"Why were you always such a mystery to me, Charlie?" I asked. "Why couldn't we ever really reach each other?"

313

"Because I didn't understand myself," he said. "All I knew was that I was always afraid of people, afraid to be hurt. I couldn't ever quite believe that anyone could love me. I was sensitive about being a small man with an oversized head and such small hands and feet. I never understood women. I mistrusted them. When they got too close I conquered them, but I couldn't love them for long because I was convinced they couldn't love me. Fantastic, isn't it? But there's the secret story of the self-assured Charlie Chaplin."

He paused, as though reviewing our brief years together, so long before. "Lita, if it's any possible consolation, I'll tell you that even when I was at my most abominable I knew I was disappointing you terribly, and I was wretched with it. I excused myself by saying my work was my whole life and I had to guard it *with* my life, but of course that's poppycock. I was simply determined to hold back from giving of myself. That was my pattern with you, and Mildred, and Paulette. If there were a God I'd pray to Him to not let me repeat this dreary pattern with Oona. I protected myself by hurting you, by driving you to leave me. Does it help to say I'm sorry? I doubt it."

On the way back, Charlie asked how seriously I took the doctor's warning about drinking. I said that I took it very seriously, and that that was what frightened me— knowing the consequences, I still wasn't sure I had the courage to stop.

Charlie's sense of order took over. With an edge of anger he declared, "That's the speech of a child. You're thirty-five and you've got your whole life before you. You've also got two sons who don't deserve to be orphaned. What do you mean, you're not sure you can stop drinking? *Stop*— that's how to stop. Pick yourself up and start fighting back. Jesus, Lita, groping in the dark is one thing, but lying down and waiting for the undertaker is something else, goddammit! You've *got* to fight! What the hell good is anything if you don't fight?"

Anyone else would just have been Knute Rockne giving

a pep talk, squeezing the bellows of vim and vigor into his players. But I was listening Charlie, who was, at long last, force and sensitivity and compassion.

Charlie drove me home. Before I got out he repeated how necessary it was to think of myself affirmatively. Then he touched my arm and said, "Just a moment, Lita. For what it's worth after all these years, I've really loved only two women—you and the girl who's my wife now. I'm sorry I wasn't able to be a real husband."

After that meeting with Charlie, which buoyed me and made me determined to go for treatment at once, I entered the sanitarium. After a prolonged stay, which included eleven shock treatments, I emerged into a new world. I had been quite literally shocked out of a years-long paralysis of the soul.

With each visit to his office, Dr. Best assured me that I was in increasingly better health. It was he who suggested, after a time, that I think about going into an occupation in which I could make use of my knowledge of show business, and it was he who talked to me at length about opening an artists' agency. I gave the suggestion serious consideration, and in 1950, with my finances almost entirely drained through my foolish spending and self-induced illness, I borrowed some money and opened the Lita Grey Chaplin Talent Agency in Los Angeles.

The agency business is a notoriously difficult one in which to gain traction, but for a while I did quite well; I placed a number of performers in good jobs—among them David Janssen, who later went on to grab the much-sought-after title role in *The Fugitive* television series. But the business nosedived when my associate left the agency, taking many of my prospective star talents with him. The clients who stayed weren't bringing in enough to meet the overhead, and it wasn't long before I was floundering in debt. I had friends who were willing to see me over the financial bumps, but I'd had it; I closed the agency's doors in 1952.

I went back to show business, but with no better luck. The name meant next to nothing, it was worth only dates in second-string clubs in Las Vegas. I turned them down. I was forty-four now, an awkward time of life to begin a comeback, especially when one is coming back to a career that had been a shaky affair in the first place. I had no intention of becoming a replica of poor Mildred Harris.

It was in that same year, 1952, when, indirectly, my path crossed Charlie's again. I was living in a small rented house in Hollywood with Mama and Charlie junior. One day I received a phone call from a lawyer whose name sounded familiar and who turned out to be the son of a man who'd been one of Charlie's attorneys twenty-five years before. After a few moments of polite formalities, he got straight to the point. "We've got a problem, and you can help," he said. "Charlie can use all the help he can get."

He proceeded to detail some of what I had read in the newspapers and heard from friends. Charlie had recently sailed to Europe on a holiday. The U.S. Attorney General's office, which didn't like the fact that Charlie had never applied for United States citizenship, that certain circles were calling him a member of the Communist Party and that he had a penchant for sleeping with girls less than half his age without apology to the public, didn't want to let him back in the country.

"They're working to build a solid case against him so that he'll never be allowed back in," the lawyer said.

"What's that to me?" I asked. I had conveniently blotted my last meeting with Charlie from my memory and was remembering only his cruelty. How could any representative of his have the nerve to reach out to me?

"They're going to subpoena you," he answered. "They're going to go after him for moral turpitude, and they'll use both barrels. You're involved mainly because they got hold of that divorce complaint from back in twenty-seven. They were intrigued by phrases like 'improper sexual practices' and 'degeneracy.'"

"Oh God," I sighed, fumbling urgently for a cigarette. "All that was so long ago. Why bring it up now? I've got plenty of unpleasant memories of Charlie, but he's certainly no menace to America."

"That's why you can help," he said. "No one's asking you to picture him as a saint. You *are* being asked to stand up for fair play, though. Personalities aside, it's a grave moral injustice for the Department to do what it's attempting to do. It didn't simply kick him out of the country, which might have made some grotesque sense. It waited for him to leave on a vacation, and then hurried to build a legal case to bar his re-entry. That brand of conduct is understandable in a totalitarian country, but it's indefensible in ours." He offered to furnish me with good legal counsel.

There was melancholy irony, I thought, in the fact that of all the women in Charlie's life I was the only one the government would be able to subpoena to testify for or against him. The lawyer had told me that Oona O'Neill could not testify against his moral character even if she wished to. Mildred Harris had died at the age of forty-three from alcoholism. Paulette Goddard, who was now linked with author Erich Maria Remarque, whom she was eventually to marry, was in parts unknown. Joan Barry could not testify, for following the paternity trial she had been committed to a state mental institution. The other women meaningful in his life were either dead or helpless. Edna Purviance was ending her own drastic bouts with alcoholism but entering the first stages of the racking decline that would end, a few years later, in equally racking death. Red-haired Merna Kennedy was dead at thirty-five from what the papers had called a heart attack. Only Lita Grey was available to condemn, and with that yellowing divorce complaint in hand, who else could better serve their needs?

On October 20, 1952, I went to the Immigration and Naturalization Service section of the U.S. Department of Justice Building at 458 South Spring Street in Los Angeles. The lawyer who was to represent me as Attorney for Witness spent a solemn half hour with me in the corridors before the testimony was to commence. He informed me of my rights as a witness at this governmental hearing, which was to determine whether or not Charles Spencer Chaplin should be permitted to return to the United States.

"Nervous?" he asked.

"Very," I said.

"Try not to be. These fellows know their stuff, but the minute they seem to be rowing you into muddy waters, I'll jump in. Where it's at all possible I'll say, 'This is a privileged communication between husband and wife at that time and if you do not wish to answer it, you do not need to do so.' Then you say, 'I would rather not answer on the basis that it is a privileged communication between my husband and me when I was married.'" He handed me a card on which that statement was typed and which, he said, I had the right to keep in front of me.

He was so highly organized, so apparently sure that I was going to jump through his hoop, that something made me say, "You know, I just might fool you and your smooth-as-glass law firm. I just might decide to crucify Chaplin." He looked at me as if I'd slapped his face.

One examining officer and two investigators sat at a long table. A stenographer was in attendance. The examining officer began: "You are advised that I am an Acting Immigrant Inspector of the United States Immigration and Naturalization Service, and as such I am authorized by law to take testimony under oath from any person regarding the right of an alien to be, enter, re-enter, reside, or remain in the United States. I desire to take a statement from you under oath regarding the right of one Charlie Chaplin to enter, re-enter, or remain in the United States. You are advised that any such statement you make may be used against Mr. Chaplin in any proceedings."

I was sworn in and answered the routine opening questions the panel asked me, such as how old I was, where I made my home, and so on. Then, quite abruptly, the kindly Dr. Jekylls turned into hard, grim Mr. Hydes: "Before your marriage to Mr. Chaplin, did you have intimate relations with him?"

"Yes," I said, a bit taken aback that they were getting down to brass tacks so fast.

For the remainder of the hearing, which lasted an endless three quarters of an hour, they didn't let up. They were skilled inquisitors, and they took turns at putting questions to me that were clearly designed to see that Charlie would be slaughtered. The lawyer was in my corner—or I should say Charlie's—and when the going got rough he reminded me of privileged communication between husband and wife, but even so they were determined to wear no velvet gloves. They had done their homework prior to the hearing; they knew the charges in my divorce complaint by heart, and they obviously had tracked down a great deal of additional information from other sources. They knew that I was fifteen years old when the intimate relations with Charlie began. They knew that Charlie and I were married only after I had conceived and had refused to have an abortion.

They came out of the bedroom for a brief period to tackle politics:

Q. Prior to your marriage to Mr. Chaplin in 1924, did you ever discuss with him political ideology?

A. No, I don't think I knew anything about politics. I still don't.

Q. Did he ever tell you or state in your presence that he was sympathetic to the Communist movement?

A. No.

Q. Or to the world Communist movement?

A. No.

Q. Do you have any knowledge that Mr. Chaplin contributed money to Communist organizations?

A. No, I knew nothing about his business.

Q. Do you know if Charlie Chaplin ever met with known members of the Communist Party?

A. No, I wouldn't have known who they were. I don't think anything was said about Communism at that time, that I remember.

Then they returned to the bedroom, and stayed there. Examining Officer Albert Del Guercio said, "Let me read you an allegation contained in the complaint which you filed on January 27, 1924: 'That approximately four months before said separation defendant'—meaning Charlie Chaplin—'named a girl of their acquaintance and told plaintiff'—yourself—'that he had heard things about said girl which caused him to believe that she might be willing to commit acts of sexual perversion, and asked plaintiff'—yourself—'to invite her up to the house some time, telling plaintiff'—yourself—'that "they could have some fun with her." ' Do you remember that?"

The lawyer cleared his throat and called it privileged communication. But Del Guercio wouldn't give up; he got on the issue of so-called degeneracy: "In your complaint for divorce filed in the Superior Court at Los Angeles you alleged among other things that Mr. Chaplin's conduct and manifestation of interest in sexual relations between you and he (sic) were abnormal, unnatural, perverted, degenerate and indecent. Did you so allege?"

Up till this point I don't think I had completely made up my mind how I was going to treat Charlie in my testimony. Much of the once unrelenting bitterness had faded over the years, yet I was far from ready to forgive him for the heartache he had caused me and others. But Mr. Del Guercio, who was only doing his job, was nevertheless beginning to get under my skin. This business of trying to hang Charlie—or anyone—for actions of a generation back seemed shameful.

"I don't know," I said coolly, "because the attorneys prepared the complaint. They asked me the questions and I told them what I thought was abnormal at the age of sixteen."

"Are you familiar with the provisions of Section 288a of the Penal Code of the State of California?"

"I don't think so."

"I will read to you the provisions of Section 288a of the California Penal Code: 'Any person participating in the act of copulating the mouth of one person with the sexual organ of another is punishable by imprisonment in the state prison for not exceeding fifteen years.' Did you have any such relations with Mr. Chaplin during your married life?"

I told him I would rather not answer. What I didn't tell him was that I knew he probably felt like a damned fool trying to find a crime in anything done a quarter of a century ago between a confused child-wife and a man whose complex personality she had not yet begun to understand.

After forty-five minutes, the investigators thanked and excused me. I hadn't helped Charlie, evidently; he never returned to the United States. But I hadn't hurt him, either. Word later reached me that Charlie had cabled from Europe, expressing sincere appreciation that I hadn't been, in his phrase, "heartless and vengeful."

The message, oddly enough, thrilled me.

Chapter Twenty-two

Although Charlie hasn't made a movie since his bitter and badly received *A King in New York* in 1957—not shown in America—he continues to make news. It is news when he announces plans to create a motion picture for Sophia Loren and our son Sydney. It is news when his lovely daughter Geraldine leaves his and Oona's home in Switzerland to pursue a life independent of him and accomplishes it. It is news when Michael, his first son by Oona, leaves home and turns up in England as a bearded and long-haired beatnik. It is news when Charlie takes a vacation, when he flies to his brother's funeral, when he speaks, when he refuses to speak. Whether he is Chaplin the comic genius or Chaplin the stubborn ingrate, the whole world knows who he is, and cares.

Millions of words have been written about Charlie, lionizing him, damning him, sincerely attempting to assess him; no doubt countless more words will be written about him in the future. Unfortunately, in discussing the man himself, his biographers—including his autobiographer— have a tendency to take a rigid point of view; Charlie emerges as either a carnivorous monster or the Son of God. Neither characterization is fair to the public, or for that matter, to Charlie. There are books which ascribe his every act since birth to base motives, just as there are books so dazzled by his greatness that the weaknesses in him are explained as strengths. Both do him a disservice, because he is far too human to be seen in a single dimension.

Charlie and I were linked together, for a variety of reasons, over a period of twenty years. During the brief years of our marriage I saw him in every conceivable mood, from the peak of elation to the nadir of prolonged depression. I was witness to his compassion and his cruelty, to his explosive rages and about-face kindnesses, to his wisdom and his ignorance, to his limitless ability to love and his incredible insensitivities. Others are much better equipped than I to evaluate his genius, which will endure a thousand years after his detractors are forgotten. But I believe, neither modestly nor immodestly, that I know him—the basic, human Charlie—as well as any human being will ever know him. And perhaps, if his own auto-biography is any measure of his capacity for self-revelation, better than he knows himself.

I have, in this recollection of forty years, passed judgments on Charlie. I pray that I haven't, at the same time, portrayed myself as a storm-tossed waif, innocent of guile or sin. Psychologically shaky people have the all-too-human tendency to hurl blame for mutual failure on others. This Charlie and I did to each other. Each of us was wrong, and each of us was right. I cannot speak for Charlie, but the widening gulf of time and the mellowing of years help me to look back on our life together and its aftermath with more understanding than I once would have imagined possible.

There is no denying that our marriage was doomed to fail. At the time I did everything a scared, bitterly confused, romantic young girl could think to do to not only save the marriage but to have it grow into a positive, productive one. Even so, I did not do enough, and what I did do was often wrong. Even today I find myself reflecting on what I might have done if I'd had the sense and spirit then that hopefully I have now.

My answer inevitably is that nothing would have helped, because every imaginable card was stacked against any chance for success. Charlie was a legend at thirty-five and thirty-six, and I was an overwhelmed, ungifted child of fifteen and sixteen, and the chasm between us was bottomless from the beginning. Yes, many things he did are as reprehensible now in retrospect as they were then in act, but my hands were scarcely clean. I couldn't have saved the marriage. But perhaps I could have been a wiser and better person.

Now I live in a house in Laurel Canyon and I can look through a window and see, across the Hollywood Hills, the same native hillsides I saw when I was a child. They haven't changed; everything—the natural growth of brown brush, the wild flowers, the tall, white, stiffly erect Spanish bayonet, the towering eucalyptus, the way the sun plays hide-and-seek in the hills' deep crevasses—is still the same. All around, and on either side of these hills, lie the great freeways. In the distance there is the steady hum of heavy traffic, but here it is peaceful.

And here, though I regret much of the past, I live in the present. I am proud of Charlie's sons. Charlie junior has had more than his share of frustrations and defeats, as he has manfully admitted in his autobiography, but his future as an actor—and an excellent one—is assured. Sydney's success in the theater is solidly and deservedly established.

In a more mature way, I am closer than ever to Mama, whom the years—she is well up in her seventies—have also served to make less dependent, more mature. Gladys, wonderful Gladys, still calls me "Skipper" and still scolds me if she catches me going out in damp weather without a coat.

I am home.